"Compelling, moving, honest, L mother's story of bringing up a so ing the parental experience with styl narrative of transcendence moves fr to a state of acceptance of autism and .... and their contribution to both family and the wider society."

– Dr Michael Fitzpatrick, author of *Defeating Autism:*
A Damaging Delusion

"Sheila Barton's vivid and lively writing draws a picture of the ups and downs of family life with a child with autism. The overwhelming love she feels for her children and her spirited responses to setbacks are a joy."

– Clare Coombe-Tennant, trustee of Ambitious about Autism

"We all wonder how we would cope if our child were disabled, looking on in admiration as others do, seeing only a tiny part of the story. Sheila Barton tells it all, with honesty, humour and self-knowledge, making this an outstanding and ultimately uplifting memoir. Autism is a word many of us use often but understand little. *Living with Jonathan* offers much-needed enlightenment."

– Peter Stanford, broadcaster and writer

"Parents whose children have just received a diagnosis of autism experience a whole range of emotions – and often come to terms with them by hearing about other parents who have shared the same experience. Sheila Barton's book gives an insight into life with an autistic son – importantly it highlights the joy that her son has brought to her life. It makes an important contribution to our understanding of living with autism."

– Mark Lever, CEO National Autistic Society

"A moving, enthralling, personal account of life with an autistic son. Sheila Barton is unflinching in her portrayal of the power autism exerts – the beauty and the terror, the joy and the pain. Highly recommended."

– Charlotte Moore, author of *George and Sam*

Sheila Barton took a first-class degree in theology at Cambridge and then worked as a teacher, lecturer, social worker and manager in the charity sector. She has published articles about autism and disability equality in *The Observer*, *The Guardian*, *The Times*, *Nursery World* and *Disability Now*.

Living With Jonathan is her first book.

LIVING WITH JONATHAN

Lessons in Love, Life and Autism

SHEILA BARTON

WATKINS PUBLISHING
LONDON

This edition first published in the UK and USA 2012 by
Watkins Publishing, Sixth Floor, Castle House,
75–76 Wells Street, London WIT 3QH

Design and typography copyright © Watkins Publishing 2012
Text copyright © Sheila Barton 2012

1 3 5 7 9 10 8 6 4 2

Designed and typeset by Paul Saunders

Printed and bound in China by Imago

British Library Cataloguing-in-Publication Data Available
Library of Congress Cataloging-in-Publication Data Available

ISBN: 978-1-78028-383-8

www.watkinspublishing.co.uk

Distributed in the USA and Canada by Sterling Publishing Co., Inc.
387 Park Avenue South, New York, NY 10016-8810

For information about custom editions, special sales, premium and
corporate purchases, please contact Sterling Special Sales
Department at 800-805-5489 or specialsales@sterlingpub.com

To my son Jonathan, in admiration and with love.
And to Will who made me finish it.

Acknowledgements

I wish to express my thanks to Graham Maw Christie and to Mike Fitzpatrick for believing in my book, and to Shelagh Boyd for all her helpful suggestions. My gratitude goes to all the people in this book who were kind to Jonathan and to me and who treated him with dignity and respect.

My heartfelt thanks go to my husband Will for his constant encouragement, to Cornelius for being a friend to Jonny, and to our granddaughter Caroline for giving me love when I most needed it.

Most of all, my thanks go to Jonathan, who lived it and came through.

All names have been changed except for mine, Will's and Jonathan's.

CONTENTS

FOREWORD

by Jon Snow

THIS IS A SEARINGLY honest and open account of living with a 'difficult child' and is a compelling read. For whilst Jonny is diagnosed with autism, and his world is especially removed from ours, there are few families on earth where a parent does not, at least from time to time, suffer the frustration of living with a child who seems somehow 'other'. Indeed the closer you get to know other people's families, and your own, the more aware of this you become.

But Jonny is autistic and profoundly so. What is so very remarkable about this lyrical account of 'living with Jonathan', is the degree to which Sheila, in particular, and her family is general, come to penetrate the weird and occasionally wonderful world that Jonny and his autistic self inhabit.

The utter, exhausting, all-consuming energy that pours through Jonny's autism threads through this book like a torrential stream strewn with rapids. He never stops. Neither does Sheila, craning across her husband's dormant form to reach the coffee maker to fuel herself up at dawn to cope with Jonny's wet bed, and woeful, demanding wakefulness. She pauses briefly to go to the loo, summoning one of Jonny's siblings to keep him going with yet one more nursery rhyme.

Sheila's reward is the sheer normality of her two other children and their capacity somehow to live their lives around Jonny's constant disruption. They are exceptionally understanding children. Far from being disturbed by Jonny's howling, fixations, demands and more, they are in some way enhanced and rounded out by it.

This is a book we all should read. For whilst it may not necessarily expand our understanding of ourselves, it will vastly increase our understanding of a human condition which is expanding exponentially before our very eyes. Perhaps too we shall realise that so many more people in our lives – people we work with, live with, intersect with – are on some continuum of the very acute condition from which Jonny suffers.

As Jonathan's story unfolds, and the complex interactions with him coagulate, I find myself marvelling that Sheila – Jonny's mother and our very present informer – has not gone completely mad.

'Pussy's in the well...' she intones. It is the umpteenth quickly delivered nursery rhyme in a few minutes. And whilst the couplets spew, Johnny somehow relaxes. Any break in the flow, and the demons of his world begin to rebel. The screeches return, the damp patches appear in his trousers, and the whole ritual of hosing down, both verbal and actual, begins all over again.

I have no doubt that writing this book has been for Sheila a cathartic experience. It is also one to read it. A remarkable human story, a remarkable piece of writing.

Jon Snow
October 2011

INTRODUCTION

WHEN MY SON was diagnosed with autism, I refused to believe it. I knew about autistic children – they were cold and unaffectionate, unable to relate to other people. Their problems were often caused by pushy mothers, obsessed with their children's success. As babies, they were indifferent to stimuli and difficult to feed; as toddlers they didn't learn to speak or to play pretend games. This couldn't possibly be my son. This was a child who had barely let go of me since birth, a voracious breast-feeder who had chuckled his way through his babyhood and who sat placidly every day looking at books or pushing play people round on their roundabout. This was a boy who smiled continually; who spoke precociously early and who knew all his colours at 18 months; who sang songs and recited nursery rhymes.

Well he *had* done all those things. Now he usually sat staring at his books, which were opened at particular pages featuring food. And the speech had largely gone too. Now it was repetitive and functional, interspersed with stra inappropriate phrases copied wholesale from someo

– echolalia I learned later was its proper name. Then there were all the things he had *never* done. He had never asked a question or thrown a tantrum. He was slow to crawl and slower to walk – not because he couldn't but because he just didn't want anything that much. It was an overwhelming desire to get hold of the cat that had got his older brother moving. What Jonathan was short of in his early life was curiosity and desire.

Jonny's journey into autism was a relatively unusual one. Most autistic children don't develop speech at the appropriate age. They are often difficult, unsettled babies who struggle with feeding. The timing of our diagnosis was pretty standard though, at three years old, following expressions of concern from a health visitor. Most people's diagnosis results from the failure of their child to acquire speech. Ours came after the loss of it, coupled with increasingly difficult and obsessive behaviour. I was right about one thing, though. My son wasn't cold or unaffectionate, and I wasn't a pushy mother. We had, and have always had, a strong and loving relationship. Nowadays, people are less likely to hear this nonsense about cold mothers and children who can't love when they get the devastating news that their child is autistic. But they still hear an awful lot of drivel.

Autism is hard. It's hard to have and it's hard to live with. But our beautiful children are still just that – beautiful children. We may have to fight for them and, quite often, with them. But they are individuals like anyone else, part of the family with ties and attachments just like anyone else. They might have a different way of showing them, but autistic children have feelings and emotions like the rest of us – some so strong that they can barely cope with them.

Jonny is now in his 20s. This is our story so far.

Chapter One

———

A DAY IN THE LIFE

Dawn. A thump on the wall and the desolate cry of a wounded animal. I am in there almost before the sound waves hit the eardrums of the other sleepers. 'One at a time,' I pray, 'and this one first.'

He is banging his head against the wall, Thomas the Tank Engine quivering on his chest, blond curls preparing themselves for another masochistic assault. The smell of urine is overpowering. You might think the best thing I could do is to gather him in my arms, comfort him, get him out of the sodden bed. But you would be wrong. We are in another country here, where the customs are different, the language strange. I don't actually speak at all. In here words can be dangerous, adding to the heady cocktail of terror and bewilderment. In here a word of kindness could ignite it, send the whole lot up in one ghastly conflagration. He's only nine but he has made windows fly. I crave coffee. Did I lean over my husband and start the machine? How they all sleep! Fear is out with all his knives and only we two are awake.

I don't touch, speak or look. I sing. Sitting on the stinking bed, just out of his reach, looking away from him at the wall, I start on *My Bonny Lies Over the Ocean*. Twice through and he's still banging, though watching me surreptitiously. I move onto *Ding, Dong Bell, then There was an Old Woman* and *Hush Little Baby*. For a minute I think I've won, as the prettiest little baby in town watches for a second or two before the next resounding crash. But I move on. *Little Boy Blue, Oranges and Lemons* then back to *My Bonny*. He stops banging his head and starts to cry. It's over.

I still don't look, but I hand him a tissue. He uses it to smear snot from his nose across his cheek. I give him a biscuit and go to run the bath. The crying has ceased and the flipping of my heart settles to its customary ache. When he sinks that neat row of teeth into your arm, you think there can't be anything worse, until he cries like this and sorrow washes the walls. I run into my bedroom and press the button on the coffee machine. It gurgles into life and the smell alone is enough to fill me with pleasure.

In his bedroom, he is watching the morning light through fingers splayed open in front of his eyes. I undress him and take off the saturated nappy.

'Bath,' I say, 'bath, sweetheart.'

'Bathy, bathy.' A sudden squeal of delight and we are home.

Ten minutes later he is in the bath, pouring compulsively from a plastic tub. The puddles on the floor are mating and mutating into a lake. I don't care. It's heavy-duty vinyl, the bed is stripped, and I have glorious caffeine flooding my system. The trick is to get washed and dressed before the tidal wave which will mark his exit. People who talk about multi-tasking don't live with autism. It is a jealous companion.

It's 8.30 and the first desert has been crossed with the aid of breakfast, cereal and videos. We have worked our way through a box of spinners and flappers and will need to move on soon. One sleeper has left and the other two are stirring. It is the school holidays and I must produce a day like a stream of brightly coloured ribbons from my sleeve. I'm halfway through the second book of nursery rhymes when Ben appears at the door. He looks in, dressed and ready to be off, but hesitant. Wanting to go, worried to leave. What disasters might occur in his absence? The fair hair is darkening, the voice veering between high and low. He hovers in the space between childhood and adulthood, pausing at the cliff edge that is adolescence. In his case, there are extra fears. If he leaves us watching at the top, will we manage? Is it safe to launch himself off? Who will carry Jonny over when his turn comes? He's his brother, and he is heavy.

'Joe's going down to the woods on his bike. Can I go?'

'Yes, of course. Have you had breakfast?' He looks at the bag of crisps in his hand. 'Go on then. We'll be out, I expect. Take a key.'

He looks for a second or two. Jonny is agitated by our conversation, irritated that the nursery rhymes have stopped. His 'Peesa, peesa' has become an ever more persistent back-drop to our conversation.

'He's saying "Please".'

'He wants more rhymes. Could you read a couple while I go to the loo?'

Ben eases himself between us and takes the book. 'Come on, Jonny, let's do *There Was an old Woman*.'

A ghost of a smile flits across Jonny's face as his brother sits down to read to him. You're not sure you've seen it, but you have. Feelings of pride and despair accompany me to the toilet.

He's persuaded to leave, reassured that we're all right, just as the last sleeper awakes and appears on the landing. She's five years old and dwarfed by one of my old t-shirts. Rubbing her eyes, her face framed by a waterfall of curls, she smiles and my heart sings just to look at her.

'Hallo, Jonny.' She talks to him as she talks to her dolls, with careful kindness, adult tones overlaying the play. He ignores her but flaps his plastic spinner even harder. He's pleased to see her.

Hannah is dressed, after a fashion, and eating cereal while I try to think about the day. Thinking is tricky in this sleep-deprived, pared-down place. What do they both like? How can I get one through without trauma and the other without boredom? Well, he loves water in any shape or form – droplets catching the light, the shimmering sheet flowing from tub to floor, the ribbon of liquid from jug to cup to table. He loves wind and the feel of air on his face. He loves food. He loves tall structures, leaves and large spaces. He loves his sister, his brother and his father. He loves me, even when his forehead crashes into my face. He loves the play of angled light on oblique movement. He loves that place we all love, where it is comfortable and safe; the place we fit into, the space made in our own image.

I will take them on a walk through the woods to the stream. I will take wellies and pourers, toy people and a picnic. What are the logistics? The forward movement required to get us there, passing, as we will, all number of flappable objects; the confidence that we will get back, walking all the way there and returning without major incident or refusal to move; the making of the picnic at a time already stretched thin. I decide to risk putting him in the garden.

He's on the climbing frame, rehearsing the repetitive jump he's been working on for two years. The bars on one part of the frame buckle regularly. I turn them round until they are fatigued and then order new ones. They tire, but he never does. He looks all right. She's standing on a chair, a huge apron covering her ill-assorted clothes, ready to make the picnic and chatting as she spreads enormous amounts of butter on the slices of bread I hand her.

'Can we have little sausages, Mummy? Sadie and Tammy like little sausages 'cos they're little. They don't like cheese, they certainly don't. We devastate cheese, ugh!'

We wrap up the sausages and I slip in some cheese anyway. It's almost normal. Then I remember to go and check. I don't want another neighbour at the door asking me if I have a child with a green sweatshirt because he's up on their shed roof, and, no problem, but they're a bit worried for his safety. The worst I expect is his perfect balancing act on the topmost bar, but he isn't there. I rush out to look, stilling the panic. Then I see it – the arc of banana skin through the air, an accomplished lob followed by one of eggshell and another of tea bags. Each item of compost falls in perfect sequence onto our neighbour's garage roof. He is squealing with delight. I fetch chocolate.

In the lane our progress is slow. There isn't any point trying to hold hands. She has a companion in each, with whom she is earnestly conversing.

'Now, then, Sadie, we are going for a picnic in the woods, and you must be good. No, we don't have ice cream, I've told you before. How could we keep it freezing? Now, don't sulk, or I'll take you back home. Tammy is being a delicious girl. So you must be abiding too.' They stare blankly back at her like sad giraffes, with their felt-tip make-up and their long, deformed legs.

He will only scrunch up his fingers and whimper if I take his hand. I don't want to upset him. All the behavioural therapy in the world won't alter the fact that there are other lives to consider, other childhoods happening here. I watch intently for the sign that he is about to run. But he is concentrating on the leaf he is flapping. One finger is in his ear, though, just in case. Sound is a tricky enemy, bursting upon you suddenly and invisibly. He is quietly providing his own barrier.

'Ticka, ticka, ticka,' he says. Just like a time bomb.

The grey has faded and the sun is breaking through. It will be an early summer's day like the ones in the storybooks we read, with flat expanses of primary colour and unblemished skies. Trees and houses will sit square and confident in this world of certainty and exuberance. Everything and everybody will know their place and be happy in it. Children will be laughing. These days I'm ambivalent about laughter. I listen like a code breaker. When she laughs it's like a shower of sunlight in clear air, a firework fountain of silver brightness, and with Jonny it's sometimes like that too; the pure unsullied joy of high winds blowing through his hair, or the ecstasy of raindrops on his face. Fairground rides, where I cling on to rough metal and the jagged edges of fear, move him into a place beyond happiness. But the surfaces are thin, membranes that can be pushed with a little finger into something else. When he was in his buggy and the laughter started in supermarket queues or at the bottom of the playground slide, everyone would smile and nod at this beautiful child giggling at his private thoughts – for the first few minutes. As it stretched into the unacceptable length and the hiccoughing into sickness, the smiles would freeze and I would move on. That's when I learnt that laughter is like crying. You can simply have too much of it.

We cross the road and move slowly into the wood. They can't run in front of cars now and I relax a little. We're stopping a lot, but progressing. The wood is blissfully quiet, with no sound louder than the rustle of leaves and the crack of twigs underfoot. There is birdsong and the buzzing of insects. Sunlight drips through the trees, landing in little pools at our feet. Aconites and primroses are scattered around and we seem to be alone in the world. We walk carefully. Sadie and Tammy are still complaining about the absence of ice cream. They are difficult children. The path slopes downward through the wood, with leaves and ferns that can be flapped till they break and then easily replaced. There are stones that can be thrown with no danger to neighbours. There are all manner of things that can be put in the mouth. This is an enormous joke. We know we aren't supposed to do this. I spoil the joke by ignoring it, but she remonstrates.

'Jonny, take it out, silly boy.' He is better practice than dolls, a true innocent.

We come to a tree felled by April storms, lying across the path. Its fall has crushed the ferns underneath and the cracks in it are crawling with insects. There has been no time for the moss that covers other such casualties to form, and it is easy to climb onto. He scrambles on and she sits for a rest, poking at woodlice with a twig. I sit beside her and watch Jonny jump off the log over and over again. He sits down.

'Bumpy.'

'No it's not, Jonny,' she says, patting the tree, 'it's smooth.'

'Bumpy.' He takes my hand.

'Oh, he wants *Bumpity, Bumpity*.' I sit him on my knee and sing. 'Bumpity, bumpity bumpity bump, as I was riding my charger. Bumpity, bumpity, bumpity bump, as proud as an Indian rajah.'

It's how we used to get down the stairs. He laughs and laughs and I notice a wet patch on the front of his trousers.

'Quick, Jonny, wee wee.' I pull down his pants and try to get him to lean forward. We have spares, but I'd rather leave them till later. I pull the trousers up again and he whimpers a bit so I grab his hands and move them both on.

At the stream, I take off the heavy backpack and get out their wellies. I give him a spade, and her the box of little people. And for a while I sit and watch them. Somewhere else in these woods, my other child is recklessly biking or swinging on carelessly tied rope. I wish sincerely for his safety and close my eyes for a second. These two are deep in their games, he sending an ever-higher spray of water from his spade into the air, she creating an entire metropolis of miniature waterside life. Occasionally people walk by. They stop and smile, consulting the maps in plastic wallets round their necks. I hold his hand to stop the spray of water from his spade drenching them. I try to chat about the fascinating old footpath and the rare orchids, all the while hoping they won't stay long.

We eat our picnic, the giraffe women with their own little plates. I change his clothes. I discuss with my daughter the difficulties of bringing up these women-children with their permanently arched feet and ridiculous breasts. She sits on my lap and we watch him together. I let myself off the usual pastime of wondering what she and her other brother think of it all, whether it be for good or bad. I just hold her and know I'm glad for her, glad for all three and the little bit of space they occupy in the universe.

Getting back is harder. The path is steep and we are tired. In the end we resort to *Ready, Steady, Gody*. It involves a lot of stopping and starting and a great deal of pulling heavy children up the sloping path. But it works and soon we are back in the lane. I am tired, tired, tired. I would like to lie down on the pavement and close my eyes. Maybe I would never open them again. Maybe I would lie back in the sweet arms of rest and sleep forever and ever.

'Look, Mum.' She grabs my arm, pointing upwards and I look.

There, arched against the sky is a tree overflowing with white blossom. It shimmers with whiteness, sings and shouts with it. It dances before my eyes, taunting me with joy, flaunting its beauty. I reach out to touch it and it fills my cupped hand with fragrance. It is the most beautiful thing imaginable. She holds up her arms and I lift her to touch it. She puts her face right into the blossom and grins. We drown in its scent and brilliance. Then she kisses my cheek and says, 'Shall we go home now?'

Chapter Two

———

DIAGNOSIS

It was a day entirely drained of colour. I remember thinking, when she took us off into another room to take details and move things on, that there should have been branches tapping on the window, intimations of disaster, signs and portents. But there weren't. It was quite still outside – midwinter, but not even particularly cold. She felt sorry for us. I could feel the pity oozing from her, the not knowing what to say. Poor woman, I bet she wished she'd never asked to come. She will have to get used to it, though. It will happen to her over and over again in her career.

Jonny is ignoring the bricks he's been given, preferring to flap his boat. He holds it up, just to the side of his eyes watching. The little blue plastic fish taps on the side of it. Tap, tap, tap. There is no other sound. We're sitting, in the corner of a large room, on chairs made for children. Dr Lomax, who is writing, is tall so she must be very uncomfortable. I am comfortable on children's chairs but my mind keeps flying away.

'Sorry, could you repeat that?' She remains patient, telling me again, writing things down.

In the assessment room, she has watched and listened carefully. She is only a locum and wants the old paediatrician to answer the question that has puzzled her. What is wrong with this woman's son? Why is he in the room with them, but oddly not? He can walk, he can talk, he sits quietly on his mother's knee. But it isn't right. Something about the quality of it is all wrong.

The secretary, told to bring an extra coffee, smiles kindly at me, 'Milk and sugar?'

'Oh, it isn't for her,' says the old paediatrician, 'it's for Doctor Lomax. She's going to sit in on this.' Once their coffee arrives, the assessment begins.

Jonny whimpers as I sit him at the little table, and displays a complete lack of interest in little dolls and teddies that might want to move here or there, or give each other this or that. He doesn't care whether they are under or on the table. He wants to flap his boat. And why does he have to line up four bricks to make a 'train'? Everyone knows a train doesn't look like this. He loves trains, watches them every day from the window. He plays with toy trains, wants train books read to him, looks at pictures of trains, has birthday cakes of an Intercity or a Thomas. He doesn't like this woman who asks such pointless questions, and he isn't going to give her the benefit of the little bit of speech he has left by naming the pictures she holds up to him. He wants to go back home with me and line up cars. Or sit with his books, open at pictures of food and spread around him on the chair. He wants me to push him in his buggy by the canal, stopping to throw any bread he hasn't eaten to the ducks. He wants to wait outside the school for his brother to rush out, full of curls and enthusiasm, and then sit with him in front of the television, drinking juice and waiting for tea, bath, bed; familiar rituals, getting more rigid by the day.

And once it is over I sit in another room with Doctor Lomax, on chairs made for children, with the tap-tapping of the boat and the little boy labelled and explained, while the grey sky seeps into my soul and she tries to tell me what will happen next. Once she has finished, we put on our coats and leave. I lift Jonny into the car, strap him into his child seat, put on a tape of nursery rhymes and start the car. His eyes are still wide and blue, his blond curls still beautiful, his lovely little podgy hands still clutch the boat. Nothing new. But all is new. There is a word in the car with us that wasn't there this morning. It will never leave us now. It will direct, inform and bind our lives from this moment on.

At the hospital whole trains of events have been put into motion. The quality and content of our lives for months to come is set. But just at this moment in time, no one else knows. His brother and father are ignorant of our new status. We can carry our secret with us for a few hours yet, like a bomb that will blow everything apart and must be carried very carefully. Once it explodes, it will leave a permanent crater in our lives. A parent's worst nightmare has just begun and a whole lifetime of telling and explaining is about to begin. Jonny smiles as the tape plays and I edge home through the traffic.

'Ding, dong bell. Pussy's in the well.'

'We're going home now, darling.'

'Home, darling.' Tap, tap, tap. I hold jealously onto the last few hours before I let it start.

And that's a question I'd like answered. When did it all start? This isn't how it is supposed to happen. Jonny didn't fail to acquire speech, he had no difficulty with feeding, didn't cry with distress. He was the sunniest baby on the planet. He talked, he laughed, he cuddled. He didn't walk or ask questions, though; didn't complain when I had to sit and prepare lessons instead of amusing him. Rather, he sat happily looking at books or setting his cars to run down the ramp of the toy garage before bringing them back up in the lift. Ping, ping, ping. He didn't seem to be interested in crawling or walking, and preferred his buggy to exploration. But he gazed up happily at me from his changing mat, singing the songs I had sung to him earlier in the day. We thought he was going to be an academic, a plump professor, uninterested in physical activity but glued to books. Or a musician. His intonation and retention of rhythm and melody were remarkable for a child of his age.

But where had all that speech flown? Why had the singing stopped? Why were the books that we had read with such delight permanently open at pages of food? It was as if we were moving backwards through something strange and frightening. People liked to reassure. They had known babies who hadn't been breathing at birth, been slow with crawling and walking. He would catch up. And listen to him talking – all those colours – he couldn't possibly have any problems with intellectual development. Give him time. Look at him with those piles of books. Even the doctors said the same – his breathing problems at birth hadn't gone on long enough to cause damage. The jolly orthopaedic consultant who had seen him on his second birthday, because he was still showing no sign of walking, had examined him carefully and smiled at me.

'Absolutely nothing wrong! He's overweight and flat-footed. Just give him time. He's obviously fine mentally. Clever little boy.'

The changes in speech – from sentences to reversed pronouns to single words, and in behaviour – from delighted laughter at books and songs to rigid lines of cars that mustn't be moved, were incremental and hard to explain. The health visitor, though, watching Jonny climb onto the table as she drank her coffee, said gently, 'There's something wrong, Sheila. Let me make an appointment for you. That isn't normal behaviour.'

In the evening the telling starts. At home first – before it spirals out into the wider family. My mother-in-law gasps and clutches me.

'Oh, no.'

She wants me to comfort her, but I have nothing to give. I am numb with shock. Then we must tell friends, and then the world at large. It's exhausting. A few days later, we get a babysitter and go out for a meal. We are dressed nicely, and the food is good but we don't know what to say to each other. We don't really know what it all means. We can't quite believe it will be that bad. Jonny is such a lovely boy. A profound sadness hangs over the evening, but we have hope. We can do things to stop deterioration, we think. As the days, weeks, months and years stretch on, we find out just how bad it can be, just how little we can do.

A few days later my own sadness develops into a nightmare that will last for the next few years. My husband Bob, just home from work, says casually as I come down the stairs, 'Joan asked me today what trauma Jonny has suffered.'

'What?'

'She says that's what causes autism – trauma, or a cold upbringing. She told me about some books.'

I feel the world spin round again, as I did in the room with the little teddies. Coldness? Trauma? I sit on the stairs to steady myself, feeling utterly betrayed. I do not just have an autistic son to care for. I do not just have developmental delay, degenerating speech, difficulties with social interaction, a whole lifetime of interventions from people I do not know, but certainly need. I do not just have another child, and later a third, whose needs will at times get pushed to the margins, who will have to try to love someone who screams and head-butts if they touch him at the wrong moment. I do not just have all this. I also have blame. It is all my fault.

I read books – Kanner, Bettelheim, Tinbergen. Some of my contemporaries – the intellectual mothers of my acquaintance, steeped, as we all were in theories of insanity caused not by nature or chemical imbalance, but always by environment, life, our parents – are sold on the whole mad theory. I plough through accounts of ducks and rats. I learn about autism and about my place in it. I must be a 'refrigerator mother', someone who puts intolerable pressure on their children, or perhaps just one child from the family, scapegoated to set the others free. I cannot believe what I am reading. I adore children. I cuddle and talk to my sons. I play and sing and laugh with them. Seeing them happy and secure is the most important thing in my life. The world continues to spin. Jonny has not changed. He is still odd, affectionate, plump and lovely. But everything else has. For the first precious seconds of every day, it has not happened. Then I remember who and where I am, and the nightmare resumes.

Autism – the word – I learn from Kanner who first coined the term, comes from the Greek *'autos'*, meaning 'self'. It describes children locked inside themselves, unable to relate to other people, completely self-absorbed. They have no social abilities, frequently have difficulties with speech – always with communication – cannot, or do not want to, 'read' people in the normal way. They sound to me like changelings, magically appearing in normal families to infect and subvert. I cannot think of anything worse than a child who cannot love. I begin to look with envy at families with Down's syndrome children or those with cerebral palsy. Until one day in a toy shop, while Jonny happily pushes a wooden train round a track, I watch a beautiful young woman lift her beautiful son out of his wheelchair to play and know that her slight body will be broken in a few years time. But how can I have caused this perversion in my son? I am ashamed, but even then a little rebellious. Why one child in the family? Why a good mother like me? It doesn't make sense.

Deciding that perhaps some 'normal' intervention might help, I make an appointment with a local nursery. I want to enrol Jonny, see if we can't encourage him to socialize, get him doing the things he won't do – paint, model, build things. The owner sees us after the other children have gone. It looks nice and I'm feeling optimistic. He's bound to make some progress here, regain some speech. There are paintings strung across the room, mounds of play dough, boxes of Lego.

'Sorry to keep you waiting,' she says and her smile is bright. She looks at Jonny, impassively beautiful in his blue dungarees, sitting in his buggy flapping his boat.

'Um, I don't think he'd fit in, to be honest. I don't really think we have the facilities. Sorry – I mean he'd probably be better off somewhere else, wouldn't he?'

Walking home, we stop to feed the ducks. Jonny eats the bread whilst I stare at the water.

The playgroup is better. Social services pay for them to have an extra member of staff on his three mornings. He sits quietly looking at books, or cuddles up to the helpers when songs or stories are on offer. His speech almost disappears and the flapping gets more intense. I read and talk to him, spend time with our other son. In between, I torture myself. I had really wanted a girl. Maybe I showed this disappointment at the moment of his birth? What I remember, though, is what most mothers remember as they emerge from the maelstrom – relief that it is over, that this miracle has occurred, that the baby is safe and well and the most beautiful child you have ever seen. At that moment all trivial hopes of gender were subsumed and burnt away by the inferno of birth and the desire that I and my baby would survive it. What about the abrupt weaning? Could it have been that? I remember that hot, hot summer, feeding my voracious baby day and night. He, growing rounder and rounder as we sweated together, joined at the nipple. I was reduced to watching television indiscriminately and apathetically for hours on end, the housework left undone; or cooking one-handedly, my other arm holding my baby on my hip and nipple. My older son decided on guerrilla warfare. He needed the toilet always at the exact moment his brother latched on. A tummy upset in my fat baby gave me the excuse I needed. Milk made him vomit and cry in pain. I didn't feed him for a day, gritted my teeth against the bullet-hard breasts and never fed him again. He didn't

seem to mind. He was ready for cereal and took to it with equal gusto.

People didn't seem to want to talk to me about it. They didn't exactly cross the road because I wasn't exactly bereaved. But they were uncomfortable; worried that I might start a conversation they didn't want to be part of. I wondered if they had all read Kanner, were wondering which part of me was frozen solid. Later it occurred to me that it wasn't that at all. It was because there was no reason for it – no reason at all. These were people who didn't smoke, and ate carefully so that they wouldn't get cancer, made sure their children's food contained no artificial colourings, bought skimmed milk. They knew how to protect themselves and their families from life's vicissitudes. And here I was – one of them, a good mother, responsible, careful. Like them, I made play dough and cardboard models, read stories and sang songs. Though liberal in our middle-class ghetto, we knew that disturbed children lived somewhere else. My funny little boy, still reluctant to walk anywhere and squawking and flapping in his pushchair was a great worry to them. Because there was nothing at all wrong with me. And if it could happen to me, it could happen to them.

The wheels set in motion on that grey, still day, cause help to arrive almost immediately – speech therapy three times a week and a teacher coming to our home. Thus begin the years of matching and sorting. Jonny never reaches Key Stage 1, a fact of which we are reminded annually until he leaves school at 19. The home teacher has been forced to return to work because her husband has left her for another woman. She cannot believe that this has happened, that

suddenly she must work to earn money. She gets out bricks for Jonny to build and pictures for him to name. I listen to the divorce story again, while Jonny creeps away to his line of cars. I should be grateful for the help. I am grateful. Grateful and hopeful, as a mother should be, ready to work and try, try and work. There are days though, when I wish with all my heart that they'd all go away and leave us alone.

It's a nice sunny day when we start speech therapy. We're upbeat. Jonny is happy and I have decided to be optimistic. He used to be able to talk – although he's never asked a question in his short life – why shouldn't he again? Speech therapy takes place in the old clinic. I've brought the children here for their tests and injections, waited for my contraceptives. We're used to the place. The therapist is bright in yellow; enthusiastic, Japanese, lovely.

'Hallo Jonny, it's good to see you. Come and see all the lovely things I've got in here.'

He doesn't look at her as he flaps his boat. Out come the teddies and dollies again. And again they don't know if they're on or under the table. Jonny couldn't be less interested in their dilemma. He rallies a little when they want food and mumbles a couple of answers. We have to be quick to catch them – they are quiet and indistinct. But suddenly, when a picture is held up for him, we get a wonderfully clear response.

'Fire engine.'

It's a ball. I sink down, the magnificent wave of will-power on which I have carried us, ebbing more quickly than the evening tide.

'No, listen,' says the therapist. In the distance I hear a siren.

Walking home, it is as if all the beauty of the city is flooding down on us. Sunlit slopes rise from its golden heart. Trees line the horizon and, standing in the middle of town, I can see sheep grazing in the skyline fields. Jonny is clutching a beautiful little green-and-white bus which we got in France. I always slip it into his hand when I prise out the flapping boat. I like us to go out in disguise – mother and good-looking toddler with bus. Pushing the buggy, I try to listen to the sounds on the periphery of my hearing – things I would normally blot out so that I can think or talk to the person next to me. It feels overwhelming, a melee of sensa-tion bathing me in indistinguishable stimuli. Is this what it is like for him? Or did he just happen to hear something he is very interested in and decide to tell us about it? The speech therapist has given me exercises to try. I'm weary just thinking about them. I know he can, but won't. Or maybe could once, but can't anymore. Who knows? We turn into our street, and I look forward to forgetting for 20 minutes while we cuddle in front of children's television. When I unstrap him from the buggy, I see that he has lost the bus, dropped it but didn't say a word. He looks puzzled as I sit on the floor and sob.

Jonny is getting into his stride now. Each month brings a new aspect of autism to our lives. Far from turning back the tide, I am powerless and astonished by the inexorable strength of the waves. We are queuing at a checkout, moving towards the bright rows of sweets at child height, when Jonny, who had been sitting quietly in his buggy, begins to laugh. People smile at him.

'What a beautiful little boy!'

'What's tickling you, then?' But, as we move slowly

forward, the laughter goes on and on. There is nothing funny as far as anyone can see and Jonny is staring oddly into the distance. He starts to hiccough and gag. People who were smiling a minute or two ago, turn away, embarrassed. We make our purchases and hurry off. He laughs all the way home, eventually making himself sick.

But that is as nothing compared to the distress and anger he begins to exhibit. Jonny has always been placid and happy, an easy baby. But one morning, just when we have a houseful of children on a sleepover, he isn't happy. He isn't happy at all. I think he may have tummy ache or a sore throat. But how would I know? He won't point and he rarely speaks these days. He doesn't speak, but he does scream. He screams and screams. He hits and bites me, throws himself around. I bear it for a few hours, then call the doctor.

'Sorry, I don't know what to do.'

'I can hear him. I'll come.'

Bumps and thumps come from upstairs. They're playing He-Man and Skeletor. I hope for Ben's sake that their noisy play masks the wailing of his brother. The doctor is kindness itself. He has seen disability in children before and knows so much more than I about what is in store. He gives me some Valium, which I must try to give to Jonny. It sits in the cupboard for several months, reproving me. I make one attempt to get some into him, but don't succeed and never try again. Over time we find that getting him into the car and driving round is more effective. One such marathon lasts for five hours. Later, he is too big for this and we must manage as best we can.

Our house begins to show signs of autism. Lumps out of doors, breakfast cereal cemented to walls where it has been thrown and then set hard, watermarks on the ceiling where the bath has overflowed. Precious things are broken – vases and bowls bought for me by my other children, necklaces that have been yanked from my neck. We bear the signs too – teeth marks on our arms, scratches on our faces. Jonny's rage and distress seem to know no bounds. My usual stock in trade for soothing upset children is completely ineffective. Nothing could be worse than cuddling, stroking or gentle talk. I learn to practise the exact opposite of good childcare. I don't touch my distressed son, because that makes him wild with anger. I don't talk more than necessary because that makes him more distraught. I keep stimuli down to a minimum. I learn to get him into a safe place, stay on guard but not within reach, and wait. It is the hardest thing. I learn to watch and listen to my son. I know the books are wrong, but I'm not at all sure what is right. I have to learn to understand his world from the inside.

We're waiting at the hospital. We've seen the paediatricians again. There's nothing more they can do. I learn quickly that the medical profession loses interest quickly when cure or physical treatment is not an option. A sense of failure hangs over the appointments, a feeling that they would like us to go. Eventually they cease. What I need is help with management of an incurable condition, help to help my son. This, though, is not available. They've suggested some tests, so we're waiting for an encephalogram. We're called into a room and the technician, a middle-aged woman in a white coat, smiles at Jonny who is moaning softly. She speaks gently to him.

'Hallo darling. It's OK. We're not going to hurt you.' She looks at me.

'We need to put these on his head and lie him down.'

I look doubtful. 'He hates things on his head.'

'Does he like Smarties?'

'Loves them.'

'Let's try that, then.'

Nothing abnormal shows on the screen. Later I learn that autism never does.

'Happy birthday, Jonny.'

It's his third birthday and he's lying in bed in his train pyjamas, under his Thomas the Tank Engine duvet. His walls are festooned with train pictures – many of them drawn by his brother. He smiles, his chubby face sleepy, his golden hair dishevelled. He still has enormous blue eyes.

'Let's get you dressed and go and see what you've got for your birthday.'

I get the nappy off, clean him up and dress him in trousers and a new Thomas jumper. Then we do *Bumpity, Bumpity* down the stairs, he on my knee and laughing. Downstairs are his presents. His brother opens the presents and cards for him, patiently showing him each one, putting cars into his hands and reading him books. We have splashed out on the plastic ride-in car that he has always loved to play with in the toyshop. He doesn't seem as thrilled as I was expecting him to be, but he gets in. Ben has a friend staying and together they push Jonny round. They are so encouraging.

'Isn't it lovely, Jonny? Aren't you lucky?' Over the next few weeks, Jonny takes to sitting in this car for long periods of time, getting in it before he is dressed, drinking his morning juice from his Tippee cup. He doesn't move, but likes to be in it, at least.

In the afternoon we have a party with jelly and biscuits, crisps and a Thomas cake. I've taken a lot of trouble over this cake. It is blue and quite magnificent, standing on liquorice rails scattered with hundreds and thousands. I think Jonny likes it. Friends arrive and we play games, dance and pass parcels. I hold Jonny's hands and dance him round to some of his favourite music, but I know he wants me to stop. He eats crisps and biscuits with the others and we all chat and laugh. He blows out his candles at the right time, but returns quickly to his jelly. Ben and his friend take turns in the car. Eventually everyone leaves with pieces of cake and I bathe Jonny and put him to bed. When I come into the dining room to clear up, Ben has both hands in the hundreds and thousands. His mouth is smeared with colour and he grins widely.

I decide to beat the autism. I decide to teach my son to do things. We start with simple jigsaws. He learns to put the wooden pieces into the cut-out shapes. Then he learns to sort the cutlery, putting it in the right compartments. I read and read to him. I get him to finish sentences that I start. I set up pretend play and lead him through. I am exhausted, mired in denial and a complete refusal to believe what I have been told. I cuddle him and note every emotional response triumphantly. I teach him to count. I get him clean and dry in the day. Later on, I realize that it isn't the diagnosis that's wrong – it's the whole way autism has been categorized and described. This isn't caused by trauma or coldness. It isn't psychosis caused by emotional deprivation. They may not be able to see the damage in his brain, but I know it is there. My son is disabled. As time goes on, I read much better books. Books that tell me about the theory of mind – that my son cannot understand that other people may hold different views or knowledge from him in their minds.

Suddenly his frustration, and his lack of interest in telling me what he wants or that he has tummy ache, becomes comprehensible. He thinks I already know. How obtuse of me not to give him what he wants! I read about sensory overload, and the inability to order sensory information. Then I understand why my touch may be too much for him, why his fingers are in his ears again. I read about the inability to predict situations, to learn from the past. When he is screaming, I get close enough to feel the rapid beat of his heart. And finally I understand how very frightened he is.

We are by the canal at the back of our house, watching a boat go through the locks, when I realize what the central problem is. Jonny is, as usual, in his buggy. The canal here falls into a basin, forming a little lake before flowing under the road and down to the other locks. Jonny is excited by the sudden rush of water from the lock as the water level drops. He flaps the boat even faster, arms and legs quivering. He watches till the flow of water stops and then loses interest. But I stand looking for a while. There's a Georgian terrace behind the lake with a white wrought-iron bridge leading up to it. Afternoon sun falls on the golden stone, reflected in the water. I never cease to wonder at the beauty.

'He lacks imagination,' I think. And it all falls into place. All the problems with predicting events, the fear of change, the comfort in sameness, the social and communication difficulties stem from this. I think about how many times a day I imagine what is going to happen; how I use this ability to manage the future, the events of everyday life. I start to understand that fear will be reduced if all this uncertainty is reduced. I start to try to fill in the gaps

for my son, to tell him what will happen, to provide for
him the pictures his own mind won't produce in order to
make his life tolerable.

It's 7.30 pm on a warm summer's evening. The children's
rooms are at the front of the house and sun streams in at the
end of the day. We are tired, but we have them in bed at last
and sit down to eat in peace. We have the window overlooking the garden wide open. There's a soft breeze and a view
of flowers and trees; behind them, the sky is still blue. The
scent of nicotiana wafts in. Halfway through the meal, the
doorbell rings and I'm surprised to see a neighbour on the
doorstep. She lives across the road and runs a guesthouse.
She looks a bit embarrassed.

'Um... sorry to disturb you.'

I look enquiringly at her.

'It's just your little boy.'

'Sorry?'

'I mean, did you know – well he's balancing on the windowsill. I mean I don't want to interfere, but it'd be awful
if he fell.'

I race up the stairs and open the door as quietly as I can. In
Jonny's room the curtains are billowing in. I left the window
open because it was so hot. I thought he was asleep. He's not
asleep though – he's perched on the windowsill, leaning outwards, laughing. I stand completely still and think. I mustn't
shout or rush to him. I mustn't do anything suddenly.

'Jonny?' I almost whisper it. He ignores me completely.

'It's all right, darling.' I am walking very slowly towards
him as I speak. When I am close enough, I grab him and
pull him onto the bed with me, clutching him tight. He's still
laughing as the curtain billows in with the evening sunshine.

I left the window open. For days I ask myself whatever sort of mother I can be. As for Jonny, he is quite happy. Not as happy as he was balancing on the window ledge, but completely unaffected by the event. The love of heights doesn't leave him till he is in his mid-20s. Over the years it manifests itself in different ways, developing from excited balancing on the top bar of his climbing frame to the thrill experienced from the edge of a cliff or the summit of a hill. I usually try to hold onto the back of his tee shirt or coat, but he shakes me off. If there is wind – or even rain or snow – the joy is even greater. He never acquires any awareness of danger. Luckily his sense of balance is acute. He has never fallen.

It's mid-afternoon and the room is a mess. We're having building work done – a kitchen extension, and a loft conversion to provide another bedroom when the baby arrives. It's dusty and there is constant banging. There are bare floorboards and exposed pipes. There are only garden chairs for us to sit on. Then the builders finish for the day and suddenly it's quiet. I say goodbye to them and lie back in one of the canvas chairs, tired by my pregnancy. I know my baby doesn't have Down's or spina bifida. As far as they can tell, all is well. They wouldn't be able to see autism, of course, but I feel I've done all I can. I know she's a girl, so that immediately reduces the chances. Jonny, sitting on the floor playing, looks at me and then leaves his traffic jam, climbs onto my knee and lies against my swollen body. I close my arms around him and sing. His long eyelashes flicker, then close, and I close my eyes and sleep too. His body is soft and warm against mine and for half an hour we are completely at peace.

Chapter Three

BIRTH

I'M DETERMINED NOT to go too soon. I time the contractions and guess at the dilation. Unlike some of my contemporaries, I have no desire to give birth at home. They might find the technology threatening, but I find it extremely reassuring. I'm not, however, planning to go to the hospital a minute before I have to. Once my contractions are strong and regular, we drive to the maternity unit and it all seems a bit chaotic. It's a short night – the one when the hour goes on, and a large number of women have gone into labour. The suite is fairly new – it's modern and bright. I'm in a little room, up on the bed, ready to lie down and give in to it, go down the long tunnel. There is no sense of when the end of it will come, only of the walls of pain that close around you until it's over. The dilating women now outnumber the midwives and a nurse runs in to check me. Seven centimetres.

'Right Mrs James, I see this is your third.'

'No,' I howl. 'No, no, no.'

'Sorry, sorry. Wrong notes. I'll get the right ones. Don't worry.'

But I do.

I've been moved into the delivery suite. My legs are open and there are people around me. The pain has changed and I know I'm near the end.

'Nearly there. Well done, Sheila. Pant, that's it. Don't push for a minute. Easy, easy. Here we go. Don't push. There – it's a boy, a lovely boy.'

But even in that moment, that dislocation of pain, gas and air, I hear them muttering together. I'm straining to hear in my fog. I want to know what is wrong. The cord was round his neck, and they cut it before he was quite delivered. Now he's safely out and they lay him on my stomach. It's how you're supposed to do it these days – gently, bonding. Vernix-covered, he is white and still.

'Is he dead?' I ask.

'No,' they say, but he is whisked away.

They suck out the mucus that is blocking his nasal passages and get him breathing before giving him back to me. I hold him and get him on the breast. He takes a couple of sucks and I am happy. But his tubes fill up again and he gives a little cough before they take him again to get him right. All newborn babies have blue eyes, I know that. I know it's nothing special. But his are huge and fringed with long, long lashes.

'Just like his brother,' I think. 'It's going to be all right.'

It isn't really all right, though. They are fussing far too much.

'He's cold,' the midwife says and I look puzzled. 'He's in shock.'

I expect them to take him away to an incubator, but they don't. So many women giving birth on the shortest night of the year. I worry, but they seem amazingly competent. I have a bath and the nurse tells me it's not that unusual for a baby's tubes to be blocked, or for the cord to be round the neck. They just need to keep an eye on him. They're so reassuring. I think it will be all right. Down on the ward, he's put in the little crib beside me. They've tilted it so his head is low and the mucus can drain out. His hair is dark and starts far back on his head. His little fists are clenched.

'Try to get some sleep,' says the nurse.

'Not likely,' I think.

You can't sleep on maternity wards anyway, even little four-bed ones like this. All through what is left of the night, the baby opposite cries.

'Feed him. Feed him,' I think.

But the young mother changes him, pats him, tries to soothe him, anything but get out those sore, cracked nipples to give him what he wants and endure the pain again. I ask for a plastic tube to suck out the mucus, and watch my baby. They have put on a little hat and bootees to try to get him warm. Blue for a boy. Periodically, the breathing stops and I clear the mucus. Eventually, one of the midwives comes in and sits on the bed next to me and I realize they've been discussing the situation.

'Would you mind if we kept him with us till the morning? You could get some sleep, then.'

I agree and he's wheeled away. But I can't sleep and I wander out to look for him. He's lying by the nurse at the desk, asleep in his Perspex crib, head down, breathing properly. He is wearing the little old-fashioned nightie I brought in and has a blue, cellular blanket and blue Humpty

Dumpty quilt wrapped round him. They have put a fan heater next to the crib to warm him. I'm not quite sure what to say, so I say nothing. Where on earth did the fan heater come from? Shouldn't he be in special care? I'm too dazed and exhausted to articulate my thoughts. I suppose they must know what they're doing. Later, I sleep, and in the morning they bring him in.

'His temperature's perfect now. Everything's all right.'

They're busy all day with the young woman next to me. Her baby is jaundiced and every few minutes someone else comes in to give her a different piece of advice. Eventually she breaks down and cries.

It's visiting time and I'm listening. Several seconds before he arrives at the ward, I hear my other son running up the corridor, chattering, excited. He comes into the room and stops dead, suddenly quiet. Ben has masses of blond curls and is clutching a tiny teddy. Jonny and I are by the window, clean and tidy – he's wearing a clean gown and the bootees; I'm in a pink striped nightie. We're sitting in a big armchair.

'Over here, sweetie, here's your new brother.'

He approaches shyly, excitement drained away, over-awed. He holds up the little teddy.

'Hallo, baby. I've brought this for you.' Jonny lies impassive in a pool of sunshine. Ben tucks the teddy under his brother's arm and I hand the baby to his father, and take my three-year-old onto my knee.

'When are you coming home, Mummy?'

'Tomorrow, darling.'

'Is the baby coming too?'

'Yes, he is. He's our baby, your little brother. Remember, we talked about it?'

'Yes.' Ben snuggles into me. Later, when they go, he looks sad.

'See you tomorrow,' I say and he brightens.

'Bye, bye, Mummy. Bye, bye baby Jonathan.'

On my second day home we watch Playschool and make a big cardboard car out of the box the fridge came in. Ben has been cutting and sticking. He's painted the car and I have used split pins to attach cardboard windscreen wipers to the front. Ben is happy. Mummy is home and she isn't that different. We still watch Playschool every day and then make something. Although I have no artistic ability at all, my older son has a precocious amount and my days as a primary school teacher stand me in good stead for all the painting, drawing and model making I encourage him to do.

For the first few days Jonny is very content, carried from room to room with us in his Moses basket, causing very little distraction. On this second day, we carry the box car outside and Ben plays in it under an apple tree heavy with buds. The garden is full of daffodils, the days are getting longer and I am experiencing postnatal elation. Pregnancy always makes me feel vulnerable and anxious. This particular nine months was a nightmare, and I am very glad it is over.

I remember thinking, 'This isn't good, this can't be good for the baby.' But as people told me, women go through all sorts of things when they are pregnant – even war and famine – and produce perfectly healthy babies. I'm yawning in front of early morning television with Ben, when I notice it. The nausea of early pregnancy has passed, but I'm permanently tired, desperate for sleep that is in short supply. Ben has a large, almost finished, Lego boat in front of him whilst he keeps an eye on the cartoons. It's 6.30 on Sunday morning and Bob is having his weekly lie in. Ben's boat is impressive. Every morning he amazes me with the intricacy of what he produces, the concentration, the magnificent result. Most of all, though, I'm amazed by the way he casually takes it to pieces the next morning to start something new. I've been rubbing my arm and when I look down, I see a patch of red, peeling skin. By the evening, I find large areas of my body are covered in similar patches. The doctor tells me it's a skin condition that will take six weeks to clear up. It leaves me feeling embarrassed and debilitated. Luckily, the six weeks are up just as it reaches the edges of my face.

When my body begins to look normal again, I start to sneeze. My temperature rises and rises but I steadfastly refuse to take a single painkiller in case it damages my baby. I am feverish, delirious in the night, waking with no idea of where I am or what is happening. We call out our doctor, but a locum comes.

'You've got 'flu. It'll go. Bed and lots to drink. Any problems with the pregnancy?'

'I have high blood pressure.'

'Well, nothing like a week in bed with 'flu to bring blood pressure down!'

The influenza is accompanied by blinding headaches and nosebleeds, followed by weeks and weeks of coughing. One morning Bob, ready for work, says 'goodbye', leaving our son in bed with me.

'You aren't going, are you?' I ask feebly.

'Oh, you'll be all right,' he replies. 'Get my mum to help you.'

I step out of the bed, dazed with fever, and fall straight back into it. I lie there for a while, as the room spins round, then I make a supreme effort to pull myself together and get on with the day.

My own doctor tells me he thinks I may have whooping cough. Every day is a struggle. I wake weary and go to bed beside myself with exhaustion. Eventually, eight months into my pregnancy, I wake and clear my throat, producing a large amount of infected mucus. I can hardly get out of bed. I take my son into town and, coming out of a toyshop, I know I cannot go another day like this. I go to the doctor, who examines me and then speaks gently.

'I'm going to give you some antibiotics.'

'You can't. The baby. I can't take them.'

'You've got pleurisy.'

'What does that mean?'

'That you'll have pneumonia within two weeks if we don't get you well. It'll be dangerous for you to go into labour like this.'

I give in, take the drugs and recover quickly.

Now, at home, with a lively toddler and a baby, feeling well, I am in my element. I'm sure I can cope with it all. And Jonny seems to have survived my unhealthy pregnancy and his unhappy birth without any ill effects. I'm dropping Ben off at playgroup. I park the car and take him in holding his hand, and my baby close against my shoulder. The playgroup is in an old church. It's dark when you go in, until your eyes get used to it. The big hall – once the main body of the church – is kept for the climbing frame and big toys. Toddlers in cars and trains circle the pulpit. The 'quiet' area, where you first come in, has been separated from this with a stud wall. It's cluttered with easels, tables with play dough, and little carpeted areas with books or boxes of cars and dolls. The other mothers come to look at my baby.

'How's it going? Isn't he lovely?'

'Oh fine, he's a clone of his brother. I've got another lively one on my hands.'

We get on with life and I forget all about the night the clocks went forward.

I'm sitting up at the dining-room table, preparing lecture notes. My part-time teaching job turned into a full-time one, and so I resigned. But we're short of money and when one day a week teaching music comes up at Bob's college, I take it. I start off teaching the same thing six times in succession to six different classes on my one day of work, and know I will go mad if I do this every week. I can't remember, halfway through the third lecture, what I've said and what I haven't. I'm working hard, preparing lessons, so I can vary the day. Jonny is sitting quietly on the floor amusing himself with a basket of books. Outside, it rains steadily and the bare branches of trees are blown about in the wind. Jonny is no longer a clone of his brother. I cannot remember when the change started, but he is placid and easy, perfectly content to amuse himself. He shows no sign of wanting to crawl and, at eight months, is still sitting propped up with a cushion. I look at him 'reading' his books and feel guilty. I ought to be playing with him, reading or singing to him, stimulating him. But he is so happy. In contrast to his late physical milestones, his speech is advanced and complex. People tell me that children who are not breathing at birth are often slow with crawling and walking. His other abilities make everyone sure that there are no major problems. He'll catch up, they tell me.

He's still within an acceptable developmental timeframe. He's happy. We spend plenty of time doing things together. I get on with my work.

It's early morning. Jonny is lying on his changing mat whilst I take off his nappy. He smiles at me and waves his arms in excitement. His face is round and his thighs are rolls of fat. He really ought to be moving about by now. But he's still beautiful. The blue eyes got bluer and the black hair fell out to be replaced, just like his brother's, with a mop of curls the colour of sunlit corn. He's excited because I'm singing – learning by repeating over and over again the songs I plan to teach my students. Their placements are in multicultural settings and I'm teaching myself some Caribbean songs that are new to me.

'Pull away, me boy,' I sing. 'Pull away, me boy.'

My fat baby looks up at me, blue eyes clear, singing, 'Pull away, me boy, Pull away, me boy.'

He has the words and the tune – amazingly accurate for this young child. 'Well,' I think, 'he may not be crawling, but we might well have a musical genius on our hands.'

It's Christmas Day and time to see what else Santa has brought. The stockings have given up their treasures so we get dressed and go downstairs. I open the curtains to a morning crisp and clear against a luminous light-blue sky. Outside is like a different world today. It won't impinge on us. The lounge is magical, lit only by Christmas lights and smelling of pine. By the tree are piles of presents and plastic sacks full of surprises. I prop Jonny in the corner of the settee. He's nine months old and still needs support just to sit up. He's happy – his tongue stuck half-out as it always is in these days of constant teething. I've dressed him in dark-blue velour dungarees and a navy-and-cream striped jumper. He looks lovely and laughs constantly. A ring of bells was in his stocking and he's shaking it enthusiastically. Lots of his presents are musical and a wooden xylophone soon emerges. Ben is unwrapping as fast as he can and showing his brother each new toy.

'Look Jonny, look what Father Christmas has brought you!'

I put a cushion behind Jonny when I sit him on the floor. He has the xylophone beaters in his hands, legs stuck out, hitting the instrument and repeating the words that are said to him. His brother takes the other set of beaters and they hit it together, laughing.

Eventually a sea of paper covers the entire floor. Every present is unwrapped. Bricks, cars, dressing-up clothes, things that tinkle and ring and chime and roll are scattered everywhere. Dinner needs to be served. Jonny will sit in his highchair, happy with turkey and mash, gravy and carrots. Both children are high with excitement. Jonny sits surrounded by all this Christmas chaos, with a plastic barrel rammed into his mouth. He's my funny little boy. He loves his brother. He loves his presents. Who cares if he can't crawl? He's perfect.

Chapter Four

———

SCHOOL

W HAT'S REALLY WORRYING me is that he might not be able to walk across the playground. He's never gone this far without the pushchair, and maybe they won't want to take a four-year-old who can't walk such a short distance. This is the only provision for autistic children in the city. I know for certain – despite the current fashion for integration – that Jonny cannot cope with, and will not get the help he needs at a mainstream school. This unit, for children with autism and language difficulties, is attached to a local primary school. If they decide to take him, we're told, then he'll mix with the other children here anyway. I hold Jonny's hand, willing him to make it, and smile brightly at the two women who run the unit.

'He has a diagnosis of autism, but I'm not sure about it. He used to have very good speech and he still has some. I mean, sometimes he really surprises us and says something we thought he'd forgotten...'

I look to Bob for verification and he agrees.

'We wonder if it's all still there in his head somewhere. He doesn't speak for days, then he'll come out with a really long sentence – words we didn't think he knew any more.'

'Oh, might well be. We could probably get him talking again here. Who did the diagnosis?'

I tell her and she exchanges a look with the other teacher.

'She said he couldn't learn but I've taught him to do jig-saws and some sorting and to count to ten.'

They nod and smile.

It's another colourless day, mild and grey, early spring. Jonny manages the walk, although it's slow, and once we get into the unit we all relax a bit. There are two classrooms, one for infants one for juniors, with a lot of nice equipment. Between them there's a little foyer where we sit. Jonny is given some books to look at.

'Tractor,' he says, beautifully clearly, and I could kiss him. 'Lovely tractor.'

'Oh, we'll be able to get him going,' says the main teacher. 'We'll certainly be able to do something with him.'

A secretary comes out of her office and makes us coffee. Everyone is so kind, so understanding, so in agreement with my assertion that the diagnosis was wrong.

It's break time and we're invited to stay for it. The chil-dren in the junior class, all in school uniform, join the infants, who are not. They all sit in a circle and we sit with them. Jonny flaps his boat and I see the two teachers exchange glances again. There are four girls and ten boys, including identical twins. The classroom assistant smiles warmly at me as she gives the children their cups of milky coffee. They all take them obediently. The twins don't speak as they gaze at the ceiling. They start to slip out of their seats, but are swiftly put back.

'No, Richard. No, Robert. We know we sit till everyone has finished, don't we?'

They shuffle, but stay. There's a girl from the older class – probably nine years old and very pretty, who gives out biscuits. She speaks carefully to the children. 'Here is your biscuit, Carl. Please take it.' I wonder for a moment why she is here. She seems nervous, though, and the speech is stilted. After she has given out the biscuits, she stands for a moment, her arms held stiffly up at her side, elbows uppermost.

'Sit down now, Sally. Thank you.'

There is a split second before she faces the speaker, and then she sits.

After the coffee break, the children go back to their activities. Some of the junior children are reading and some of the infants are colouring big pictures. The classroom assistant sits with the twins. She has her hands over theirs, gently guiding them to touch pictures as she speaks. They are both looking the other way. We get ready to go, and the teacher in charge walks us to our car. Outside the unit there is a little playground, separated by a fence from the one used by the main school. It has an expensive safe surface covering the tarmac and a wonderful wooden climbing frame.

'This looks lovely,' I say.

'Yes, the local rotary has a fete for us every year. They paid for it. We've got lots of friends.'

Another charity brings a big bouncy castle for the children every week, we're told. This is enjoyable and very good for them.

'We don't give in to the autism here. Some of the parents let them get away with it at home. The twins' house, for instance – it's completely bare. There's nothing out in case they break it or climb on the furniture.'

'Oh dear.'

I feel quite flattered that she's talking to me like this.

'We can see you're not like that.'

'Well no – I just don't think they've got it quite right with Jonny.'

A couple of weeks later, we're invited back again. I make sure we leave the boat at home. Jonny holds a toy tractor instead, which he sucks. But I'm frightened that he'll scream if I don't let him have something to hold. It's a warm, sunny day. Driving up, we pass verges full of daffodils and trees in blossom. At the unit people, including some of the parents, are outside on the grass. They greet us cheerfully.

'He can sit here,' says the woman who teaches the infant class.

She takes Jonny's hand very firmly and before he knows it, he's sitting on the grass with the others. 'Please stay,' I pray, and to my amazement he does. They are giving out swimming trophies and certificates. I can't believe the distances these children have swum. It's so impressive. Everyone is clapping and some of the children grin. The twins are still impassive but they are taken up, hands held, to get their certificates. 'How on earth did they get them to swim?' I think. Afterwards – Jonny has been taken off into the classroom – I chat with one of the mothers.

'They're wonderful here. Carl has made loads of progress – unbelievable really. They told us not to expect anything much at the hospital, but he's really getting on well. We think he might be able to move into the proper juniors next year. We never thought they'd get him into the water, either. He used to be terrified of it!' She's clutching a 25-metre certificate.

'That's fantastic,' I say.

'When did you get your diagnosis?' We talk and she explains that the teachers here have friends at the university, where they use the pool. Later, the teachers say that Jonny's brother can go with them if he has an in-service day any time. In fact, he can come up to the unit anytime he's free. I'm so pleased.

'They both love swimming,' I say, 'Although Jonny's still in armbands.'

'Oh, he'll soon be swimming. You'll see.'

Every morning, I wake hoping; hoping that I'll hear today. After a couple of weeks, we get a telephone call. They'll take him after the Easter holidays, once he's four.

A taxi comes to take Jonny to school every day, and the nice classroom assistant is his escort. He starts off with a couple of mornings. I go too, but they seem very keen to get him in full time and without me. It's a much shorter introduction to school than my other son was expected to manage but they obviously know what they're doing. They talk a lot about their success with autistic children. And, they don't think Jonny really is properly autistic. He's got autistic tendencies, but really not much more than that, they say. They can certainly sort him out. I start fantasizing that we'll get him into mainstream school in a couple of years. This is clearly just what Jonny needs. They don't like children to miss school, they explain. Even if he's a bit under the weather, I should send him. They can give him an easy day.

We're getting into the swing of things now. Every morning I get both boys up and try to get Jonny to dress himself. He still wears a nappy at night. It's hard, slow work to get him to pull up his pants, put his feet into his shoes. There's no question of his managing zips or laces, buttons or even poppers. They have made a couple of disparaging remarks at the unit about the way I do things for him and I know I ought to try to make him more independent. We're in the bathroom, nappy off, bottom clean. His hair is dishevelled, his face sleepy.

'Pull your pants up, sweetie. The taxi will be here soon.'

You wouldn't have thought he'd heard me. By this time, though, we've had a hearing test and can be pretty certain that he has. He gazes at something in the far distance and flaps his boat. That's a struggle, as well. He absolutely mustn't have the boat at school. I gently prise it out of his hand, replacing it with a sweet, every morning. The escort helps me. She knows there'll be trouble if he appears at school with it.

He goes off happily every morning, but isn't really making any progress. On the contrary, the deterioration continues. He speaks less and less. Even the echolalia is infrequent. His moods are now completely unpredictable. My placid baby has disappeared completely. It's a struggle to get him to do anything for himself in the mornings, and the pressure is always to have him ready in time for the taxi. It's the same at night. He's usually sweet, flapping and squawking. He loves his bedtime books and mostly complies happily with dressing and undressing. But he does not see any role for himself in the process. I am pregnant with my third child. I am tired. They want me to stop him indulging in any autistic behaviour. They want us to fight the autism, purge him of it. I'm happy to try to do that, but it's very, very hard.

It's a beautiful sunny Saturday for the summer fair at Ben's school. We have gone to a lot of trouble with his fancy dress. It's on the theme of television characters and he's an inspired Edna Everidge complete with gladioli and card-board twirls which Bob has made, stuck to a pair of glasses and painted. We try it out in the garden and the students living next door come out to laugh and admire him. One of his favourite TV actors will be presenting the prizes – taking a few hours out from appearing at the theatre – and he's very excited at the thought that he might win. I'm very pregnant now, and wearing comfortable dungarees. Jonny's in a little pair of shorts and a yellow striped tee shirt. He'll like the roundabouts and bouncy castle, I think. It's always a good day, especially in weather like this. There'll be lots of our friends there, ice creams, games, plants to buy. The children will be running around, safe within the school grounds. I'm going to make Jonny walk – no more buggy these days. I've got to stop babying him.

It all goes well. Ben wins the fancy dress. Both the children have ice creams. I get some nice plants and Jonny laughs as he swings round on the roundabout. The sun shines all afternoon on the big field. Looking up, I see trees filled with green on the skyline. We chat with friends, updating them on the pregnancy and Jonny's school. He's having a go on the bouncy castle when someone speaks to me and I turn away for a moment. As we chat, I feel a hand on my arm.

'Sorry to disturb you, but is that your little boy?'

I turn to look. Music is playing and children are bounc-ing in time to it. They laugh and scream in delight, holding hands, seeing if they can fall on their bottoms and bounce up again.

'It's just – I mean, he might get hurt, they're falling all over the place.'

In the middle of the melée, surrounded by bouncing children, one little boy lies on the plastic, his body moving up and down as the other children jump and run from side to side. He is holding a toy boat, which he gazes up at, ignoring the feet landing close to his head. A blue plastic fish sways backwards and forwards above his face as the children bounce and the music plays.

The doorbell rings and I go to open it. Jonny's on the doorstep holding the escort's hand, and I can see all is not well. She grimaces.

'Bit of a bad day. You might want to change him.'

Jonny is moaning softly, often the prelude to an evening of distress and violence. His brother has started to give him a bit of a wide berth which saddens me beyond measure, although it's the sensible thing to do. I just pick Jonny up. I know I'm not supposed to. I'm not supposed to treat him like a baby. I'm not supposed to pick up anything heavy at this stage in my pregnancy. He can really kick and scream when he's unhappy. But I just want to get him in and sorted out before anything starts. In his bedroom I change him and see that the insides of his legs are red and sore. He smells a bit, so I wash him and put cream on. I suppose he must have wet himself, but he doesn't usually get sore like that. I give him biscuits, read him some stories and he calms. We're back from the brink this afternoon. It isn't always like that.

It's a cool summer evening and I'm at home alone with the children for the night. Bob has gone on a college trip to London and won't be back till the early hours. My baby daughter sleeps in her pram in the hall, which is almost dark. She's a couple of weeks old and, although she makes little noises from time to time, I hope she'll sleep till her next feed. The two boys are upstairs in bed, Jonny dozing after his stories and Ben listening to his tape player. I'm tired, just finishing the washing up and pouring a glass of wine, hoping to sit quietly for a while in the fading light; hoping for a few minutes peace. I'm halfway through the glass when I hear, from Jonny's room, the soft moaning that I have come to dread so much. I always hope it will come to nothing. It always comes to something. The moans become louder and are accompanied by thuds as he moves into the howling stage. In a moment I know he will begin to hurl himself round the room. As I stand at the bottom of the stairs in the gloom, listening, hoping for a silence that I know will not come, my daughter begins to cry for her next feed. It's a whimper at first, building to the full-throated cry of a hungry infant. Upstairs the howls and thuds grow louder and more frequent. In his room, Ben turns his story tape up to full volume. I stand at the bottom of the stairs, completely alone, with my baby crying for a feed and my autistic child in enormous distress, trying to decide which of my children must be left to cry.

It's a big day for us today. We've been offered some respite care by social services and have been up to see the home several times; Jonny has spent some time there by himself. It's a big house at the end of a country lane, with a climbing frame and a trampoline in the large garden. Some of the children who come here won't be using those. They lie on blankets, dribbling and clutching toys with which they occasionally hit their faces as their arms flail about. Some are strapped into wheelchairs so they don't fall out. All are lovingly cared for and spoken to with humour and care. The bedrooms are cheerful and there are lots of toys. The staff has gone to an enormous amount of trouble to find out what Jonny likes and doesn't like, what his routine is. They've been to our house, seen his bedroom, talked to us and to his brother; taken time with him, played with him, read to him, got his trust. They've been to see him at school and to talk to his teachers. They know what music he likes, what juice he prefers. Now he's going for a night. I've talked to him about it. I've packed his bag. His teddy, boat and favourite books are all in there. The plan is that he will go to school as usual, be taken on to the respite care from school and be picked up again in the morning. Bob has bought steak for a special treat, and we have a bottle of wine. We're looking forward to a whole evening without stress, an uninterrupted night's sleep.

By 8 o'clock, Hannah is asleep and Ben is reading in bed. We've set the table with candles, put on a tape of jazz. There have been no phone calls, so all must be well. Everything feels peaceful, calm, strangely quiet. I finish the clearing up whilst Bob cooks, putting away clothes and toys. In Jonny's room it is quiet, the last rays of the sun giving just enough light to make out his Thomas the Tank Engine duvet and pillowcase, his train pictures, his toy cars. I have tidied his shelf of books full of tractors and diggers. His trousers and jumpers hanging on the rail are shadowy in the fading light. I sit on the bed for a while, eyes closed, wondering if he's OK. And then I find I am crying, crying and crying, thinking about my beautiful little boy, wishing he was all right, wishing he was here.

Halfway through the next morning, the phone rings. It is Linda from the respite care, the young woman who will be Jonny's key worker there, the one who would have tucked him in last night, read to him, cuddled him. She sounds agitated and I feel the waves of alarm that so often accompany news of Jonny.

'I wanted to tell you what happened yesterday. Don't worry everything's all right. He was fine, not upset at all. He's gone off to school really happy.'

'So, why the phone call?' I think. 'It's nice if she just wants to reassure me about him.' Something tells me, though, that it's more than that.

'When we unpacked his bag, his boat wasn't there.'

'Really?' I can't think what could have happened. It was the one thing I was quite certain went in. 'I did pack it. I made sure.'

'I know. I knew you would have. I rang the school.' Her voice is stiff with suppressed anger. I'm puzzled, full of unease.

'They had it there.'

'What?'

'They went through his bag to see what was packed for him, and took out the boat.'

'What?'

'So, we went up and got it.'

They don't meddle with his things again. Jonny settles into a pattern of going to his respite care one evening a week and one weekend a month. He goes on trips, and plays on the climbing frame. He seems happy there. They have a good supply of incontinence pads and are happy to use them. They make care plans and try to identify and avoid triggers to distress. He often shares a room with Euan who's the same age. The first time we see Euan, I wonder why he's in respite care. But each time we see him, there are changes; his face a little fatter, his speech a little less distinct. He and Jonny giggle together, long into the night. One day they smear their poo on the walls. They both, I'm told, think it's hilarious. I meet Euan's mum, who is nice but sad.

It's Jonny's fifth birthday and we are going to have a joint birthday party with his 'friend' from the unit, whose birthday is a couple of days later. I've made a teddy cake, and Tim's mum has made a train with 'Tim and Jonny' iced on it. Tim is small and quiet, speaking very rarely. He comes over to our house with his mum, dad and older brother. The garden's full of daffodils, but there's a cold wind, so we stay inside. We have jelly and ice cream. I light the candles on the cakes and we stand the boys on their chairs.

'Blow the candles out, boys,' I say.

They hesitate and Tim's mum says the same.

'Come on boys, blow them out.' They blow without looking at the cakes, as we all sing *Happy Birthday*. The brothers and sister all make tremendous efforts to do a birthday properly – encouraging their brothers to take part. They open presents and exclaim. They pass a parcel, holding Jonny and Tim's hands as they help them unwrap a layer when the music stops. They play with the toys. They are so very, very sweet and we all do our best.

The children always get a birthday at the unit as well – a party and a cake.

'You don't need to do one, if you don't want to,' the two teachers say. 'He can have his birthday up here.'

We do, though, all continue to have parties for our children, make cakes, light candles. Quite a few joint parties are held, one at a city farm where Ben does a magic show, another at someone's home where Sally leads the children in running down a slope, holding their hands tight, saying 'Come on now, don't be babies.'

We mothers exchange glances – she has caught the intonation exactly. Later, as the children eat their tea and we
drink coffee, Sally's mother tells me she thinks things will
be easier for me in the future than for her. I'm dumbfounded

'What?' I say, thinking, 'What does she mean?' Sally can
talk, dress herself, read, for goodness sake.

'Sally'll never be independent, though, will she? She'll
always need to live with us and she'll never be bad enough
to be looked after. She knows she's different, as well. That's
already starting – wanting to know why she can't go to
school with the other children in the road. She knows that
she doesn't understand what they're talking about, that she's
always getting things wrong.' I look at Jonny spooning jelly
into his mouth. Quite a lot of it is down his jumper. He's
absorbed in it, smiling. Perhaps she's right.

The doctor recommends a referral to the family support
service. I am very, very resistant. I don't want my family to
be branded a 'problem'. But I need help. I am exhausted,
torn into three pieces and desperately unhappy that the support and care of my children is such a struggle. I decide to try
it once. A woman contacts me and assures me that it will be
quite appropriate for us to see her. We won't get branded as
anything. It's hard to manage an autistic child. It transpires
that she has worked in London with an eminent psychologist on a project for families with autistic children. She is
nice, Irish, intelligent, on my wavelength. First, she sees us
as a family and then visits Jonny at school. Fairly quickly,
she homes in on me. She offers to see me once a week, to
talk about managing Jonny's behaviour and anything else I
want to talk about.

'I'm babying him too much. I do too much for him.'

'Yes, they seem to think something like that. I think you're doing a magnificent job.'

'Do you? What did they say?'

'They just kept looking at me when he couldn't do things.'

'He's still in nappies at night.'

'He's five and autistic.'

'Is he?'

'Yes, you've done really well to get him dry in the day. When did you last have a proper night's sleep?'

'About three years ago. But he could talk – autistic children never start to talk.'

'Three years – good God. How are you managing?'

'Don't know – I just do. What about the autism?'

'I have a paper for you to read about late-onset autism.'

She comes to the house and we sit on the squidgy sofa in the living room, surrounded by toys, while the children play. Ben and Hannah regularly come to show her books and models, dolls and teddies. They draw her pictures of us sitting together talking. She says 'thank you' very solemnly. Jonny lies in the canvas playhouse, flapping his boat, tired from school.

'You've got a lot of toys,' she says. Ben tells her a joke, and she laughs.

I start to have weekly sessions with her. We talk about Jonny and we talk about me. I continue to manage, knowing that my session with her is only ever a few days away.

Every year the two teachers take the children to 'camp' at an outdoor centre on Exmoor. There are beautiful photos up in the unit – one of the children at the base of a cliff, wild with joy as enormous waves crash in around them. I want Jonny to be able to go.

'We can't take anyone still in nappies.'

'It's only at night, he's OK in the day.'

'We aren't changing nappies. If you want him to come, he has to be out of them. We can't be expected to undertake nursery duties.'

Strictly speaking they're not nappies – they're incontinence pads for disabled children. Once a month I go up to the continence service at the local hospital and get another carload. They're always kind and helpful there. I've tried a few times to get Jonny dry at night, but it results in broken nights, enormous amounts of washing, frustration and exhaustion all round. I must have another go, though. I can't have him left behind because of this.

I explain to him what we're doing. He gazes out of the window. I tell him I'm going to wake him up and put him on the loo every night. Sometimes I do. Sometimes I just can't face the hours of screaming and crying that follow. He's always wet, anyway. I change sheets four, five times a night. Jonny becomes exhausted and continually fractious. It feels like living on the edge of a volcano. Sometimes he erupts; sometimes I manage to calm him. I wash and dry bedding continually. Jonny gets a cold and then a cough. He coughs and coughs for weeks on end. One day he can't stop. I decide he's too ill to go to school and tell the escort I'm keeping him at home. An hour later, the phone rings.

'Where's Jonny?' It's the teacher in charge.

'He's really bad this morning. I've kept him here.'

'We told you we can always manage.'

'I didn't think he could.'

'You baby him.'

'I'm sorry. I thought he was too ill.'

'Send him tomorrow. He'll think all he has to do is sniffle to get a day at home.' In the background Jonny coughs away.

The family therapist has contacted the continence service and an advisor comes to see me. She asks some questions and I tell her the story. She's quiet for a moment.

'Your son's five?'

'Nearly six.'

'And autistic?'

'Yes.'

'Can he talk?'

'Not much.'

'Dress himself?'

'With help – not shoelaces or buttons – anything like that.'

'He's dry in the day?'

'Yes.'

'Then why does it matter about the nights? You've done really well to get him dry in the day.' I explain about the camp.

'Well, he doesn't have to go.'

'I don't want him to miss out.'

Her voice is very gentle. 'I think you should use the pads at night. Neither of you can go on like this. You're both exhausted and what's the point? He's got serious problems – this is a really small thing.' The next night I pick up a turd from the floor. The night after that I put him back in the pads and we all sleep.

I talk to the educational psychologist. He arranges to meet me with the unit staff and the head teacher of the main school. It's the first time I've met this woman and she doesn't know who Jonny is. The unit staff feel 'their' children are best kept away from the main school. The psychologist introduces everyone and asks me to explain what I'm concerned about.

'I want Jonny to be able to go to camp with the others.'

'We can't be expected to take a child in nappies.'

'Incontinence pads. I've been advised to continue using them at night.'

'Well then, he can't come to camp.' The head teacher looks alarmed at the way things are going. She says nothing.

'That's not fair on him – the others go.'

They look at each other. 'We'll take him but we won't use nappies.'

'OK,' I say, and I think, 'You try'.

Jonny's away for five days and on Friday we all go to collect him. I'm very excited at the thought of seeing him again. I hope so much that he had fun, that he got to see the big waves. I imagine him laughing as the spray showers him, his arms and legs wobbling in excitement at the huge, huge sea.

'Maybe they got him dry at night,' I think. 'They got a child terrified of water to swim.' We go into the unit. The children are in another room, allowed out, one by one, as their parents arrive. Jonny is let out of the room and I am astonished when he runs over to me. He looks absolutely exhausted.

'How was he?'

'Fine.'

They turn to other parents, greeting them warmly. Ben hugs his brother. We pick up his bag and all get into the car. After we drive out of the school gates, I turn and give him his boat, which he holds tightly. When we turn into our road, he says, 'Home.'

He wets the bed five times that night. The next night we go back to the pads.

Then night after night it is the same. I drift off into a fitful sleep and wake to the low moaning that heralds the start of this night's session. There is absolutely nothing I can do. Night after night my son experiences terror and distress, rage and self-harm for several hours. I try every night to lessen and stop it, to help him and myself, but nothing avails. I get into his room while he is still moaning, hoping he will not wake Ben. His light is kept low with a dimmer switch; the effect is quite eerie. He is writhing in the bed.

'Jonny. Jonny, darling.'

I keep my voice quiet and calm. He ignores me. The noise level rises and rises and the quality changes. Moaning becomes screaming. He is no longer half asleep in the bed, but sitting up banging his head on the wall, clawing at his stomach. I try to hold him, comfort him and he bites my arm, throws himself onto the floor, kicks me, screams and screams. Every night, my little boy, fair-haired, blue-eyed, six years old, hurls himself through a journey to hell and back. And he takes me with him, head-butting and scratching if I get too close. I close my eyes. I know it will end, as it ended the night before, and the night before that, but at this moment I cannot believe it. I love someone who is in complete torment. I love someone who is attacking me for trying to help. I cannot help; cannot reach him.

Eventually it blows itself out. The howling decreases, then stops and changes to normal crying. For the first few nights, I try to hold him at this point. Soon I realize that this pushes him back into torment. He cries wretchedly for some time. If I touch him, speak, even, it makes things worse. I must leave him to ride the wave alone. After the crying he is quiet and I lift him back into bed. Sometimes I read to him till he sleeps, sometimes just sit, not touching, just there, until his breathing becomes even. I return wearily to my own bed, never knowing if my presence has made any difference or not. I lie awake with pains in my chest and despair in my heart. One morning I wake and realize that we have slept all night. I get him ready for school and I decide that they will never take him to camp again.

Ben's been up to the unit quite a few times now. I think how lucky he is to be able to go swimming when his school has an in-service day; how nice it must be for Jonny to have his brother there with him. Jonny has learnt to swim really quickly. I can't think how they've done it. He loves water, but I was never able to get him to give up the armbands. Ben has another day off and I assume he'll want to go. He's a bit quiet when I mention it and then, in the morning, as I am putting swimming trunks and towels into a plastic bag, he says:

'I don't want to go.'

He looks down and mumbles. It isn't like him at all. I'm really puzzled. Perhaps he's beginning to get embarrassed by the situation. It was bound to happen.

'OK. Are you sure?'

He nods.

'Are your friends doing something? You don't have to go with Jonny if you've been invited to something else.'

He shakes his head. Jonny goes off in the taxi on his own and Ben plays in a desultory way with his Lego. These days it's spaceships, made with tiny bricks, and even smaller lights and controls. I make a cup of coffee and sit down, watching him for a while.

'Why didn't you want to go? Is it embarrassing? It's OK if it is. You never *have* to go with Jonny.'

'They threw me in the deep end. I didn't like it.' He doesn't look up from his model. 'They said if I can swim then I shouldn't be frightened of the deep end.'

We don't speak for a minute or two.

'Did they do it to anyone else?'

'Yes, they do it to get them to swim.' There's a pause whilst he puts together a particularly fiddly bit. 'And I don't like lunch.'

'The food's bad?'

'I don't like it.'

I'm quiet, torn between wanting to hear and wanting never to know.

'They hit their hands with a spoon if they don't use their knives and forks properly.'

'That's bad.'

'Yes. I'm going to watch television now.'

I stand in the kitchen, looking out at the garden, not seeing.

We're up at the Christmas play – *Jack and the Beanstalk*. They've been rehearsing for weeks. The children who can talk are doing well with their parts. The staff has gone to enormous trouble with the costumes. Jonny's playing one of the money bags and he's doing well. He comes in at the right moment and stands where he should. He's wearing a costume made of sacking with a green pound sign sewn on, and a hat made of the same sacking and with the same sign.

'How did they get him to keep that on his head?' I think. It must have taken weeks and weeks of drilling to get him to stand like that. He's holding hands with another 'money bag'. I think how beautiful he is, with his big, blue eyes, blond hair, open face. He isn't fat any more. He looks up, and sees me. His hands flap a bit and the other money bag holds on tight till it passes. I wave surreptitiously. The sun shines.

Afterwards we parents have mince pies and drinks, while our children are in another room. I'd like to give my money bag a hug – although he'd probably squirm and hate it. There's a new boy at the unit with striking dark curls and plenty of speech. His mother comes to say hallo. There's something of the old hippy about her, colourful clothes, beautiful red hair. She has five children. I like her.

'How's Jack getting on? He did well, didn't he?'

'Mmm.' She doesn't seem impressed. 'It ought to be good, they've spent weeks on it. They're getting children up from the main school to watch it tomorrow.'

'Jack's got a lot of speech, hasn't he? Jonny hardly talks at all any more.'

'Yes, he's got the speech, but he's really got the autism too. Very obsessive, doesn't have a clue what's going on half the time.'

I still find it surprising to hear her refer so casually to Jack as 'autistic'. There are one or two rebels, but mostly it's a dirty word up here.

'Is Jonny all right?'

'How d'you mean?'

'Not distressed about coming to school or anything?'

'No.' I don't really want to continue this conversation.

'You aren't worried about what's going on up here?'

'No, I mean I know they're a bit funny sometimes, but they do seem to help the children.'

She grimaces. 'I don't think they're helping Jack. He hates it here. I'm looking for another school for him.'

She wanders away to get a mince pie and I just stand for a moment. The unit head comes to stand by me.

'Jack's mum's got quite strong ideas about things,' she says.

I don't reply.

'We can't work with children if their parents won't co-operate.'

It's said with a smile but suddenly I feel very cold.

The escort invites us round for lunch in the holidays. Jonny's very fond of her and I'm happy to go. She's laid out just the right sort of toys for him and made us a nice lunch. We sit in the garden watching him play with pourers and a bowl of water, absorbed in the flow of liquid, happy. His golden curls catch the sunlight. It's a lovely day, a light breeze gently moving the branches of a row of huge beech trees at the end of the garden. But I've decided – I made up my mind before we came – I *will* ask. It seems such a shame to spoil the peace, but I can't pretend any more. These questions have to be put.

'At the unit...'

'Yes?'

Suddenly I know she was expecting this. It's why we were invited. She's in a difficult situation but she *wants* to tell me.

'Do they... I mean... do they ever... hit the children?'

'Yes.'

Straight out, no preamble, no excuses, quite clear. The world shifts a little on its axis.

'At lunchtime?'

'They tap them on the hands with a spoon if they don't hold their knives and forks properly.'

Oh Ben. 'What else?'

'If they wet themselves, they leave them in the pants all day to teach them a lesson.'

The sore legs.

'In fact, they make them wait a really long time before letting them go to the loo. They go on these long walks.'

'Yes, I know.'

'And they aren't allowed to stop for a wee. Jonny's all right. He doesn't care. He just ignores them and goes against a tree.'

I thank God for my wonderful son.

'But Sally, she's pale with worry and holding it in by the time they get back.'

'They don't like you, do they?'

'No. They'd like me to go. They make things quite difficult for me. But I don't intend to give them the satisfaction.'

The next day I take Jonny up to his respite care. I ask if Euan will be there and they tell me that he has died.

Jack's mum is on the phone. 'Can I come round?'

I feel really afraid, but I say yes. She's very agitated. They've just had another 'camp' – this time a real one under canvas, and only taken the junior children. Jack went. I have a bad feeling that this visit will be about that. I make camomile tea and we sit down.

'You used to be a teacher, didn't you?'

'Yes.'

'How d'you make an official complaint?'

'Against who?'

'That bloody unit. Those bloody women.'

'You'd have to go to the education authority.'

'They'll just cover it up.'

I feel faint. 'Cover what up?'

In her hand is a packet of photos.

I've arranged a meeting in my house. I have to run back from taking Ben to school and I'm out of breath, but I left the other two there to wait for the woman from the education authority. Jack's mum – the old hippy, laid-back, permissive, colourful, keeping Jack at home till she can find him a place in a Steiner school. And Stephen's mum – churchgoing, older, hair in a tidy bun, neat skirt and jumper. Between them, there's me, a sort of average. This woman isn't going to stand a chance. She's going to have to listen to a story told from very diverse angles. I get my breath back, make us coffee and then I start on my story. The camp, the nappies, the hitting with spoons, the throwing in the deep end, the sore legs. She blanches a little, but I can see she's not convinced. Stephen's mum, though, once she starts on her account, has evidence. She's taped her son sobbing and begging not to be sent to school. 'No, not Miss Smith, not Miss Smith. Please Mummy, please Mummy, home, home. Please stay home.' Stephen's mum is quietly spoken, not used to making a fuss or challenging authority. Usually she doesn't like drawing attention to herself. Today she's quiet but full of rage.

Then Jack's mum – our pièce de résistance – begins the final round. Jack was taken on the camp. Jack can talk. Jack can tell you what has happened to him and now his mum is going to tell the lady from the education authority. They went on a walk – a long walk. Jack was wearing his favourite wellies – the ones with duck faces on the front. Miss Smith says, 'They're baby wellies, Jack. Look everyone, look at Jack's baby wellies.' Jack has a tantrum and stamps his feet. He cries. He pulls off the wellies and throws them into a bush. And there they remain. Jack must walk in his stockinged feet all the way back. He is in agony, crying.

His feet are covered in cuts and blisters. The woman from the education authority looks doubtful. She's obviously got a bit of background on us all from the unit.

'Jack doesn't always tell the truth, does he? I mean, I know he's autistic and can't help it, but some of his stories…'

Jack's mum ploughs on. In the evening they make a campfire. Jack trips and falls into the edge of the fire. He burns himself.

We are all watching the young woman from the education authority. She's probably very nice and went into education because she likes children, is interested in their welfare. It's a bit irregular, coming to my house. Somebody must be worried. We know we have her within our sights now. We can see how anxious she is. Nothing they told her about us tallies. We don't seem like obsessive mothers who can't let our children go, won't let them grow up. And a campfire with such young children! What can have possessed them?

Jack's mum is on a roll now. She continues with her story. Jack is burnt but they don't contact his family. Instead, they take him up to casualty themselves. Jack's burns are dressed and he's taken back for another night under canvas. The first she knows of it is the next day when she comes to collect him. Jack is unbelievably distressed. He hasn't been to school since. The story is at an end. The woman is clearly shocked. We know and she knows that the A&E department will have records. We are all quiet for a few moments.

'It's possible they'll deny it all.' Stephen's mum holds up the tape. Jack's mum gets out the photos.

They let them take early retirement. We don't care. Just so long as they never get near our children – or anyone else's again. Not that this sentiment is echoed by all the other parents. Not at all. We feel the wall of hatred every time we go up there. We have been instrumental is taking away their saviours, their miracle workers, the women who will save us all from autism. One evening I see the saviours across the auditorium in the theatre and look away. In the interval, I lie low, afraid. A couple of years on, in the supermarket, I just glare back. The unit is soon re-staffed with kind and skilled special education teachers. No more miracles, but no more cruelty either. Jack never goes back to the unit. His mother keeps him at home till a place comes up at the Steiner school she's found for him. Stephen's mum and I start to look for other schools.

I don't remember what happened to the boat. Maybe we lost it. Or did the fish come loose and disappear down a drain or the back of a chair? Did he chew through the cord that attached it to the boat? It wouldn't have been any use for flapping without it. But whatever happened to it, he didn't have it with him when we took him to his new school. He'd become more adaptable about things to flap by that time. Outdoors, leaves and twigs would do nicely and were easily replaced. Indoors, slinkies – those colourful plastic springs that 'walk' down the stairs – were, and still are, a good staple. They tangle easily – but as long as you have a new one to hand it doesn't really matter. Jonny doesn't walk them down the stairs, although I showed him what to do. But he loves to sit or stand and let the spring fall away or to get someone to hold the other end and swing it. When it tangles, he gives it to me, saying, 'Fix'. The whole family has become very good at picking up cheap 'flappers' from markets and pound shops.

So I'm sure he's sitting quietly in the back with something to flap, listening to tapes, as we drive the 65 miles to his new school – a weekly boarding school for autistic children. He is, by this time, a truly beautiful child. All the fat has gone, and he's as leggy as any other eight-year-old. His hair is now light brown and very curly. His eyes, though, are exactly the same – huge, deep blue, fringed with extremely long lashes. His squint has largely disappeared and the general lack of symmetry in his features moderated. We, from the autistic fraternity, often discuss the outside world's view of us – the myth that all autistic children are beautiful, for instance. We know it's that faraway look that gives the impression of serenity, the lack of expression that leaves their faces pure. They are our saints or madonnas; with us in body but not in soul, lost in a holy trance, thinking higher thoughts. Jonny has everything he needs for the week in his holdall. He's has been away from home for more than a week by this time, when we've taken holidays with the other two children whilst Jonny goes into respite care. All the same, we're taking an eight-year-old who can barely speak, and who finds change distressing, to board at school from Monday to Friday, school terms, for the fore-seeable future.

This is how it goes: I am run ragged and I have two other children who are suffering neglect and constant stress because of the level of care their brother demands of me. Jonny will have to be looked after by strangers during his life, come what may. If I hang onto him, it will happen suddenly – when I have a breakdown or become ill. If I really endure it for a long time, it will be when I become frail or die. If it happens suddenly, it will be an emergency placement – unsuitable probably – for a person who has never become used to care. I decide that we must begin now. Slowly and incrementally he must learn to live away from us. And if we start now, then I can exercise a level of control over the kind of care and education he gets. Jonny's flapping happily in the back – he loves car journeys – something that persists to this day – but I gaze out of the window, consumed with sadness.

We've been to look at quite a few schools and this one is easily the best. There's no question that there will be any cruelty here; any belief that with enough willpower autism can be driven out of a child. They won't leave children in urine-soaked pants or force them to walk barefoot because they've thrown their shoes away in a tantrum. Stephen is already here, as well as a couple of others from the unit. They go by taxi on Monday mornings and come home on Friday afternoons. All the school holidays are spent at home. Jonny can join them in the taxi with an escort who seems very nice. We've done all the usual stuff – been for the day on several occasions, introduced Jonny slowly, talked endlessly about it to him, taken his brother and sister to see where he will be. It's a momentous September for them all; Hannah starting school, Ben starting secondary school and Jonny starting weekly boarding. And I, after four years of rarely leaving the house without children in tow, of giving up work and reading and singing and seeing friends and visiting family, of being a mother and nothing else at all, have found a part-time 'no work in the school holidays' job.

It was supposed to be perfectly straightforward – there's no provision for children like Jonny in the county – so they pay for him to go to a school outside it. That's what every-one told me. It's always like that. The other children from the unit were assessed and the places at the weekly boarding school were quickly approved. The funding followed as a matter of course. Once a week, the placements board of the local authority meet and approve all of the recommended out-of-county placements. The law says they must meet a child's educational needs. If they can't do that themselves, then they must find somebody who can. There's something in the air, though; something bad for people like us. There is constant talk in the press and on the news of 'over-manning' and waste. Stringent cutbacks are to be applied. Local authorities have been profligate with our rates, hospitals with our taxes. There has been a war. It's time for a bit of backbone in society, which, of course, doesn't actually exist. We must all take responsibility for ourselves a little more. The recommendation of the educational psychologist that the county cannot meet Jonathan's needs and should fund a placement for him at the school for autistic children named in his application is turned down, as is every other child's before the placements board on that day. It's never happened before.

We start a dance together. Bob contacts a pressure group that helps parents appealing against such decisions. So, we are well briefed. At the beginning of the dance, we circle each other. I tell the educational psychologist that Jonny's statement of special educational needs is severely lacking in many sections. I quote Department of Education Guidance, with references. The statement is rewritten by the next day. We get reports from everyone we can think of to be added to the statement. They are clear. Jonathan needs a school specifically for autistic children on a weekly boarding basis. He also needs transport and speech therapy. The local authority recommends a number of schools within the county for children with severe learning difficulties, which we go to visit. We ask at each one. 'Do you have any autistic children here?'

'No.'

'Do you have any staff trained in teaching autistic children here?'

'No.'

We take Jonny to one of these schools on another grey afternoon. It's in new buildings and has been strongly recommended. They have places. We go in to see the head teacher, Jonny squirming as I try to hold his hand and get him to sit down. Not that it matters. Every now and again I'm more than happy for him to show people his full range. We tell the head about Jonny's difficult behaviours and he smiles kindly at us.

'We don't know much about brain damage, do we?' he says gently. 'I often wonder if our children are in pain.'

There's an air of kind resignation about him. He knows Jonny won't come here, but, like us, he must join in the dance.

We go into one of the classrooms. It is new. It is light and airy. It is calm and warm. There is soothing music playing. On the floor are mattresses and blankets. On the mattresses and blankets are children. Some are quiet, others make noises. One little boy is crying, being soothed by a young woman, who is gently stroking his head. He looks about four. Jonny runs to the window, his feet dangerously near the head of the four-year-old boy.

'I'm sorry,' I say. 'He's not always aware of other people. And he's not very co-ordinated.'

'It's OK.'

I decide to keep a firm hold on him if I can.

'You take the children quite young then?' I'm looking at the little boy. His head is large, his legs bent. He's wearing a bib, dribbling as he cries.

'David's 12.'

Jonny has started squawking. Sometimes, because he rarely talks now and is often silent for long periods, I forget just how much noise he can make. In here he seems huge, loud, larger than life. He seems robust and healthy, which is exactly what he is.

'I think he might be a danger to some of your children, if he came here.'

'I'm sure we'd manage, but perhaps he needs specialist help?'

'Yes,' I think. 'That's exactly what he needs.' Although, of course, he will spend his life in the company of people who increase his stress levels, people who squawk and cry and hit and scream; unpredictable people who might suddenly head-butt or bite him. People to whom you'd like to give a wide berth if you don't like sudden and violent surprises. People just like him.

The dance becomes more intimate. Now it's a little more like a fencing match. We meet representatives from the authority. I've sent them a long document outlining, point by point, why the schools they have recommended do not meet Jonny's needs. I've cross-referenced it to the Department of Education Guidance. We sit in a circle. We are all courteous, calm. I go through my document, my face sweet reason, my voice low, the only one aware of the thumping of my heart. I am not sure how many more months I can hold things together. He's my child, but I cannot give him what he needs. And held within that failure is the knowledge that

I am also letting down my two other children. The education officers listen. They read what I have written. Then one of them tells us that we are right. They cannot meet Jonny's needs. He can go to the school we have asked for. The man who tells us this smiles amiably.

'I've taken a personal interest in this case. I'll be recommending to the placements committee that they approve funding for your son at the school you've identified.'

A favour, then. His special favour to us. Something they'd decided before we walked into the room. I don't care. We have won.

The sun has come out by the time we reach the school. It's a lovely, mild autumnal day. Jonny will sleep in a room with three others, where we unpack his things, name tapes carefully sewn on them all, even his flannel. We put his teddy on the bunk bed, and show him everything as he looks out of the window, or up at the ceiling or at his flapper. It's very hard to tell if he understands any of it at all. At a tub designed for water play, he suddenly comes to life and pours happily for a while before we go round the classrooms again, the play area and the field outside. We go through what he will do every day, the book that will come home every Friday to tell us what he's been doing and for us to write in an account of his weekend. We see the classroom kitchens, where he will learn to cook, the soft-play room where he will get massages or listen to soothing music. We look at pictures of walks and canoeing, of the centre where he can abseil up a gym wall or bounce on a trampoline.

'Look, Jonny,' I say over and over. 'You can swim here, or go in a boat. You can do cooking.'

'He likes cooking,' I tell them again. 'We make birthday

cakes. We have to hide them, though, once they're made. Once he ate all the icing off his grandmother's cake.'

We all laugh. All except Jonny. The head teacher is a very good-looking, middle-aged woman, blonde, well made-up, in smart but practical clothes. She is lively and friendly, her northern accent making her seem down-to-earth, approachable. Finally she looks at us and says quietly, 'It has to be done. There's no way to make it easier.'

And I know we must go now. I must leave Jonny and go home to my other children. On the way, I sleep.

It's Friday afternoon, warm and sunny. Jonny's been at the school for nine months now and it's time for him to arrive home in the taxi. He's last in on Monday morning; first home on Friday afternoon. I keep an eye on the lane so as not to keep anyone waiting once they arrive. We live in a cottage now, very old in places, much extended. It's down in a hollow; detached, with a very big garden. You'd have to come looking for it to find it. On the day we moved in, we had a thousand pounds' worth of fencing put round it to keep Jonny in, including large gates with a heavy lock. It's all too high to be easily climbed over. We went round to the nearest neighbours to explain to them we aren't unfriendly, that there are special circumstances. Our old neighbours, whose children leant over the garden wall to jeer at Jonny, are a thing of the past; as is the woman who parked her car in front of our taxi one morning. There were often no spaces where it could park, so it was in the middle of the road with the engine running. Other taxis and ambulances needed to get down to the other end of the road, where there was a special school for children with severe learning and physical disabilities – one of the ones we were later sent to look at. When the taxi didn't move off, I looked up and saw this woman's car in the way. She scowled as she wound down the window to speak to me.

'Sorry about that' I said. 'There's nowhere for him to park while I get my son in.'

'What's he need a taxi for? You're causing an obstruction every morning.'

'He needs it to get to school. Could you just back up a couple of yards and then they'll be out of your way? Thanks.'

She got out of the car, which was completely blocking the road, and slammed the door. 'There's a perfectly good school for children like him at the end of the road. I'm sick of you and your taxis. I'm going to see my daughter.'

She returned 20 minutes later and Jonny got off to school.

So now there are no obstructions for Jonny's taxi. The lane is narrow but we are right at the end of it. Tucked away. Private. I see it coming and go out to meet it. The escort opens the door.

'He's gone to sleep again.'

It was a regular occurrence. Poor Jonny – back and forth every week. Tired out on a Friday afternoon, getting comfortably asleep only to be woken up in a completely different place. We wake him gently.

'Hallo, sweetheart. You're home now. Come with Mummy. You can have a drink and a biscuit. Come and see Hannah. She's home from school.'

He shakes me off and settles further down into his sleep. The other two boys are getting restless. It's another hour home for them. I lift Jonny out and he wakes. I hold him as the taxi backs out and he starts to scream. He fights me. He wants to get out of my arms and I am no longer strong enough to hold him. As he flails around, punching me, I let

go of him and he lies down in the lane kicking and screaming, the noise growing and spiralling away into the summer
afternoon air. I try to soothe him, to move him nearer to the
house. I am scratched and bitten. Streams of words come
from this child who rarely sees the need for them.

'Pasta, curtains, curtains closed, jumper, drink water.'

'We can get you a drink, sweetheart. Just come inside.'

The stream of words continues, screamed, ever louder,
less and less distinct.

'Taxi, jelly, biscuit, seatbelt on, bread, water.'

It takes an hour, during which time he is moved slightly
nearer the house, only to lie down again. Eventually I get
him inside. There he lies on the doormat and it all starts
over again. My daughter stands anxiously by my side as he
screams and I sit at the kitchen table and cry. There's a knock
at the door and our neighbour stands there.

'Are you all right? Is there anything we can do?'

I hastily dry my eyes. There isn't anything anyone can do.
He looks at me, worried, helpless.

'No, no, don't worry, we'll be fine. Honestly.' I smile.
'Really. He's just tired. He'll calm down in a minute.'

By the time the other two get home, Jonny's sitting at the
table eating his tea, smiling.

The weekend is warm and on Saturday afternoon I get out
the hose for them to play with. The garden is wonderful for
this – it would be very hard to do any damage. Its greenery
reaches up through terraces and trees to the outside world,
high above us and screened from view. The lawn is huge,
scattered with daisies. The gates are locked. The children
scream with pleasure, running around in their swimming
gear, getting out umbrellas, squirting each other.

'Your turn, Jonny.' They put the hose in his hands, and he swings it around, screeching with pleasure. He squirts the climbing frame, the slide, the little house, his brother and sister. He swings the hose and flaps his hands in the stream of water. When they take it off him again, he claps with pleasure and runs into the spray of water over and over again, laughing.

On Monday morning we go out to wait for the taxi. Our big garden, ideal for Jonny to play in without bothering anyone – big enough for a climbing frame, a trampoline, a large paddling pool, bouncy castles on birthdays – has trees at the far end with a path winding through to the lane. Our driveway isn't that easy to navigate, so to make it easier for them, we walk up to the road. People pass us and I nod at them. Jonny flaps and squawks. For nine years I have been learning to lose embarrassment, to be out defiantly with my son in public places. To take him swimming, to parks and playgrounds, to firework displays, on buses and trains; to make it clear to the world that he lives in it and will not be hidden away. I have, though, developed my own strategies for dealing with the looks and stares, the comments and disapproval we regularly elicit. Jonny may be the one with autism, but I'm the person who avoids eye contact.

Jonny boards weekly for three years. The transitions are always difficult, and the weekends and holidays always hard work. It's a strange life – one where weekends are harder than the week – where there are no breaks, no oases. I suppose this is what it was like when women had one child after another, on and on through their lives. Jonny swims and canoes, abseils and trampolines. He has foot massages and lies in a Snoezelen room – full of optic fibres and cushions, soothing music and essential oils. His loss of speech and difficult behaviours plateau. We have reached the end of the deterioration and know what we are dealing with. He is cared for kindly and calms a little. He gets plenty of practice at social interaction, at managing the world, which is just what he needs. He goes out shopping and learns to wait for change. He goes out to cafés and knows how to wait, to sit, to eat. He has practice at crossing roads. He learns to do some cooking and a little bit of sign language. He can get dressed, but still needs to be encouraged to do so. He never learns to tie shoelaces. He still chews his toothbrush rather than using it to brush his teeth. He barely brushes his face with his flannel. He overwrites his name, if someone puts a hand over his. He never learns to count further than I taught him. But why would he need to count?

In December we go down for the Christmas show. It's a foggy, evening drive, but we're determined to go. All through Jonny's school career, we go to everything, show support wherever it is possible, try to give something back to the people who care for him. The show is ambitious – a sort of pantomime with many different scenes, music and comedy. The staff has joined in with gusto, pushing it along in their funny costumes and willingness to throw dignity to the winds. I wonder, as I always do, what they will get Jonny to do. The sort of coercion that kept him standing still in his 'money bag' costume won't have been used here. Eventually he appears, with a troupe of clowns, in a beautiful costume and clever make-up. No one has tried to make him put anything on his head. The clowns run or walk in. Jonny's hand is held, and I'm not at all sure that he is a willing participant. Circus music plays and they throw around large balls and tumble.

Then his teacher brings on a little trampoline and I see what they have done. It's clever; inspired really. He loves to jump, is never happier than when bouncing on a trampoline. And that's exactly what he does – bounces to the music in his beautiful clown costume – happy. At the end of the show, the children and staff all come up onto a crowded and chaotic stage. Some of the children know what has been achieved and some don't. What does Jonny think? Is it just one more strange event in a life full of them? Tonight, and in every Christmas show and carol service, he shows us what he can do, and what he can't. The staff look exhausted, and as we crawl back though the fog Jonny sleeps soundly in the back of the car under his Thomas the Tank Engine duvet.

On Christmas Day, the usual chaos ensues. By lunchtime, the floor is covered in toys and paper and the children are over the top with excitement. Hannah is trying simultaneously to listen to a bright-red personal stereo and play with a huge doll, while a Doctor Who video plays loudly in the background. Ben is watching the video and fiddling with a Rubik's cube. Jonny sits quietly, surrounded by his presents – he always gets an enormous number of them. Ben and Hannah watch anxiously as I manipulate his hands to open their present for him. 'Does he like it, Mummy? Does he like it?' This as he stares away from the enforced unwrapping.

'Yes, darling, he likes it. He's a bit overwhelmed. Later he'll play with it. Don't worry.'

Later, what he will do is sneak back to eat the chocolate decorations from the tree, leaving the foil hanging, as he spins the faceted red balls and laughs. When the sun shines this is a particularly good experience as red chips of light spin round the room. Once he has eaten a large dinner while the other two pick at theirs, waiting for the next round of sweets, I get out his present from me – a video of *Fantasia*. I keep trying, even though it's so hard to get it right. I want something he will watch, something to engage him for a while.

'It mustn't have words,' I think, 'it must have music, colour, movement, the effect of lights and spinning.' But Jonny can subvert the very best of intentions.

The other two are watching an afternoon film in the front room, taking the occasional break to play again. Their grandmother sits with them. All three are wearing the hats from their crackers. Under the tree, empty now of presents and looking strangely bare, is a pile of pine needles. We are clearing up in the kitchen. I've put the video on in the back room and left. Jonny, I think, hates to do what you want him to do. It's important to appear casual, not to display hope or express encouragement. I look into the room from time to time to make sure all is well. I've persuaded the others to leave him there, alone and holding up an old book by its cover, flapping the hanging pages. His head is bare. We finish the clearing up and I peep in, ready to move him on before he gets bored, not expecting much except the flapping of the book. But he's kneeling in front of the television, the book quite still in his hands. On the screen is colour, movement, the effect of lights and spinning. Music plays. And Jonny watches, mesmerized, 'playing' with one of his presents.

When he leaves his school, there are many fond farewells; and also a strange sadness, expressions of regret from some, that they have not helped him as much as they had hoped. I feel uncomfortable, but do not know why. Jonny's autistic. This is part of who he is. This will not change. Often, when people are sympathetically regretful, I feel that their sadness is being pushed onto me. They want him to be someone else – beautiful little Jonny without the autism. There's something about my son – something about the way he looks at people, can suddenly do or say something out of the blue, which is never repeated, something about the way he laughs and enjoys himself, the way he cuddles up on occasions, something which makes people think that he is suddenly going to forge ahead. They are always disappointed.

We move on to termly boarding. The weekends have become increasingly hard for us all to bear. Jonny arrives distressed and disorientated, calming just as the time comes for him to go back to school. I spend evenings with him in his room, skilled by now at managing the distress, keeping it to a minimum, not getting hurt. He's 11 now and will soon be bigger than me. I make sure that the violence is contained, do my very best to stop it spilling into the lives of his brother and sister. Mostly they get on with it all, behave with amazing compassion and good humour. From time to time we talk. I wait expectantly for the day they will say they are embarrassed, don't want friends round when he is there. I make sure they know that this is allowed, that they won't be letting him down. That day never comes. He is their brother, they say. Any friend who can't deal with this is not a friend. The friends, amazingly, seem to agree, take it all in their stride. No, they tell me, they don't need to keep people away. The thing they're really worried about is that I will get hurt.

Jonny has been with his schoolteachers and classmates to visit his new school. They have made a photo album for him. On the day that we go, we also take pictures. Photos and video are becoming the way we help him to predict what will happen, the way we lessen the fear of the unknown. Jonny loves them and will still sit happily for a long time watching himself and his family on video, or browsing through photo albums. Bob and I go to see the new school when it is half finished – poised between the brutish décor of a deserted prep school and the luxury that is a new boarding school for the hardest-to-place children. We like it very much. We know that this is a very good time to try to get him in – before it's ready – when there will be a few places up for grabs. And his current school will only keep him till he's 16 – just at the age other schools don't want to take children like him, teenagers embroiled in an adolescence with extra features. Special education goes on till the age of 19, and those three years could be really hard if we don't get it right. We decide to move him sooner than planned. An opportunity like this doesn't come up very often. Local government reorganization means that a newly formed local authority assesses us this time. Recommendations are made. We are not required to jump through any of the old hoops. They give it to us freely, a gift.

Once the school is ready to take pupils, the whole family goes to look. It's a longer drive than the old one – through winding country lanes that elicit car sickness in our youngest child and our dog every time we visit. The destination is an old-fashioned seaside town with beaches and ice creams, hills and an old castle, a steam railway and slot machines, nature reserves and a ferry. And there is a school for Jonny, high on a cliff, with playgrounds and gardens, individual care plans, staff who for the first time do not regard Jonny as a problem with a boy attached, and – out of almost every window – the huge, huge sea. We look at bedrooms and bathrooms, classrooms and playrooms, kitchens and a gym. Most of the furniture has been made by a local carpenter – robust pine, nice to look at. On the walls are Impressionist prints. The teachers chat to all three children and two of them respond. But Jonny isn't unhappy, only irritable for a few minutes in the gym when a ball is thrown to him and he doesn't fancy catching it. He likes the wooden slide and climbing frame, he looks out constantly at the sea. The other two cannot believe his luck. School at the seaside!

That isn't the best thing, though. The best thing is Julie. She is a light switched on in a darkened room; curtains thrown back to let sunlight stream in. Jonny is 12 when he starts termly boarding. And the day we all go to look at the school, we meet his new personal tutor. We meet the first person in his education who regards him as a person rather than a problem – and a person she likes very much. Julie writes things down in her notebook, she jokes with Ben and Hannah. She watches Jonny and, at lunch time, sits quietly by him, waiting for him to be comfortable with her before she says anything. She is a miracle. As time goes on, she and Jonny form a bond that many experts on autism would deny is possible. They giggle together as they play. She reads to him and teaches him to look after himself. He smiles when she comes into the room. And Jonny is no longer just a case of autism. He is a great little boy, with a fantastic sense of humour, a will of iron, and a love of music. He likes to do things his own way – but who doesn't? Who isn't getting fed up with being treated like a child as they enter adolescence?

The children are divided into 'family' groups, and Jonny settles fairly well. There are bad days and good days of course, things that don't go so well, but Jonny's years here are largely happy and full of progress.

Later on, once I have started a kind of a career in middle age, I go to a training session. The trainer talks about dementia – normal behaviour in an abnormal world, she calls it, and I think of Jonny's time at this school. It isn't all good. Care workers come and go and some are better than others. But most of his time here is spent with two exceptionally gifted people who take precisely this view. Jonny's world is his world, and what he does makes sense inside that world. The key to helping him live with dignity and happiness is an accommodation with the autism; helping him to control its fears and excesses; helping him to manage behaviours that make his life, and the lives of those around him, difficult. But never, never is it trying to force him to be someone he isn't, or to pretend that autism isn't always going to be a big part of who he is.

In the classroom, they are trying a new system from the States. It works well. As soon as you stop thinking of autism as a psychological condition and start to look at it properly, help with managing it emerges. This scheme takes account of Jonny's need for control, for clear systems, for order, and particularly for finishing things off. This last is very big in his life. Jonny sets up all sorts of mechanisms for finishing off – including washing and throwing things out of windows or putting away every single thing in sight. He now has a desk with a board above it. Every morning, he's helped to put on the board symbols of what he will be doing that day, in the order they will happen. Each task is followed by a reward activity. Breaks are illustrated. On the left is an in-tray containing the day's tasks – each one packaged into a plastic case, nicely delineated with all anxiety-inducing confusion eradicated. Once the task is completed, the material is put back into the plastic case and then put in an out-tray on the right side of the desk. Jonny responds well to this system. He doesn't always want to do what is required of him – but who does? He knows, though, what he's supposed to be doing. He understands the beginning and the end. He understands that when he finishes, something nice will follow. What's more, he begins to take pleasure in the knowing and the doing. He experiences his first sense of achievement.

Nowadays, we still reap the benefit of this breakthrough. We see when Jonny recognizes a situation and knows what to do. We see the pleasure in his face, the clear indication that he is thinking 'I know this one. I can do this.' He oversees the washing-up now, making sure we do it properly and put *everything* away after he has dried it. He wipes the placemats, giving himself his own reward activity of squeezing water onto them before putting them in the drawer. He wipes the table and puts the cloths away, all the time beaming with pleasure, calm, happy to see something finished properly, allowing him to move on.

In his living area at school, similar systems are in place – pictures put up in order to show what will happen during the day, a clear routine with tasks and leisure activities mixed. Jonny learns to make his breakfast at the weekend, supervised of course, but mostly by himself, and to set out the places for everyone during the week. He learns to brush his teeth, wash his hair, vacuum his room. He gets inordinate pleasure from knowing how to do things and doing them well. He relaxes and starts to indicate what he wants, many of the old fears dissipating in this new environment. As he becomes more confident at showing people what he wants and getting control of his world, his anxiety lessens, his behaviour becomes calmer and his sense of humour and individuality comes to the fore.

When he moves in with the older pupils, his personal tutor sends us emails with digital photos of what he has done during the day. It is wonderful to turn on the computer and see what Jonny has been doing just a short while ago. I see him grinning happily in a burger bar, playing pass the parcel at a birthday party, making his breakfast. In one sequence of pictures, he is initiating play with a fellow student, sitting next to her and trying to make her laugh by putting a book on his head. Eventually she does, and they sit companionably for a while giggling together as Jonny puts the book on his head and allows it to fall off time after time. This initiation of play, sense of humour and interaction with someone else is regarded as so unusual in autistic teenagers that it is featured in magazines. You can almost sense the held breath of the photographer, standing quietly, catching forever this wonderful sense of humour and awareness of someone else's pleasure. Walking to the classroom in the mornings, Jonny leaves the group to walk the other way round buildings, balances along walls, gets there using his own route, his different path.

He starts a paper round, shadowed discreetly, but competent, folding the papers, putting them into the letterboxes, receiving a small wage that he takes to his building society. He goes for walks, takes part in birthday parties, gardens, cooks, sails, trampolines, goes horse riding – an activity he has always loved. In many ways, his education is one of privilege, of activities that many children can only dream of. Meantime, he continues to want to 'finish' every toilet roll, regularly blocking loos. Once all the toilet paper is down the loo, he washes the cardboard tube, rips it to shreds and puts it in the bin. And he loves to watch liquid – pouring till the jug overflows onto the table and then the floor. On the occasions when he can be persuaded that full is enough, each cup is filled completely – so that it is almost impossible to drink from.

It's 11.30am, and we've just arrived. We do this every three weeks – visit Jonny and take him out for the day. We've got a funny little van – can't run to a people carrier – with three rows of seats. The back row has no outside door or window. In this way, we can all go out with Jonny and know that he cannot hit anybody, open the door to get out whilst we're moving or throw things out of the window. The sight of the pages of our road atlas and a couple of fleeces flying down the dual carriageway behind us has taught us that we must be tidy when Jonny is in the car. The two-hour journey is pretty but frustratingly slow, and getting everyone up and ready by 9.30 on a Sunday morning is not easy. I'm driven though, largely I suspect by guilt, and we always get there. He is ready and waiting by the door, happy to see us all. He puts on his coat and climbs into his place in the car. We all get in and slide the doors across.

'Seatbelt, seatbelt.'

'Yes Jonny,' Ben answers. 'We're putting on the seatbelts. Shall we go to the park before lunch? Swings?'

'Swings.' He's happy.

Ben's getting a bit old for swings and slides. He'll push the other two and anxiously watch over Jonny, worried that he might run off or become upset and violent. 'Soon,' I think, 'he'll need to stop doing this so often.' He'll need to be with his friends, get on with revision, rest on a Sunday before the frenetic exam and assessed work schedule that constitutes his education. For the time being, though, we all come. After the park we go for lunch. Jonny continues to love his food and this restaurant is a real find. We're in a relatively small seaside resort and not that much is open out of season. This place, though, looking out over the sea if you get a window seat, which we almost always do, is open and busy all year round. They know us now. It seems that many of the townspeople are accustomed to the young people from the school, happy to accommodate them and the business they bring. A waitress we often see is there and she smiles as she shows us to a window table. We eat a good lunch, Jonny happily watching, from his seat next to the window, waves splashing against the sea wall and seagulls swooping.

'Chips or baked potato?' the waitress asks him. He's having gammon and pineapple. He continues to watch the waves.

'Jonny,' I say gently.

'Bub!'

He's irritated by my interruption.

'Do you want chips?'

'Bub!'

'Or potatoes?' I'm sure people think I'm unkind, abrupt with my son, uncaring. I do not have the time or energy to explain over and over again that words confuse him, distress him even, that fewer is better.

'Chips or potatoes, Jonny?' Ben asks.

'Bub!'

'You have to choose, Jonny,' persists his brother.

'Bubub!' Getting angrier now.

'We'll have chips,' I say.

I choose the same meal with potato so that all the bases are covered. But he's happy with chips, especially when they are covered in tomato sauce. He eats them all first, then the pineapple, then the gammon, then the peas. I take the other two to look at the display of desserts and guess at an ice cream for Jonny. He is not able to leave anything, even when he is clearly full or not that keen. Sometimes he throws up on the carpet afterwards to rid himself of the excess.

In the warmer months we go on the beach or, best of all, for a boat ride round the bay. Jonny and I both love boat rides, especially on a sunny day, when the sea is blue and the spray bright white against it. Jonny quivers with excitement when we are splashed by the water. Finding activities in the winter months though, especially when the wind is bitter cold off the sea and almost everything is closed, can be daunting. Today is a mild autumn day and we will go on the train.

'Come on, Jonny, train,' says Hannah. 'Steam train.' The only reaction is faster flapping, but we know this means he's happy to be going, that this renovated bit of track running stream trains at the weekend to the castle and back will be right for us today. The station is fantastic, replete with 50s' posters and piles of authentic-looking luggage. In December, Father Christmas comes round and gives the children sweets and the adults sherry. Today, it's just the enthusiasts in boiler suits and the travelling public in evidence. We get into the train as the whistle blows and settle in a little carriage we have to ourselves. The sun comes out as we watch trees and fields in the five miles to the castle, mellow in autumnal colours and wreathed in steam from the engine.

'Tickle, tickle.'

Jonny has become excited now – he can go from complete inertia to hyperactivity in a split second – and wants his brother and sister to join in his favourite game. They oblige and soon Jonny is wriggling and giggling as they tickle him.

'Tickle, Jonny, tickle.'

I smile but watch anxiously. He is much bigger than Hannah and this excited mood can flip over into anger very quickly. Not today, though. Today everything is fine. We get to the station and persuade Jonny that he does want to get off just as the doors are slamming for the return journey. There'll be trains every half-hour for a while and we have some time to kill.

'Come on, darling.' I'm more or less dragging Jonny, and now that we're out here with no car it's important to keep him moving and happy. 'Shall we get some sweets?' Ben and Hannah are enthusiastic.

'Yes! Yes please!'

They all quicken their pace, even Jonny, and choose sweets in the shop. I buy a packet to keep in my pocket for bribery on the walk back to the train, and we climb slowly up the slope of the ruined castle. It stands dramatically, what is left of it, high above the surrounding countryside, well preserved and looked after by the National Trust. This also means that there are good disabled toilets. Taking out a boy who is no longer a little boy is hard for me. I can't take him into the gents, get funny looks in the ladies, and cannot leave him to go himself.

'You go ahead with the others,' I say to Bob, and the

children run off, planning to climb to the very top. Jonny is always slow – unless he suddenly decides to run – and I don't want to feel pressured to get him to keep up. We two have just made it to the drawbridge – Jonny's happy just to stand looking over at the drop, flapping a leaf he has found – when the others get back.

I get one sweet out at a time for Jonny on the way back to the station, walking just in front of him so he has to take a few steps to get it. In this way we get back to the train and steam our way back.

'Come on, Jonny, we're back now. Let's get off.' The children speak to him so patiently always, but he doesn't want to move. He is starting to groan, shaking off their hands irritably, so I tell them to go ahead and get the door open so we don't find ourselves returning to the castle. I manage with the aid of the sweets to get him off. Once on the platform, he sees a bench and runs to it.

'Can you go and get the car?' I ask Bob, and he goes off while I sit with the three children. I give the others money to buy ice creams and they go off, returning triumphantly with three cornets.

'It's dripping, Jonny,' they tell him, and I wipe the ice cream from his coat and face with baby wipes. He likes the wafer and always eats the cornet from the bottom. Getting messy, though, can cause distress so I do my best to control the inevitable flow of melting ice cream.

Once back by the sea, we sit and eat the sandwiches I've bought, watching dogs, allowed on the beach out of season, and children throwing Frisbees and flying kites, as well as the occasional treasure hunter complete with Geiger counter. Then we finish the day in our favourite place – the amusement arcade on the front. It's been a haven for us in some of the winter months when the waves crash over the sea wall onto the esplanade and the rain is torrential. The arcade is quite small and family orientated – not too expensive if we're careful. There are a couple of small rides that Hannah likes and a pinball machine for Ben. For Jonny, though, it's the slots we're after. We give in our pound coin and take the cup of two-pence pieces to the machine, where I stand by Jonny, handing him a few coins at a time. Quickly he feeds them in, absolutely mesmerized by the journey of each two-pence piece onto the bank of coins which is sliding backwards and forwards. The overhang gets bigger and bigger till we hear the sudden sound of coppers falling and pouring down into the reservoir at the front of the machine.

'You've won some, Jonny,' I say, and he tears himself away from watching the movement to gather up his winnings. He leans with his face right against the glass, watching obliquely, rigid with excitement. Probably we don't really need the two-pence pieces; we could just stand and watch it go back and forth. But we like to do it properly if we can.

After that, we take him back to school. Night staff are on duty now and he goes in quite calmly.

'Goodbye Jonny.' His brother and sister try to kiss him, give him a hug, but he wants us to go now. He doesn't like these transitions, these times when two worlds collide.

'Bubye,' he says. 'Bubye.'

So we go, and start on the winding journey home, playing tapes for the children on the way. Hannah falls asleep. I watch trees and fields, a crescent moon rising over hills and villages, feeling sad. It's been a happy day, tiring but successful, a day spent together as a family without incident or fear. I cannot though, ever, shake off the guilt, the yearn-

ing to have all my children together at home with me. It is
years before the grief of leaving my son to other carers every
time I visit becomes tolerable.

Another day out is rather different. As time goes on, I get
back into employment, starting with part-time jobs and then
eventually getting this demanding full-time work. It involves
a lot of travelling – driving to far-flung parts of the West
Country where groups of disabled people meet as part of the
charity I work for. Even though Jonny boards for the school
terms, it's still hard to manage. The school has organized
its terms so that they are of equal length and each holiday
about three weeks long. In this way, the long summer holiday, distressing for pupils and their families, is avoided. All
the same, there are plenty of school holidays, and this isn't
a teaching job where I get them as well. I work long, long,
hours, often driving home in the small hours so as not to be
away from the children too much. The subsequent build-up
of time off in lieu allows me, with the help of some respite
care, to manage in the holidays. I feel as though I am working or caring almost every minute of every day.

On this particular Friday evening, I am speaking at a
meeting close to Jonny's school. So I get up early, take him
out for the day and then go on to the meeting. I get home at
half past midnight but the day has been good. I could not
have been down the road from Jonny without seeing him.
A year later when I am running a rural awareness week and
cannot fit in a visit, even though we drive past the castle and
along the back of the town, I am reduced to tears and have
to leave my colleagues talking to our clients. On this day,
though, it has been warm and sunny – quite beautiful. The
beach is fairly quiet and we settle on a stretch away from

the road. I'm sitting reading whilst Jonny digs with a spade, when he says quite clearly, 'Swimming time.'

He grabs my hand – an almost unprecedented gesture – and we run to the sea. We're both in blue – he in little trunks and me in a bright swimsuit – and we wade in, laughing. He throws himself in, happy to go under the waves and come up again, hair dripping, in a way that the other two would definitely find disturbing. For a while we jump over the waves until he says, 'Picnic', and then we sit on our mats with the row of beach huts behind us, eating cold sausages and drinking squash. Later on, I tell people at my meeting about my day and they look sympathetic, despite their own difficulties – a progressive, degenerative disability which they probably knew little about and certainly did not expect in their lives, until the day they found they could not move properly or could not stop shaking. There are times when people are incredibly kind.

When Jonny is home for the holidays I try to think ahead, plan activities for every day. We need to get out and do things. Staying in the house, or even the garden, does not work for very long. Boredom sets in very quickly and with it, difficult and distressing behaviours. I try to map out each day before he comes home – it's hard to find time to think once he's with us. The life of a carer is difficult to describe to others – the sense of your life dissolving into another person's, the way you are hardly aware of your own existence.

At school, Jonny's life is crammed with activity. He goes swimming, trampolining or horse riding. In the holidays, I long for a day sitting in the garden, but it never works when I try it. There are some things that will keep

Jonny occupied for a few minutes at a time, and these are precious to me. At the moment, I can hear the sound of marbles shooting down plastic tubes and clattering into the reservoir at the end of the run. Ben builds a different structure for him every day and he sits on his bedroom floor, feeding in the glass balls, mesmerized by their progress. This allows me ten minutes to make lunch. Earlier, he has played for 30 blissful minutes in the bath, giving me time to get dressed and ready for the day. This is after he has washed his bedclothes in the bath and thrown them out of the window.

Every day starts with this gathering up of wet pillows, sheets and duvet if I don't get to the bathroom in time. If he wakes in the night, I may be retrieving these things from the garden at 4am. Our days are punctuated by the washing and throwing away of items of clothing. I have to come to an accommodation with this behaviour.

Every morning, I put out his clothes, encouraging and cajoling him to dress himself; then giving up and helping him on with them. I've sewn his name into everything. If he notices these labels, he rips them out with his teeth and spits them onto the floor. We go to the park, feed ducks, walk on walls, watch trains, jump off benches. He is old for some of these activities and other children stare. He loves high buildings, so we drive to Wells to look in the cathedral and feed swans by the bishop's palace. We eat in the café there. We go swimming, visit adventure playgrounds and fairs, fly kites. Jonny lets go of the end of the string regularly and we watch as another one makes its escape. I try tying the string around his wrist, but he unties it. Our lives are a ceaseless round of activity. I try to think of ways we may stay at home. I fill the paddling pool, but it is empty within ten minutes. He steps on the side and watches, fascinated as a deluge of water floods the shed. Or, if I put it on the lawn, he steps in and out until it is a pool of mud. I put out a table of plastic containers and a bowl of water. He pours the water away and throws everything else over the fence.

When we move house again, I am consumed with anxiety. How will he cope? I know we must do it while he is at school. It's enough of a chore, packing the boxes, taking almost every spare minute of my days. If Jonny is at home, he will unpack them as fast as they are packed. So, he will leave for school for the new term from one house, and come home for the holiday to a different address. This would be hard enough for anyone to cope with, but for Jonny it could be truly terrifying. I'm inspired by the way Miles, his second brilliant personal tutor, uses photos to help him and us cope with our separation. So I make a photo album for Jonny. I photograph his room full of furniture and possessions. Then I photograph it in all the stages of being packed up. I photograph the old house packed up and the new house with the van outside, and at each stage of the unpacking. I take lots of photos of the rooms that will matter to him – his bedroom, the bathroom, the dining room. In the holidays before the move, I take him to see the outside of the new house, and to play in the fields at the back. Once the photo album is finished, complete with captions explaining each stage of the operation, it is sent to school where Miles reads it to him every day.

On the day he comes home, I am very, very nervous. I have arranged for the other two to be out, in case it's particularly difficult. But Jonny is absolutely brilliant. He comes in and looks around. Then he sits down in what is to become his favourite chair, an armchair in the hall, tucked away under the open-plan stairs, next to a table holding the phone and some books. After a while he gets up and comes into the kitchen. I show him where the bread and biscuits are kept, and so he establishes where his two most important foodstuffs can be obtained. Then he goes upstairs and tries out the loo.

Finally, he goes into his bedroom and sits in the matching armchair to the one in the hall. There are no upsets then or later. The plan seems to have worked, and Jonny, a severely autistic 15-year-old, with hardly any speech and a great fear of change, has moved into a new house without incident. I am extremely surprised and immensely proud of him. But over and over again, he surprises me like this – rising to occasions that we thought he would find extremely difficult.

Once again, we have put in fencing on our first day. And once again, we have explained to slightly doubtful-looking neighbours that we are not unfriendly. By this time, we have a dog that is also keen on escape. At the end of the steeply terraced sloping garden is a field full of sheep or goats, with two huge oak trees in the middle. Beyond the field dense woodland rises, green in the summer, fiery red and gold in the autumn months. In the summer this field is covered in a brilliant yellow haze of buttercups, and on the coldest days of winter, in the early morning snow or in the glowing, freezing dusk, a deer or fox may be seen venturing out of the woodland for a few cautious minutes.

One a hot summer's day, Jonny is sitting at the top of this village garden on a garden chair, in the shade of a tree. This stillness is unusual, and won't last for long. I am taking full advantage of it and getting dinner prepared well ahead of time. I check on him from the kitchen window every few seconds. When I look out and see that the garden chair is empty, I hurry out, wiping my hands on a cloth. What I see makes me laugh out loud. Jonny is a teenager by this time, no longer overweight as he was in early childhood, but not particularly small either. He is rolling down the slope, turning over and over, laughing. I hope he won't fall off the wall at the end of the lawn onto the brick terrace, but he skilfully slows down and stops perfectly as he reaches this barrier. Behind him, our overweight and overindulged King Charles spaniel follows, also rolling over and over, but not clever enough to stop at the edge. He falls heavily onto the terrace, picks himself up quickly, looks at me accusingly, but nevertheless follows Jonny back up the slope for another go. Later on, I look into the hall, where Jonny likes to sit, and find him sitting on the floor with the dog. Jonny is eating biscuits and the spaniel follows, with unwavering eyes, every move of the snacks from tin to mouth. Every so often, and without looking at him, Jonny hands the dog a biscuit. The spaniel wolfs it down in a trice and turns his greedy eyes back onto Jonny.

At school, Jonny's carers like him, even though he's violent and aggressive at times, as are all the other pupils. He's living in a house separated from the main school by this time, with the other 16- to 19-year-olds. There are three girls – the others are all boys, reflecting precisely the gender discrepancy of the autistic population. One of the boys was removed from his last school one night when they said they couldn't cope with his extreme aggression for one more day. He is supervised very carefully, but he seems to have settled down. Another of Jonny's housemates talks incessantly, his monologues peppered with expletives and deeply sexist phrases, parroted from God knows who in his chaotic home life. Another seems, like Sally before him, surprisingly 'normal'. It's only when you talk properly with Liam that you realize how obsessive and repetitive his conversation is; how childlike his demeanour; how very vulnerable he must be.

Jonny, though, shows a surprising amount of affection for someone with his degree of disability, and a well developed sense of humour. He'll put his jumper on back to front and then wait for a response, watching surreptitiously out of the corner of his eye. He'll balance things on his head, or put objects in places he knows they shouldn't be. His carers think he is funny, but learn not to make too much of a response. Once Jonny starts giggling, it can go on for hours, incapacitating him for any other activity. In the evenings, he'll sit next to someone and take their hand, asking for a 'tickle' or stroke. He'll take someone's arm or even occasionally allow a family member to give him a hug or a kiss.

We talk endlessly with the staff at his school, as well as attending many, many meetings, about schemes and solutions, and the whys and wherefores of his behaviour. How much soaking shall we allow? Has anyone come up with a way to deflect him from this activity? Has anyone thought of a way to stop him blocking the toilet? What about antecedents, triggers or solutions to the episodes of violence and distress? Back and forth we go. I explain how I manage to cut his toenails, holding a sweet just out of his reach for each nail. When he allows me to cut it, I give him the sweet. They tell me about the cupboard just inside the front door where he may, on occasions, be persuaded to put his coat when he comes in, instead of washing it. Often we talk and talk about a particular behaviour, finally getting, we think, to the bottom of it, just as he stops it and starts something new. I think and think and think, try new things, talk and talk.

It's Thursday and I'm waiting by the phone because this is the night Jonny 'phones home'. It rings and I pick it up.

'Hi.' It's Miles.

'How are things?'

'Fine, Jonny went horse riding yesterday and did a little canter, so that was new and really great. Not too much soaking this week. He's had his hair cut.'

'How did that go?'

'Fine. He was a bit stressed at first, weren't you Jonny?'

Silence.

'But once he sat down and got started, he did very well. Do you want to talk to Mum, Jonny?'

I hear the phone being handed over.

'Hallo Jonny.'

Silence.

'You've been horse riding, haven't you?'

Silence.

'Miles said you did a canter – that's fantastic, I'd have liked to see that... Hannah's been swimming, have you been this week?... It's been raining a lot here... Miles says you've had your hair cut. He says you did really well. I bet it looks nice... We're coming down to see you on Saturday. We'll go out and have lunch and maybe go down to the sea. That will be nice... I'm looking forward to seeing you... Not tomorrow, not the next day, but the next day... I'll see you then.'

'Bubye.'

'Hi.' It's Miles again. 'He was smiling all the way through.'

'That's great. See you Sunday?'

'I'll be there when you bring him back. Oops – better go, he's off. See you Sunday.'

'OK.' I put down the phone.

Sports day takes place on a very hot summer's day. The students are dressed in matching sports gear – well most are – some obviously have an issue with certain items of clothing and adaptations have been made. We sit on the sidelines and watch the races. Almost all the students are 'running' with a carer beside them. The field is high up behind the school, and beyond it the sea, azure blue, stretches to the horizon. Occasionally a boat disturbs its surface, scattering foam and splinters of light. Seagulls wheel above each vessel. I'm watching the field as staff, many much smaller than Jonny, virtually lift him through a race in which he has no desire to be involved. I can't decide if these attempts at normality are to be admired or if they are just sad. Other children, though, join in with gusto, and prize the ribbons and sweets they win. Everyone gets something and Jonny doesn't seem upset by anything that has taken place.

In December the Christmas carol service, held in the chapel, reminds us that this was once a prep school with a very different constituency. Jonny looks around, at the ceiling mostly, whilst the event goes on around him. But another set of parents sit with tears streaming down their faces as their son picks out *Silent Night* on the piano. The boy with the expletives has no relatives there to see him, but sings brilliantly and with great gusto, obviously enjoying every minute of his performance. I feel emotionally exhausted by the whole event, my heart pulled this way and that, glad for all the care and effort that has gone into this day, but also profoundly saddened by the fate of our children. Afterwards we eat mince pies and chat with the staff, giving them their presents and receiving cards that our children have made. Everyone is friendly and good-humoured. Then we take our children home for Christmas, and I imagine the staff breathing a sigh of relief.

Hannah has just started secondary school – it's her third day, and I'm quite worried about how she'll manage without us. I've arranged for a friend's father to take her to school and bring her back. There's nothing I can do about it – I'll just have to trust him, which I don't really. Jonny has been waiting for some time for an operation on his ingrown toenails, and now it has come up in a hospital in Dorset, near to his school. We're going down to be with him for his day appointment and then to bring him home to convalesce. These toenails have given him trouble for a long time now and, like every other ailment he has ever had, caused much more aggravation because of his autism. For one thing, he is never able to tell us that he isn't feeling well. Secondly, doctors tend to be afraid of him. He's aggressive and difficult when feeling ill, doesn't want to be examined – touched even. When he obviously has something wrong with him, treatment options are always less than or easier than what is really required. I am sympathetic really. Getting medicines of any kind into Jonny is a virtually impossible task. These nails should have been treated a long time ago, but we've been unable to find a practitioner confident enough around the flailing limbs to look at them properly or recommend appropriate treatment. Instead, he has had course after course of antibiotics, which he has spat back at me time after time. Miles, though, has seen it through this time, with the help of a GP who has had to learn to understand autism because of the location of his current practice. The referral has been made and today is the day. Jonny will be brought to the hospital by Miles and the head of care from his school, where we will meet them. He will have a general anaesthetic and the toenails will either be cut right back or removed. My brother has told me that the pain of the operation is nothing compared to the pain of the ingrown toenails. And I think of how Jonny has endured this for years, whilst people around me debate whether people with autism feel pain to the same degree as others.

We arrive before Jonny. When we see him come in, it is immediately obvious how unhappy he is. Jonny does not have a good relationship with hospitals. He clearly has bad memories of fraught appointments and unpleasant tests. Just walking in through the door is a bad experience for him and it shows. He's hungry as well, having been denied breakfast because of the anaesthetic he will have.

I shouldn't have my mobile phone on in the hospital, but we're not on the wards and I'm worried about Hannah. We're still in the waiting room despite the fact that Miles rang earlier in the week and again before they left this morning, to remind them that waiting will add to Jonny's distress and the general difficulty of the day. My phone rings. It's my mother-in-law to say that Hannah's friend's dad has failed to pick her up – just as I thought he would – and that she's too frightened to go to her new school on her own. I talk to Hannah, who is crying, worried about walking in late on her third day at big school, unsure where to go or what will happen. I feel torn in two. Eventually I persuade my mother-in-law to walk her to school. Then I ring her teacher and explain what has happened. She is very sympathetic and says she will go to the gate to meet Hannah. So I ring Hannah again and talk to her until she calms. This is achieved just as a senior nurse arrives and calls us in.

'Switch that phone off, please.'

She's old school, grey-haired, tidy. Her face is kindly but inflexible, the sort of brisk countenance permitting no nonsense, a proponent of good, old-fashioned nursing. We follow her into an examining room and sit whilst she talks through what will happen.

'He's autistic,' I say to her, and she smiles as she shows me the gown he needs to wear. 'He won't wear that,' I explain. 'It hasn't got trousers with it and it's open at the back. It will upset him, he'll want to wear proper clothes.'

'Oh, I expect he'll put it on if we explain what he's here for,' she says kindly.

'I don't think he will.'

'Well, we need to keep everything sterile. We'll give him the pre-med once he's got it on.'

'What's a pre-med?' I ask.

'Just a little needle in his hand to make him feel drowsy. He'll hardly feel a thing.'

'He won't keep it in,' I say. 'He'll pull it out straight away.'

'Mum thinks he won't take the pre-med.' She turns to the doctor, who has just come in. Miles raises his eyebrows when I look at him.

'Well, let's give it a try, shall we?'

I shrug.

We undress Jonny and he starts to groan. The sister looks alarmed. We put the hospital gown on him and he pulls it off straightaway, standing there naked. The nurse looks away.

'We've brought some pyjamas,' says Miles, and she nods.

Then she slips the pre-med drip into Jonny's hand, deftly securing it with a plaster and smiles triumphantly at me. He has it out in the second she turns away to throw away the wrapping. 'No sharps' it says on the bin.

'He's pulled it out,' I say, and she looks around in amazement as if I had removed it myself to spite her.

'What about some Valium?' says the head of care, and I feel sick, thinking of the last time this was suggested. Miles looks unhappy.

'Well surely once he has the anaesthetic, he'll just go to sleep,' I say. 'Surely we can manage without pre-med or Valium?'

The two women, nurse and ex nurse, look unhappy. 'I think we'll call the anaesthetist,' says the sister.

Jonny has calmed a little. Although the pyjamas are better than a gown, he is clearly unhappy about wearing them in the middle of the day.

'I know it's hard, Jonny,' I say, 'but it'll soon be over and then your toes won't hurt any more.'

The anaesthetist arrives just as Jonny's groans reach fever pitch.

'I think he should have Valium,' says the head of care.

'Mum doesn't want him to have any,' says the sister, before I can say a word.

'No, I agree with his mother,' says the anaesthetist. 'Some autistic people have a bad reaction to Valium.'

'But he hasn't had the pre-med,' says the sister.

'He pulled it out,' I say.

'That's OK. We'll go straight to the anaesthetic. I can do it without putting a mask on his face. Do you want to come into the treatment room with him?' he asks me.

'I think it will help,' I say.

'OK, Mum and Dad and two carers. I think we'll just about fit in!' He leaves. The sister is scowling.

'He has a young autistic daughter,' explains the head of care.

'Thank you, God,' I think.

We get Jonny onto a trolley and down to the treatment room. This is a room that very few of us ever see. If we are ever inside, it is because we are under a general anaesthetic and the only other person there is the person who administered it. It is highly irregular and way too small for four extraneous people to be in it. The anaesthetist, who probably knows more about autistic behaviour than he ever wanted to, gently wafts the gas over Jonny's face. He can guess that putting a mask on him will cause violent distress. We all start to look a little glazed, but suddenly I see that the anaesthetist is smiling and that Jonny is fast asleep. He is pushed into the operating room and his father and I go to wait in the recovery room, another place we would not normally be given access to. It feels as if a very short time has elapsed when Jonny is wheeled in, and I see that once again he has a drip in his hand. We are with a different set of nurses.

'He'll probably take that out as soon as he comes round,' I say.

'Oh, it's well taped on,' they smile.

I shrug. They'll have to learn the hard way like the sister before them. I look at Jonny, who has made the faintest of sounds, but whose eyes are still closed.

'Bloody hell, the drips out!' exclaims one of the nurses. They put a new needle in, turn to throw away the packaging, and I see my son silently and deftly remove it whilst his eyelids remain firmly closed.

The trolley is wheeled back to the little room where we established that neither hospital gown nor pre-med are to Jonny's liking. The sister, head of care and Miles are waiting for us there. As Jonny begins to regain consciousness properly, his groans and cries of anguish get louder and louder. His feet are bound in bandages and as he comes round he leans down and rips them off. Blood flows as the sister tries to replace the dressings. Jonny punches and kicks her and she is visibly shaken.

'Can you hold him down, Mum?' she says to me, her hands shaking as she tries again to replace the bandages. I try, whilst my son flails around with superhuman strength. He does not want bandages on his feet. I've never even been able to make him keep a plaster on his finger. Bob helps me to hold him, then Miles, then the head of care join us, each holding down a part of poor Jonny's writhing body. He pushes us all off and rips off the bandages again. More blood. The sink is full of discarded dressings. The sound of Jonny's distress can be heard echoing down the corridors of the hospital, and a couple of orderlies come in to help hold him down. A man pushing another trolley leaves it in the corridor complete with its patient ready for anaesthetic, and comes to help. There are eight people holding down my son as dressing after dressing is ripped off and thrown though the air.

We give up for a moment while the sister goes to ask what to do and Jonny lies still, exhausted but victorious and bleeding profusely. Miles speaks quietly.

'Why don't we get him dressed? If he has shoes and socks on he might leave the dressings on.'

'Yes,' I say, 'let's try it.' And we do. 'Could you all go now, please?' I say. 'We think he'll calm down if there are fewer people in here. Thank you for your help.'

Jonny is still wailing and they look doubtful, but they all leave and when the sister returns, breathless and with a registrar in tow, Jonny is sitting quietly, fully dressed, with a new set of bandages on under his shoes and socks.

'He's OK now,' I say. 'I think we'd like to take him home.'

Jonny's in a wheelchair, looking quite happy, as we all go down in the lift. Bob is worried that Jonny may become violent whilst he is driving the car, so we decide that Miles will come home with us and then catch a train back to Dorset. The head of care is doubtful about the whole endeavour.

'Are you sure you wouldn't like us to take him back to school?' she asks. 'We're quite happy to. We've done it before when students have been ill.'

'No,' I say. 'He'll be all right now. He's had an operation, I think he should come home to recover.'

On the way home, we stop at a village stores and Bob goes in to buy some food for Jonny. I am sitting in the back with him and Miles turns round and says, 'Are you sure you want to have him home? We could manage at school.'

'Quite sure,' I say.

'Yes, that's what I think too,' he says. 'He should be at home with you.'

We smile and Jonny does too. He seems remarkably calm and happy, watching his dad coming back with a carrier bag of food. There are sandwiches, crisps and chocolate bars as well as a bottle of water, and Jonny wolfs down every single item as we wind our way home through the country lanes. He is grinning happily. As we turn into our street, he looks up and says, 'Better.'

For the next week, district nurses come every day. I get them to show me how to do the dressings, which I replace about ten times a day. Jonny slopes off to the loo a few minutes after each renewal to remove them and flush them away. On the fourth day, someone sensible comes and I explain what is happening.

'Well, there's no point in putting them on if he takes them straight off again,' she says. And she gives me an aerosol of particularly strong, orange antiseptic, which I spray liberally onto his toes before putting on his shoes and socks. He is happy at last. Now it's only the painkillers to struggle with. In the middle of the night, I wake, hearing laughter from below my bedroom window. I put on my slippers and dressing gown and go to look. Jonny is outside, barefoot. He has unlocked the doors and found a good spot by the dustbins and drains to jump about and laugh. I bring him in and thank God for his robust health and resistance to infection. The next week I take him and his orange antiseptic back to school, handing both over with a smile to Miles.

Jonny leaves school when he is 19 and goes to live in the house where he still lives, very happily, now. I started looking for his adult placement when he was 16. I saw how few suitable places there were; how hard it was to get funding for them; what students and families went through when it was all left too late and I did not want this for us. By this time I had become very active in the National Autistic

Society and was on the management committee of a large residential community for autistic adults about an hour's drive from our home. I looked at quite a few adult residential communities but thought this place the best.

By this time, autism has emerged from the shadows, more children are getting diagnosed and a number of private providers have seen the potential for setting up schools and residential placements for adults. I go to look at one of these on a mild spring day. It's just down the road from where we live and I like it very much. The place I am involved with is huge and isolated in comparison; I can see the advantages of the smallness and the proximity of this place. I can see a few disadvantages too. How will Jonny cope if we bump into him on a day we aren't scheduled to visit? Will he want to come home with us? Will his carers be able to make him understand that he isn't going home when he passes familiar landmarks? The people there are lovely. They are learning fast about autism. But finally I decide that they should be our second choice.

The problem I foresee is one of varying fashions in private care. What will happen when something else becomes more profitable? Will the place change its use and its residents become homeless? Placing a 19-year-old is hard, but placing a 30-year-old is probably much harder. What if they go bust, become ill, get bored with it all? I decide that a charity devoted to autism is probably a more reliable provider. They won't be affected by the market or beguiled by a more fashionable disability.

And so we start on the assessment process again. Jonny is visited at school where he is observed, and his teachers and care workers questioned. Miles rings to tell me it has gone well. He was able to talk about our supportiveness as a family and Jonny behaved well. At home we fill in a very long questionnaire, thinking carefully about the answers to questions about how Jonny is likely to respond to a whole range of situations. There are, as well, the usual questions about his birth, diagnosis and schooling. I stop for a moment and try to remember just how many times I have described Jonny's birth, his early childhood, his diagnosis and his early schooling. But I can't remember. I don't tell the whole truth about events at his first school. It's important that we don't seem to be troublemakers. The whole situation feels quite precarious, really, and I'm more than aware of the absurdity of trying to play down how difficult Jonny can be. He wouldn't need to live in this way if he was easy. The managers of the residential community tell me they will let me know soon.

I've got everything organized well ahead of schedule, so I'm not worried when weeks go past. I know these things can take a long time. Meanwhile, Jonny's 18th birthday comes and goes – and with it goes all his respite care. For children with special needs, education goes on till their 19th birthday; but as far as Social Services is concerned, they become adults, and therefore no longer eligible for children's services, on their 18th. There is no respite care for autistic adults in the county. I think that I will probably have to give up my job. I don't see any other way round it – the school holidays are so long. It's only for a year, but the whole thing feels unsustainable. Two people help me. One is a colleague at work who shows me a new HR policy which will give me, as the carer of a disabled family member, a little time off if other care options fall through. The other is a social worker I haven't seen since Jonny was a little child – four years old and going into respite care for his first afternoon.

Graham has six children of his own and is as calm and kind as he was then. He suggests that the nearby private provider I have considered for Jonny's home, and which also runs a day service for young adults like him, might be persuaded to offer some respite. We go to visit. They agree, and the county pays without any argument.

Jonny's first holiday works fine, and I manage to hang onto my job. The new residential placement, where he goes for respite care, is filling up with permanent residents and I realize that several months have gone by since Jonny's assessment. So I decide to contact the place we have applied to and ask them when we will hear. They fail to return my messages for some days, but eventually I speak to the manager.

'Oh, haven't you been told? Sorry. I thought you had. We decided that Jonathan isn't suitable. Sorry, I really thought we had written to you. It was months ago. We decided quite quickly that we don't think he'll fit in here.'

I ring the kind social worker, and he promises to ring our second choice, Jonny's current respite care, straightaway. After ten minutes the phone rings and I snatch it from its cradle.

'I'm really sorry, Sheila. They filled the last place on Tuesday. We'll have to find somewhere else.'

I lie down on the floor, first of all stunned and then consumed with anger, fear and a sense that I have come to the end of something, that I have plumbed the depths of my endurance, that there is nothing, absolutely nothing left with which I can fight. The room is spinning around. I know for certain that I cannot look after Jonny at home; that I will, for certain, break down if that is what is required of me. I've thought it all through quite carefully. He must leave his parents as all young men do. As I get older, caring for him full time will become more and more difficult, and, eventually, completely unsustainable. I want him to move gradually into a situation where he lives, well supported, independently of me. I want him to be safe when I die. Into my head comes a story I heard on the news about a father who drove into the woods with his autistic son, ran a pipe from the exhaust into the car and finished it for both of them. His note said he thought it was better for the whole family. I push away such dreadful thoughts, but I am under no illusions as to whether or not I can cope with a profoundly autistic adult living with me full time at home for the rest of my life.

I do not think I can go on, but of course I can and do. I ring Bob at work and tell him what has happened.

'I'm finished,' I say.

'No, it'll be all right,' he replies.

But I don't feel that it will. Everyone, I feel, has their store of endurance. I've been lucky with mine. But just at this moment, it has run out entirely. Bob recognizes something new in my voice; that something has snapped in me, and he quickly gets hold of a book on residential provision accredited by the National Autistic Society.

Then the searching starts again. On a grey day at the end of winter, he drives me into Wales – a destination I had never thought of – to a lovely house in a small town less than an hour from our home. We ring the bell and go in. By the end of the afternoon, I am absolutely certain that this will be right for Jonny – much better in every way than what I had planned for him. Ten adults live in this house, looked after by well trained staff who understand autism. They are calm and nice. They believe in the rights of people like my son to be active and visible, to have their wishes respected, to live good lives. They are kind and understanding to us, their residents go to pubs and shops, swimming pools and hairdressers, doctors and dentists in the local community.

There is one vacancy and five people want it. We are in a good position because we know our local authority will almost certainly fund such a place without argument. Most people do not have this advantage. They have to fight for their children. They fight to find provision. Then they fight to get it paid for. They can go through the whole assessment process only to find that at the end no one will pay. We are the lucky ones.

Two staff members from the house come to see the whole family at home. It is a lovely spring day – my birthday, and after presents and photos in the morning, we make some lunch and wait for them to arrive. I am full of nerves, but the children rise to the situation magnificently. They chat and laugh with the two women, telling them about the funny things that Jonny does, and in the telling show how much they love him. We talk about Jonny's life and education, about the ways we cope with it all – what we enjoy about him.

We sit to eat lunch together and they tell us about the service – how sad it is that their local authority has decided that it is too expensive, that it is denied to the very people it was set up for. That many of their residents have lived in very unsuitable care situations before coming to them, and are institutionalized to some degree. They tell us that it would be nice to have someone new come to live there who was used to getting out and about, who could cope with change. I explain that I've tried really hard to stop Jonny falling into routine rigidity – that sometimes it seems quite mean to him.

I tell them how I make him sit at different places round the table every evening, despite the fact that he'd like to sit in the same one, that I vary the order we put clothes on, make sure he sees visitors and does different things every day that he's at home. I once heard about an autistic boy who could only turn left, that every outing had to be preceded by the plotting of a route that involved no right turns. We've been lucky with Jonathan, and I plan to hold on to that flexibility as long as we can.

They, in turn, tell us about the way their residents live, the training they provided for the staff, how they cannot cut back what it costs any more than they have. When they go we wave goodbye and smile. We like these people very much. We want this for Jonny.

Now we must wait for their decision, for them to talk about us, to read all the reports, talk to Jonny's teachers and social workers. It is a very thorough process. I float through the days, not daring to allow myself to hope, hardly daring to take a breath, screwed up with the effort of not thinking. Finally, it comes. A positive letter from the service, a phone call from social services, details of Jonny's new home and when he can go to live there. I think of the four other families who wanted the place – of how devastated they must be.

Jonny's soon-to-be key worker – Vernon – and another member of staff go down to see him at school. They stay for a couple of nights, quietly shadowing him through his days, talking to his teachers and watching him carefully. Sadly, Jonny ends his time at this wonderful school with a very poor personal tutor. Les is a former bank manager and enthusiastic Salvationist. He is tense, fastidious and determined to do good. He buys a backpack for Jonny, which

even I know is a girl's. He corners us and witters on when
we visit, talking endlessly about things that don't seem to be
very important. Jonny appears to regard him with contempt.
This do-gooder isn't happy with Jonny's morning masturba-
tion – appropriately private and unintrusive – and he tries to
stop it. So Jonny starts to wet the bed again – every morning
– a practice which continues to this day.

When Vernon and his colleague visit, Les decides to
organize a trip to the pub for the older students and the
visitors. It's a mild summer evening, and the students come
to the pub by minibus. They sit happily in the garden, some
flapping a favourite comforter, the more vocal ones talking
at someone nineteen to the dozen. It's fairly quiet at the
pub and no one bothers them. Soon they all have drinks
and crisps. Jonny has a shandy, happy as he almost always
is when food and drink are on offer. One of the young
women, though, gets up from the bench where she is sitting and starts to pace up and down. She rocks her head a
little. None of the other students seems to be aware of or
disturbed by her. Les is though. He looks at Vernon and
smiles nervously.

'Oh dear, oh dear, trouble already. We shouldn't have
come.'

Vernon looks at him in amazement, but says nothing.
He's a guest here and shouldn't interfere. Les gets out his
mobile phone.

'Bring the minibus back – quick. We've got trouble.'

Vernon raises his eyebrows as he looks at his colleague,
then they both suck in their cheeks and look at the ground.

By the time the minibus arrives, the young woman is
sitting quietly drinking her coke. The two young men who
have come back with the van look puzzled – and a bit

annoyed. They've turned round to come back and will now be late off shift. They don't mind if it's an emergency, but it's clearly not.

'We'd better go back anyway,' Les says. 'You never know when she might start again. Come on everyone, let's go back.'

Everyone ignores him. Vernon looks to see how Jonny is taking the suggestion that he return to school just as he's settled down to enjoy himself, and his expression turns to a wide grin. Jonny is sitting completely still and quiet, apparently unaware of any trouble. He sits immobile, his face impassive, his hands still. He has ripped his crisp packet to shreds, as he always does when he has finished with it, and stuffed the bits into his shandy bottle. On his head his beer glass is perfectly balanced. He waits. It takes a minute or two before it happens. But Les's reaction is worth waiting for.

It's a really beautiful, hot summer's day – August at its very best. We set off quite early because we have a two-hour drive. I make sure I have sunscreen and a bottle of water for us. Jonny has stayed the night with me and he gets into the car eagerly. I've told him where we are going, who we're going to see, and I think he has understood. I put on a tape of pop music and we set off. All around us, trees are full of green. The sky is blue, the fields full of golden wheat scattered with red poppies, waiting for harvest. Verges are crammed with daisies, hedgerows with cow parsley. Driving through circuitous country lanes, rising and falling, twisting and turning, we pass little cottages and roadside inns. We drive for several miles along a ridge, fields dropping away to either side, revealing stunning views. Jonny shakes with excitement at each new song, at the drive and, perhaps, because he recognizes a route he hasn't travelled for some time. Eventually we slow down – getting close now. On a Saturday like this, people bring their children to the long unspoilt beaches behind these villages, drive to shop in the local market town, travel with binoculars to watch birds in the nature reserve found at the end of the miles of winding lanes.

I pull into a National Trust car park, take Jonny to the loo and then get out my mobile phone. Julie answers immediately.

'Be there in five minutes. I can't wait to see him!'

We wait. Above us rises the ruined castle. Dots that are people, move up the slope to its highest point. They point out landmarks in the distance to their companions. On the café terrace people drink coffee or lemonade, eat cakes or ice cream. A hot summer Saturday in Dorset. I'm scanning the entrance to the car park. Julie has told me what kind of car to look for. 'Here she is, Jonny.' I pray that he'll recognize her, acknowledge her, show the love I know he feels for her. She pulls up beside us and jumps out. Jonny's face lights up.

'Julie.' He leans towards her as she gets into the back seat to hug him.

'Hallo darling.'

His smile cannot get any wider.

She gets back into her car and starts the engine. She checks we are behind her and drives slowly out of the car park. Directions to Miles' country cottage, it has been deemed, would be too complex for us to follow. This warren of lanes, meandering through hills and fields to the sea, sports few signposts. We follow Julie's car down narrower and narrower roads until we inch slowly down the rutted, uneven track that leads to the cottage. Finally she stops and we pull up behind her on the grass. We have arrived.

'Come on Jonny, we're here.'

For a second he just sits. He doesn't recognize the place, although he has, apparently, been here before. I haven't.

'This is Miles' house, sweetheart. Miles lives here with Sally now.'

Sally works at the school as well. Jonny looks a little more interested, but still doesn't move.

'There's lunch for us in the garden – a picnic with Miles and Sally and Julie – your old friends. We haven't seen them for ages, have we?'

He gets out.

Julie leads us round the corner. She's had her hair dyed blonde, put it up in a pony tail. She looks a little older, as I must too. A low-eaved cottage comes into view, with piles of logs stacked against it. A large garden surrounds it, with swings and mismatched chairs, a large vegetable patch and flowers. Miles and Sally come round the corner. We hug.

'Hallo Jonny, it's lovely to see you. Come and sit in the garden.'

Jonny beams and beams. I'm so happy. This is going to be a success. We sit round a table and they bring out home-made lemonade and pizza, bread, cheese, salad. Miles' hair has been cut back hard – he looks strange without the unruly curls. But Jonny knows him – and he recognizes Sally too. He eats happily as we chat. I tell them how well he is doing at his new home, about the horse riding and swimming, what he does at his day centre. I tell them about the break up of my marriage and they express sympathy, slightly embarrassed. Jonny indicates what he wants politely and waits to be told it's OK to take things. Miles' sons appear for a while, run around a bit, fill up some plates with food and disappear back inside to their computer games.

After lunch we move into the shade. Jonny settles happily into a swing seat and offers his leg to Julie for her to rub. They tell me how things are at the school.

'It's very different, now,' Miles says. 'The kids all have computers in their rooms.'

'Jonny couldn't have managed a computer,' I say. 'Nor could most of the others who were there then.'

'Yes, the children are different now – challenging, but much more able.'

'Where are all the Jonnys, then?' I ask. 'Where do they go now? There wasn't much other provision for children like him.'

They all shrug their shoulders. Sally brings us drinks. There are bits of confetti lying around.

Miles is a tenant on this pretty estate, and often used to take Jonny and the other students for walks along a private beach he has access to. We pile into his car and he takes us all there. Jonny walks well with us. It's a creek, or estuary really, that we walk beside in the afternoon sunshine. Julie talks about her new job and relationship. Jonny pauses to throw stones into the sea, watching with excitement as they plop into the water. Miles and Sally stop to look at the place they carved a tiny heart into the rock. Julie walks with Jonny and talks to him. Every now and then he says a word or two to her. There's a slight breeze, making it comfortable to walk. The waves come in very gently, scattered with diamonds of sunlight. We are alone on this little strip of sand and sea.

We walk and then drive back through the woods, sunlight filtering through the trees. Back at the house, we have tea and cake and I say we must soon be going. I am going to drive Jonny all the way back to his home – a journey of at least three hours. We've talked and talked. I've told them all about Jonny's new life; we've eaten, drunk, laughed, walked by the sea under a cloudless blue sky. These people know and love Jonny. I have relaxed and let go of my habitual tension, averted eyes, face set hard to ignore stares and comments. We have had a wonderful time.

'What do you think of him?' I ask.

'We think he's fantastic. You're great, Jonny. You've done so well.'

'He's made his own life, lives on his terms, copes with the autism really well. I'm so proud of him,' I say.

It's a long drive back. We stop at a service station and sit on the grass to have a drink. When we get back, Jonny is tired, but he runs into the house, laughing, happy.

'Did he have a good day?' they ask me.

'A really good day,' I reply. 'We went to see our friends. It was good, wasn't it Jonny? A really great day.'

Chapter Five

———

BROTHERS AND SISTERS

My MOTHER-IN-LAW and her cousin are sitting in the living room.

'We can't believe you're so calm,' they keep saying.

'Mmm. Don't worry, I'll go in plenty of time.'

I'm standing in the kitchen, in the light of a summer evening, making Ben's lunch, stopping every so often to let a contraction pass. Jonny doesn't get an option about lunch, but Ben does and he chooses sandwiches. My waters broke this morning and they say you should go straight to the hospital if that happens. This is my third birth, though, and I don't intend to go yet. I've seen the midwife; I've timed the contractions. I know this baby won't be coming for a little while yet. What I do know is that my daughter will be born reasonably soon – probably in the early hours of tomorrow morning.

It's been hot for ages. I'm big and clumsy and slow at everything, drinking juice continually. I'll be glad when it's all over. I think I've got everything covered here. My mother-in-law will help Bob with the two boys. I told Jonny's escort this morning that I'll soon be in labour and she will have let the unit know. The baby's bedroom is ready, my bag packed. I've chosen a domino delivery – in hospital for the birth – out straight afterwards. This breaking of the waters may have scuppered that, but I won't stay in a minute longer than necessary. I've come to the conclusion that hospitals are stressful places to spend the first days of your baby's life, and anyway, I'm not at all sure how things will go here if I stay in too long. Finally I decide that everyone is settled and my contractions are coming fast enough. We drive up to the hospital and a few hours later Hannah is born. This birth is straightforward – not the hours of labour and forceps delivery of my first, nor the anxiety of a baby who is not breathing that was Jonny's. I will have to stay in overnight, though. Just as I thought, the early-breaking waters mean they want to keep me there for a few hours.

I'm up, dressed and waiting by 7 am the next morning, holding my beautiful little daughter. She's been feeding well and I feel fine except that my leg is throbbing just above and behind the knee. Early this morning I asked a nurse to look at it, but she said she couldn't do anything for me. I guess she was at the end of a night shift and wanting to get off. I'm not particularly worried. This vein came up during my first pregnancy and has been getting worse with each one. I've been wearing a bandage on it for the last six months. Strangely, the vein seems to have disappeared, although the pain is persistent. I know the midwife will come to see me every day, so I'll just wait to show it to her. My baby is born, my pregnancy over. I want to get home and get on with things now. I want to be ready when my boys come home from school and meet their sister for the first time.

I have to sit waiting for two hours, but eventually Bob collects me from the hospital. Once home I sit in the sunny garden eating a sandwich, the baby in a Moses basket at my feet. My neighbour comes out to see how I am and to coo at our beautiful little girl. Hannah sleeps through it all, only snuffling and moving a little as we chat over her. She has black hair and strong features. The hair will change, I know, but the other strong features remain. It always seems so strange, this normality after birth – ordinary life that has gone on as usual while you've inhabited a nether world of blood, pain and new life.

After my sandwich, I have a bath and tidy myself up. I change Hannah and dress her in the white velour babygro with bluebirds that has been worn by all the children. I want her to look nice when Ben comes back from school with his grandmother and Jonny's taxi brings him home. Our bedroom is light and pretty, with blond wood and pink and blue fabrics. Hannah's carrycot is on its stand in the corner of the room, close to my side of the bed, so that I can lift her out quickly and feed her in bed in the night. But when her brothers come in, she is in my arms – calm, watching. Ben is overwhelmed, Jonny apparently indifferent. Ben holds his sister on his lap and smiles up in wonderment as his father takes a picture. Then I lay Hannah on the bed while Ben talks to her.

'Hallo, little baby. Hallo baby Hannah. I'm your big brother. Hallo.'

His voice is very gentle, and Hannah searches his face. Then Jonny suddenly shows a little interest. He is clutching his flappy boat as he leans over her, watching her clench and unclench her tiny fists. She doesn't cry and we get another good photo of the three children. Then the boys go downstairs for their tea and television. I hear Ben's excited chatter about his baby sister.

Later in the evening, the hot weather finally breaks and it pours with rain. I watch the raindrops race down the window in that slightly removed state of the sleep-deprived. My leg is still throbbing. The boys are getting ready for bed when the midwife comes, takes one look at my leg and rushes off for bandages and medication to treat my phlebitis.

I don't stay in bed for long. There's so much to do. My new baby is lovely – not sleeping much, just like her brothers – but good-natured, rarely crying. She lies quietly looking around her, interested in the wallpaper and duvet cover, trying hard to focus on my face when I feed her. It's peaceful during the day until the boys come home. Then it's very busy. I'm still at the stage of expecting Jonny's 'autistic tendencies with developmental delay' to sort itself out. Still expecting the teachers at the unit to effect the miracle they've promised me. It's a busy but quite happy time.

Each morning I feed Hannah and talk to her, stroking her face and getting her to clutch my fingers. Then I change her and when she's ready to sleep again, I put her in her pram in the hall and get out brushes and tins of paint. We've had a loft conversion – an extra flight of stairs leads up to a beautiful high bedroom for Jonny's and Ben's bunk beds and their shelves of toys. There are windows in the roof where you can look out on the tops of the green, green trees. The new stairs and doors need painting and it's hectic in the evenings, so I get on with it in the daytime. It takes three weeks to finish, but I feel pleased that it's done.

Bob and I get into a routine of putting Jonny and Hannah to bed – one each – and then, whoever finishes first, reading Ben his story and starting to cook the evening meal. Hannah sleeps in her pram in the hall so that I can feed her easily during the evening. I give her a last feed when I go to bed and put her in her carrycot. There are five of us now. One's autistic and needs extra support, but I am determined that every member of this family will have rights and responsibilities, that Jonny will have his place and all the care and attention we can give him, but that no one's needs will be sacrificed for him.

When Hannah is five weeks old we go on holiday to the house in north Devon we go to every year. It's owned by the kindest of couples who are wardens at a local supported housing scheme for older people. They live on site and let out their house by the sea until they need it again. The boys love the familiarity and regular routines of it, the huge beach, the corner shop with flags for their castles, ice creams and kites. It takes about three hours to get there – with me squashed in the back with Jonny, Hannah's carrycot and a lot of biscuit crumbs. Excitement mounts as we arrive at the corner of the lane where the shop is located, and turn into the driveway of the house.

'We're here, I can see it! We're here, Jonny!'

Jonny flaps the boat. The house is on the end of a terrace of four; homely, with a small, secluded, slightly overgrown garden and a double bedroom at the very top of the house, reached by a final tiny flight of stairs. The boys have bedrooms on the first floor and we have this rooftop room, where our hosts have put their daughter's old cot under the eaves for Hannah.

We unpack while Ben busies himself with the box of toys they always leave, and Jonny sits flapping his boat. Then we have tea and take the short walk down to the beach in the warm evening light. I have Hannah in a sling, strapped to me, and hold Jonny's hand tightly. He screws up his fingers, but I don't let go. The lane is quiet, with little colourwashed houses on either side, and the wonderful blue line of the sea visible in the distance. But I don't want to take the risk of Jonny running off just as a car comes round the corner.

We have a couple of mats and buckets and spades with us as we walk down the road and onto the beach. The tide is out and there seem to be miles of sand, stretching away into the distance with only the occasional dog walker and kite flyer dotted about. I settle down on one of the mats and loosen the sling. Both boys run about in an ecstasy of movement. There is so much space. Then Jonny sits himself on the ribbed sand by a little pool left by the receding tide, and drops stones in, over and over again, absorbed and happy in this repetitive movement and each satisfying splash. Ben takes his spade and draws an enormous cat on the beach. I sit and wonder. How can he tell what it will look like when he stands back to see his handiwork? He can, though. The cat is huge and magnificent. And why doesn't he mind that, while he sleeps, the tide will come in and wash it all away?

As the sun sets, the beach is burnt up in an orange glow, splashed with brightness at every little pool. We take the children home. Ben settles in front of the television while we bath Jonny and Hannah. We read stories, and put on night-lights. Soon we all get to bed and Hannah sleeps through the night for the first time.

The weather is perfect for the whole fortnight, much of which I spend feeding and changing Hannah. I'm still in that baby bubble, with time and the doings of others slightly at a distance. Jonny flaps and babbles, plays with water, seems quite happy. A friend visits us and we all go to a deserted cove where long fingers of rock reach into the sea. It's quite a long descent from the grassy cliff above, dotted with sea thrift, but it's worth the climb.

I take Hannah out of the sling and lie her on a towel on the sand. Ben rushes into the sea to jump and shout. Jonny finds a pool and throws water up into the air with his spade, a sparkling cascade of silver droplets, while we bathe in the luxury of isolation, with no other people to worry about. We eat some sandwiches and drink squash, watching the sunlight play on the waves – happy. Suddenly our friend picks Jonny up and swings him round and round. Jonny laughs and laughs. Maybe he'll be sick, I think, but I don't care. The sea is blue and white, a soft breeze blows, shifting the pink or bleached heads of sea thrift back and forth. The landscape is gloriously beautiful. My golden-haired older son splashes in the waves, shouting at us to watch him, my baby girl lies quietly watching white clouds dance above her, and against the blue sky my younger son whirls round and round, laughing and laughing.

Over the fortnight we paddle and collect shells, make sandcastles, visit the local nature reserve where we must negotiate sheep and close gates before parking by a huge beach bounded by massive pebbles. We fly kites, visit local markets and go across the estuary on the little ferry to watch children on the other side sit on the sea wall catching crabs. There is a photograph of us on this little crossing – one of our favourite activities. I'm sitting in the boat. On one side of me Ben sits, head turned slightly to watch the waves and receding shoreline. He's wearing brown shorts and a red tee shirt. On the other side of me Jonny sits, clutching his boat with one hand, the other held firmly by me. His head is also turned sideways, but not to look at anything. He's wearing blue shorts and a yellow tee shirt. Both boys have blond curls ruffled by the wind. I'm wearing a capacious chambray skirt, taken in a little since my pregnancy, but still shapeless. I have a navy-blue sling attached to my front, and from it peep two little pink and white striped socks.

I expect Jonny was difficult on this holiday – maybe crying or wailing when things weren't quite right. I expect people stared at him and that at times I was unbearably tired. I don't remember any of this, though, just sunshine and water, feeding and changing our baby, going with the flow. The tenth anniversary of Elvis' death occurs during our second week away, and Hannah lies on a blanket in front of the television, mesmerized by the recordings of his stage appearances that are shown all evening.

I join a local support group – a pressure group too, since the grandfather of one little girl at the unit is an experienced trade unionist and is determined to campaign for better educational provision for our children. He is active in local community support as well, and we start to visit the city farm he is involved with on a regular basis. Jonny's birthday will be celebrated there this year along with Tim's, and Ben will put on a magic show for the autistic children and their brothers and sisters.

Ben's love of magic began when he was very young. The Christmas he was five I made him a 'magic man' cape and top hat – complete with sequins and stars – and a 'magic man' box, similarly decorated and full of tricks. At first the trickery of it disappoints him – he thought a magic wand was just that. But after the initial shock of finding that waving it and saying 'abracadabra' doesn't make us disappear or float up to the ceiling, he takes to his new hobby with gusto.

He sends for things from catalogues, and visits magicians' shops in search of the latest tricks. He has a dove pan that he fills with paper and sets alight before putting on the lid. He waves his magic wand and recites his magic words, fixing his audience of utterly spellbound young children with a surprised expression. Then he raises the lid with a flourish, producing – not doves, fortunately – but a pan full of sweets for his delighted audience. He begins by doing these shows at his brother's and sister's birthday parties, and soon gets asked to do them for other families. He's good and he earns a little money from it.

On the day of the party we get the children dressed, Jonny in new blue cords and a blue sweatshirt with a silver robot on the front. Ben has grey cords and a yellow tee shirt under his magic man cape. Hannah's in a pretty track suit in bright primary colours. There's a brilliant rumpus room at the city farm, and I don't want her inhibited by a dress. All three children have blondish-brown curls – Hannah's tumbling down her back – and huge blue eyes with very long lashes. They are a pretty good-looking trio, I think.

'Ok everyone. We're ready. Let's get going. Have you got everything, Ben?'

'Yes.'

'Sure? Tape recorder?'

'Yes.'

We get into the car. I sit in the back with Jonny and Hannah, carefully holding on my lap a tin containing the birthday cake. I've made a sponge swimming pool, complete with blue icing, marshmallow stair rails, liquorice lanes and little plastic figures with red swimsuits iced on. Ben sits in the front with his magic show equipment. It takes 30 minutes to drive to the farm, where we park and get out.

A long table has been put out for us – most of the children from the unit have come, plus brothers and sisters. We are quite a crowd. On the table are jugs of juice, bowls of jelly, plates of crisps, sandwiches, sausage rolls and biscuits, all wrapped in cling film. In pride of place is Tim's cake – a rail track with a train. I get Jonny's cake out of the tin and put it next to Tim's. There is a lot of noise. The children – with brothers and sisters – are aged from 2 to 11. I say hallo to people, but also take a minute to watch. You would only pick out the autistic children if you knew what you were looking for.

Events like this are strange in many ways. You are spending time with people with whom you have nothing in common necessarily, except your autistic child. Like any children's event, I suppose, except that even within that milieu we tend to gravitate towards people like ourselves. It's a relief, though. Here we don't have to watch our autistic sons and daughters all the time – preparing to help them navigate, explaining, fielding stares and comments. And here, the siblings can let rip. Their brother or sister won't be an embarrassment to them. They won't be worrying what will happen. We're all in the club, like it or not.

I help Ben set out a table and hide his things – we don't want anyone knowing his secrets – and then we all go round to the rumpus room. The farm is scruffy, but that's nice too. We don't have to worry at all today. Any damage sustained will fade in with the other knocks and scrapes. A long, low room is full of soft play equipment, a little trampoline, large balls and cylinders, ropes and mats. There's a little slide coming down to a soft, safe mat. The children can run and jump, swing and roll with very little potential for damage. It's easier to pick out the children from the unit now. Jonny rolls back and forth, leaning over a ball, eyes glazed. Tim goes down the slide over and over again with no smile or screeches of delight. Sally makes a little den of big soft bricks and lies inside it sucking her thumb. Other autistic children are not so quiet. They shriek and laugh as do the other children, but the quality of it is somehow different.

Hannah runs from activity to activity, trying everything, worried there'll be something she missed. She shouts, 'Look Ben. Look Ben, Ben come on this!'

But Ben's swinging on a rope, with another older brother, and falling onto the pile of mats they've pulled into place. We parents stand at the side, watching, chatting about our sons and daughters, drinking coffee.

Some of the children go outside with Bill, the organizer, to look at the baby animals that have been born this spring. Hannah goes, hand in hand with Jesse, David's sister, but Ben and Jonny stay. I hear Hannah say, 'No, he can't be autistic. He's talking.'

'Yes, he is. He's my brother, I know.'

'No, if you're autistic you can't talk.'

'Well, David can. He still hits me though...'

They move out of earshot and I turn back to check that Jonny's all right. He's jumping on the trampoline now, absorbed in his bouncing, and Ben needs to sort his magic show so he'll be ready after tea. At teatime, the children sit at the long table, eating and laughing. The noise is stupendous. We light candles on the two cakes, and Tim's mum and I hold our sons and gently encourage them to blow out the candles. They look away as some of the children sing *Happy Birthday*. There's a lot of food on the floor. Then we put out chairs in front of Ben's table and shepherd the children onto them. Ben has covered the table with a cloth and put his tape recorder on it. He's wearing his cloak and a black bowler hat – the cardboard top hat has long since disintegrated. The music starts – he doesn't speak during his act – and he starts to produce table tennis balls from his mouth. He doesn't look at his audience, but at the balls, miming amazement and discomfort as he takes each one from his mouth. Gradually the children quieten and watch, fascinated, their eyes wide.

The music plays and the show continues. Ben changes sheets of paper into five-pound notes, makes a ball float on top of a cloth, makes coins disappear only to reappear behind the ears of the watching children. He makes ropes stand up, bricks fall down and scarves change colour. For the finale, he lights the paper in the dove pan and waves his magic wand over it. He puts on the lid and the fire disappears. Another wave of the wand, more magic words and he pulls off the lid with a flourish and shows the children the pan now full of little boxes of Smarties. They look suspicious as he hands them round, then they open the boxes and eat the sweets. Everyone claps and smiles. The mothers and fathers tell Ben how good they think he is.

Afterwards a young boy comes up to him and says, 'Magic some more sweets then – if you can.'

He's quite plump with black hair and tight shorts.

'No, the show's finished now.'

'I bet you can't. I bet it's a trick.'

'Maybe. But why weren't the sweets burnt in the fire?'

'Magic some more then.'

He's quite insistent, his face almost belligerent, and Ben looks to me for help.

'The show's finished now. There aren't any more sweets,' I say.

He looks at me suspiciously, but drifts away.

'Is he autistic?' Ben asks.

'No, he isn't. Not all bad behaviour is autistic.'

We pack up and go home. It's been a good day.

I turn my key in the lock and come into the house. I know at once that all is not well. The atmosphere is bad, although everything seems very quiet. Ben, 18 years old now and living at home while he completes a foundation year at the local art school before university, is sitting on a chair in the hall. He looks up at me but doesn't say anything. He is holding a bag of ice on his hand. I've been to choir – my one activity outside of the family, the very last remnant of an independent life. I've been singing since I was very young – in school, at university and afterwards. I've sung in abbeys, cathedrals, chapels and some quite well known concert halls. I've sung in Britain and on the continent, on the radio, television and for record companies. It's been my lifeline through some tough times, a continual source of joy. After tonight, though, I won't go to choir when Jonny is home, just as I didn't for the four years before he started weekly boarding. It won't feel safe for me to leave the house.

I look around and see there's a new lump out of the door to the kitchen.

'What happened?' I ask Ben.

'Jonny hit me.' He looks frightened and disturbed. 'He really wanted to hurt me.'

'Oh, I'm sure he didn't. I expect he was upset. I know it's rotten, but it's the autism, it's nothing to do with you.'

'No, he really wanted to hurt me. He wouldn't leave me alone. His face… He really wanted to hurt *me*.'

'I'm sorry. I know it's hard, but he does really love you.'

'You weren't here. You didn't see.'

'No, that's true.'

Bob opens the kitchen door.

'What happened?'

'He went mad. He got a bat and kept hitting Ben.'

I want to cry, but I don't.

'Where is he now?'

'He's in the bath. He's calm now.'

'Where's Hannah?'

'In bed. He didn't go for her. He bit me, though.' He shows me his hand.

I go upstairs and open the bathroom door a little. Jonny is sitting in the bath with his back to me. His hair is wet. He is happily pouring water from a plastic bottle over his head – filling it and pouring, filling it and pouring. He is 11 years old, almost as tall as me, but much smaller than his brother or father. He doesn't look round at me. The floor is soaking. I put down some towels to absorb the water.

Later, the two younger ones are in bed and Ben is watching television in his room. I am on my second glass of wine, exhausted.

'Couldn't you stop him?'

Bob looks surprised.

'Sorry, what d'you mean?'

'Wasn't there any way of stopping him from hitting Ben?'

'Well, I was busy in the kitchen. I didn't know what was going on. I can't really manage him when you're not here. You're so good with him. You can always calm him down.'

I don't answer.

Years later, Ben is away at university and Hannah has a crowd of friends staying over. They're all in the sitting room, putting out airbeds, cushions and sleeping bags. They've been to the opening of the festival – to hear the rock bands playing on the little stage at the bottom of the field, away from the jazz, classical and world music stages. It rained and there are pairs and pairs of muddy shoes on the doormat.

We took Jonny down for the opening – he likes the music, the fireworks and the glowing wands we buy for him from the street vendors. But he's overtired now, having only returned from school for the holiday earlier in the day, and now he's moaning and groaning in his room. I know that it's the prelude to violence and distress. I don't want Hannah or her friends to be aware of what is happening and I'm glad they're making so much noise. I want them to have a normal evening. I want everyone to be protected from what is going on.

I close Jonny's bedroom door and sit with my back against it so that he can't get out. This enrages him and he tries to head-butt me, his teeth clenched. His face, thrust close to mine, is full of rage. But these days I am adept at dodging these blows. It's just as well. Jonny is now bigger than me – bigger and stronger. Sometimes he gets hold of my hands and twists them, but mostly I turn quickly, moving out of the way and out of reach as he lunges at me. His shoes are downstairs and I roll away from each kick. Largely I escape injury.

The room is very small – Jonny has no love for things – it's order and compactness he needs. There's a bed – pine, half of the old bunks he shared with Ben, scratched and battered with teeth marks at intervals along the wood. Between that and the door is an old armchair where he often sits, nude, immobile. It's getting a bit smelly – he wets it from time to time. I make a mental note to replace it with a garden chair – something easier to sponge down. The brown carpet is stained. By the head of the bed a chest of drawers sits under the window, with Jonny's tape recorder and tapes, books and cup, all lined up square, tidy. There's a big poster of a man surfing on a huge wave, striking against the bright yellow walls. The curtains are yellow and blue, both at the window and across the alcove where his clothes are hung, nicely out of sight. There are marks on the wall and doors, lumps gouged out, stains, evidence of previous periods of distress.

After a while Jonny gives up trying to hit me. He sits on his bed, screaming, crying and throwing everything he can lay his hands on. Clothes, books and toys, a cup and dish all ricochet off the wall, leaving dents and scratches. There's nothing heavier in the room – I've made sure of that. I pick up each missile and shove it outside the door but I do not look at him. I try not to react at all. We are locked in here together, he and I, and we'll be this way until the storm abates. I try and try to blot the sound of his anger and distress from my mind. I try to tell myself over and over again that this rage is not directed at me, that he will be full of remorse afterwards. It's hard. He looks at me with such anger, tries so hard to hurt. I've reminded myself on many occasions of how fast his heart is beating when he is like this, of how completely terrified he is. I've told his brother, his sister, his carers.

'Remember, he's more frightened than you are.'

But in here now, in this small space that is filled with rage and violence, I do not believe this. I believe that he wants to hurt me, to cause me pain. My own son, for whom I care, for whom I exhaust and deprive myself; this child I have tried so hard to help and protect, wants to crash his forehead into my face, to punish me for bringing him into the world like this. He's right, I feel, to think this. I have failed him utterly.

After an hour, the wailing starts to wind down a little and it turns to sobbing. If anything, I find this harder. This is pure, unadulterated grief. This is the moment when I know that my son does not want this to keep happening, that he regrets what has occurred. The sadness is almost unbearable. I want to hug him, tell him it's OK. But I don't. I know that is the very worst thing I could do. I must wait, wait it out, wait for it to finish of its own accord. Which it does, eventually. It feels as if the sobbing has gone on for hours but it was probably only 15 minutes or so. He is quiet now, face stained with tears, nose snotty, and this is a tricky moment. If I react too soon then the whole thing will start again. I watch obliquely for a few minutes and then I sit on the bed, not too near, still out of arm's reach, and I open a photo album. I turn the pages slowly, looking at the pictures. After a few minutes, there is complete quiet. Jonny has moved closer and is looking at the album. I hand him a tissue without looking at him and he takes it, wipes his nose and hands it back to me. Then he leans over, his arm outstretched. I flinch but don't pull away. It's OK, he isn't going to hit me.

He turns over a page and says, 'Ben.'

'Yes, that's you and Ben on the slide. Do you remember?'

Silence. I turn another page. I don't look at Jonny or speak. I just turn the pages slowly. He is looking at the pictures. When we come to the last page, he says, 'Sorry, wite, wite.'

Another tricky moment: I must get the words exactly right; if I don't he may hit me or start wailing again. Or he may say sorry for hours, getting increasingly frustrated with my inability to answer correctly.

'It's all right, Jonny.'

'Sorry, wite, wite.'

'It's all right.'

We look at all the photos again, and then go through another two albums. Occasionally Jonny repeats the 'sorry, wite, wite' and I repeat my half of the mantra. Once I am quite confident that the incident is over, I give him his pyjamas and he gets undressed. I take him to the toilet, get him settled in the bed, read to him and say goodnight. He pushes his face towards me and I force myself not to pull away. He lays his cheek against mine and says, 'Goo night. Goo night. Sorry wite, wite.'

'Goodnight darling. It's all right.'

When I open the bedroom door, I hear that all is well downstairs. They are watching television and laughing. There is no pained, nervous silence. My daughter and her friends are oblivious to what has gone on. They are OK. I close Jonny's door quietly, listen outside for a minute or two and then go into our bedroom. Bob is lying in bed, reading the newspaper, a glass of red wine in his hand.

'Everything OK now?'

'Yes. He's settled.'

I look at my watch. Three hours.

We are in north Devon again. This year the weather isn't so good. Everyone is older. Hannah wears a little blue-spotted swimming costume and plastic shoes on the warmer days. Mostly though, I make her keep on a towelling top with a hood, which I pull up over her salty curls and she pulls down again. She paddles and jumps in the sea. Ben makes sandcastles for her. We're on the beach of the nature reserve because, although it is windy and grey, it isn't actually rain-ing. There's a limited amount of time you want to spend indoors with three children.

The beach is absolutely vast. Across the expanse of ribbed yellow, swirls of dry sands blow, getting in our eyes and clothes. The sea is wild and beautiful but very far away. We have windbreaks to put right round us – difficult to put up, blown this way and that, but once up they create some shelter. We've brought the mats and buckets and spades, as well as a picnic lunch. The beach appears to be deserted but there are a few other windbreaks dotted around, presum-ably sheltering people behind them. At each end of the bay, green hills meet the sea. I'm trying to read a paper, which is shivering in the wind, and I get quite absorbed in an article about a music project in an inner-city school. Hannah and Ben have decided to brave the wind and walk down to the sea. I watch their receding figures for a while, getting smaller and smaller. They seem to be all right. Ben keeps looking back to check that he can still see us. He'll hold her hand all the way, I know. Jonny is just lying beside me, flapping his boat. They asked him if he wanted to go, but there was no response of any sort. I'm just finishing a second article when I hear the excited return of the children.

'The sea's really crashing. You can't get near – you'd get soaked! It's such a long walk, though, we're tired, and Hannah cried because she got sand in her eyes.'

'It hurt, Mummy. It's sore. I'm not going again.'

'Where's Jonny?'

The question hangs in the air. Where, indeed, is Jonny? He's no longer lying beside me, and when I stand and survey the beach beyond the windbreak, he's nowhere to be seen.

How can I possibly have been so negligent? How quietly must he have slipped away? We stand and look around the beach. There is no sign of him in any direction, no sign of anyone walking or running, just the scattered windbreaks and the swirling sand. Both of the other children start to cry.

'Where's Jonny? Where's Jonny? We've lost him. We'll never find him.'

'Yes, we will,' I say, but my voice is shaky and doesn't sound at all convincing. They cry more loudly. 'Come on now, we need to look for him. No, no, you must stay here. No one else must get lost.' I'm panicking and they know it. 'You sit here. I'll search.'

I haven't the faintest idea what to do. I can see perfectly well that he isn't on the beach. He must have climbed over the pebble ridge and run off – please God he did that rather than run into the sea – but how can he have gone so quickly? How on earth did he go without my seeing him?

'Stay there, you two,' Bob says. 'Don't move at all. Mum and I will find him.'

We set off in different directions across the huge beach, the wind whipping sand into our faces and stinging our legs. I go down towards the sea because I can swim – not that that would be much use in this wild sea – and Bob goes towards the ridge and starts to climb. I keep looking back to check that the other two have stayed put. My heart is thumping, my attempts to push from my mind the awful possibilities quite unsuccessful. Down at the sea, I look. Nothing. Nothing and no one. Nothing but huge waves crashing in and sending a fine spray of salty water to settle over my face and hair. A strong swimmer would have enormous difficulty in here. A child would drown very quickly. I look back across the beach and see, in the distance, Bob waving and I run as fast as I can across the sand, my feet sinking in at every step. He is standing by a circle of windbreaks a good hundred yards from our own. You can't see the people inside. But as I approach I see that Bob has Jonny by the hand.

'Apparently he just appeared, sat down with them and ate some sandwiches. They reckoned he was quite happy and that someone would turn up for him sooner or later. It's OK – he's absolutely fine.'

I do not reply. My heart flips over and over. He could have gone anywhere, been taken by anyone, gone into the sea and drowned. He slipped away so quietly whilst I was reading a newspaper.

'Jonny, Jonny,' Hannah cries. 'It's all right, Ben, he's all right.'

She looks anxiously at her elder brother whose face is stained with tears, but he doesn't reply. He just sits with his forehead on his knees.

'Anything could have happened to him,' he says.

After a while I return to work and we have a little more money. So we settle into a routine of one holiday with Jonny, centred around him, and one without him. He goes into respite care for a fortnight every year, precisely so that the family can have a stress-free break.

The first time we try this, we go to Normandy for a week with a friend. We have a cabin on the ferry and the crossing is calm. We drive to the farm where our rented house is situated, and find it without any problem. The weather is good all week and the house and garden are pretty and peaceful. All around us, orchards of apple and pear trees are full of blossom. A wonderful walk through these trees takes us to a *boulangerie* for our morning bread. We sit in the garden drinking local cider and stroll around the village. We have a day in Paris, where I stay with Hannah playing in a park at the base of the Eiffel Tower whilst the others go up. We walk along the river bank to Notre Dame, where we sit in the warmth of the afternoon. On another day we visit Versailles, strolling through the formal gardens amongst the fountains of water sparkling in the sunshine.

This is a trip that I look forward to for many weeks. But once we arrive, I am continually anxious. It's so important to enjoy the break. I've put my son into care, away from his family, from his brother and sister, so that we can come on this holiday. The pressure I put on myself, and on everybody else, to enjoy it, is intolerable. Sitting by the sea at Etrètat, looking at the view that Monet painted, watching the children playing in the sea, I am utterly consumed with guilt. I needed a break from Jonny, but missing him so badly is overwhelming.

It takes me a few years to get over this feeling. Jonny seems used to being left behind, although I'm conscious that we would never know if he felt it very badly. He is taken to do lots of nice things while we are away. One year we go to Majorca with close friends and Jonny goes into respite care. We hire a villa out in the countryside – a very beautiful old house with huge ferns, a lovely pool and views of hills all around. Goats wander on these hills, their bells ringing insistently, and in the afternoons we hear donkeys braying. From the terrace we look up to a monastery. The earth around it is orange and rocky. More bells ring out from it in the morning and evening.

The heat is all-pervasive, like a hot flannel laid across everything. It is so hot it's hard to think, and we are constantly bitten by mosquitoes. In the mornings we drift out in our swimsuits and sit in the shade of the poolside shelter, drinking coffee and watching the five children jump into the water. Every now and then we rub sunscreen and insect repellent on them. The air sparkles. Later we may cram into the car and bump along the rutted lane to join the main road on our way to a local market or a beach. In the evenings the four adults sit out drinking wine, or take turns to go out to a local restaurant while the other couple babysits. I read a lot of books. One day we visit a really beautiful beach with soft, white sand under huge pine trees. I take Hannah into the sea and she swims with a bright-pink rubber ring around her, laughing, completely carefree in a way she never can be when her brother is about. At the villa I watch Ben dive into the pool with our friends' older daughter, as they compete with each other to see who can retrieve the greatest number of the plastic mineral water bottles we have sunk for them. He too is laughing, happy, carefree. We are all relaxed. And in the midst of it I feel an absence, a great hole, a persistent ache. My friends have three children. And so do I. One of them, though, is not here.

Through the years I wonder over and over if I failed Jonny's brother and sister. I tried to protect them from violence, to give them space without their brother there, to give them time and attention. I saw other siblings become angry and resentful in the families who wouldn't or couldn't get respite care, and I thought we were getting through. But perhaps there were simply too many forces at play. The worst thing about being a carer is that you have so little time or energy for thinking. You are on a treadmill with little space for reflection. You are exhausted all the time, with very high levels of stress. I know that I was emotional and depressed some of the time. I felt isolated, very, very alone, overwhelmed by a sense of failure. I look back on what happened and wonder if I could have done better. It's certainly hard to be the brother or sister of a disabled child.

I try to read books about it – although it's hard at times to keep my eyes open. I understand, I think, what the problems will be. Young children are egocentric. Everything in their world relates to them. If something is wrong, they *feel* more than *think*, that it's probably their fault. And just as the survivors of wars or concentration camps suffer guilt for those who did not come through, so brothers and sisters of disabled children feel guilt at their own health and abilities. Guilt about their brother's disability; guilt about their own ability. And that's without the sibling rivalry. Brothers and sisters are in natural competition with each other. There are times when they hate each other, many times when they want to win against each other. But what happens if you feel like this about a brother who cannot compete? You are conflicted in your feelings – guilt figuring largely alongside the desire to compete. And when there are two of you? Then, perhaps, an unnaturally strong bond will form. You are in a club of two. No one else understands your situation or your conflicted feelings.

It's a beautiful spring Saturday and all the children are in the garden. I look out from time to time, but they are fine. Luckily, our garden has no back entrance. The ground rises at the end of it where our apple tree, full of pink blossom, stands against a high dry-stone wall. At the top of the wall brambles grow, almost hiding an old green corrugated iron shed. Behind the shed there is a fence, and beyond this no-man's-land is the canal towpath. We cannot see the canal from the house or garden, and people on the towpath cannot see us. Jonny cannot get out of the garden because the house is terraced. The only way out is through the front door. There are many occasions on which I am very glad of this.

Today it is mild and the children are dressed in old jeans and sweatshirts. They are playing with a building game they got for Christmas. It consists of large bright plastic pieces – blue tubes and yellow squares, black wheels and joints. From these pieces all manner of things – slides, towers and cars – can be constructed. Ben has spent the morning making a go-cart, with enthusiastic encouragement from Hannah. She tries to add the occasional piece, which he surreptitiously removes or puts in the right place for her. I can hear the cries of excitement as the go-cart comes together. Jonny is sitting on the swing that hangs from the apple tree, chewing on the rope. He holds his boat with the dangling plastic fish in his hand.

'Look Jonny. Look at what we're making. You can have a go on it soon!'

Hannah wants him to admire their work, but he doesn't respond, except to flap the boat a little faster. A few minutes later, though, I hear excited shrieks and cries and I step into the garden to watch. All three children are on the go-cart – Hannah at the front, Ben at the back and Jonny in the middle. Ben holds the cart steady at the top of the garden and then sits on.

'Ready?' he asks.

'Ready, ready, Ben go,' Hannah cries.

Jonny sits with his fingers in his ears, somehow still managing to flap the boat faster and faster.

'Ready, steady, go,' Ben shouts and puts his feet onto the

edge of the cart. It rolls down the slope till it hits a small fence at the bottom. They all fall off, laughing.

'Again, again!' shouts Hannah. 'Come on Jonny,' and she pulls him up by his hand.

Together they run up the slope, where their big brother holds the cart steady while they get on.

Sloping gardens are a feature of our lives in this hilly city. They have advantages and disadvantages. Our paddling pool, in which Jonny and Hannah sit in the summer months – she pouring water into a spinning wheel or pushing little people round in a boat and he pouring repetitively from a yoghurt carton – has a 'deep' end and a 'shallow' end. We move, eventually, to a large detached house in a village outside the city. In some ways it is a crazy move. Ben wants to go clubbing and, in later years, Hannah too. Taxis are expensive and buses unreliable, especially the ones supposedly taking them to school. For years, we ferry children back and forth along the dual carriageway into the city. But the peace and isolation is good for Jonny.

One beautifully sunny day in the summer holiday, Hannah asks round a particularly annoying schoolfriend. This little girl hasn't been at the school long – she comes from a naval family who move a lot. She has a mop of blonde curls and a very loud voice. She and Hannah play on the climbing frame, in our huge cottage garden. She's very confident for a seven-year-old. Confidence is good, I suppose, listening from the kitchen to her strident assertions about how they should play, who should be who, what they should do and who should say what. I suppose if you move from school to school, you must get thick-skinned or go under.

I've promised this girl's mother that she can stay all day, and I wonder how long Hannah's forbearance will last. I've explained to the girl's mother about Jonny, said that he'll be here, and she's fine about it, tolerant and kind.

I take them out a little picnic to have on the lawn. They are dressed up and busy. Virginia's voice goes on and on.

'Right Hannah, you stand here. No, here. Now you ask me to come home and have tea with you. Ask me to bring my baby. Go on.'

She's holding one of Hannah's dolls – her favourite, in fact. I'm surprised she's allowed this one out of her hands. She looks at me, a bit miserably I think, but she was keen to have this friend round.

'Can she come, Mummy, can she?'

'Yes, of course she can. I'll ask her mum.'

But school playtimes are quite short and this play session has now gone into its second hour.

'Here's your picnic,' I say, spreading out a blanket for them. 'Mind the jug. Don't knock it over.'

'OK Hannah, you sit there. No, I'll keep the baby.' Her voice is high-pitched, grating, insistent. Oh well, perhaps we won't ask her again for the whole day. Her mother wanted to go shopping.

Jonny seems intent on one of his favourite games. Hannah has a little wooden house with a sloping roof, next to the climbing frame. Jonny can amuse himself for a few minutes at a time by throwing a ball up onto the roof and letting it roll down. I have to watch carefully because if he thinks no one is watching he'll throw the ball, and anything else lying around, over the fence into our neighbour's garden. He seems oblivious to the two girls, although they have commandeered the climbing frame and covered it with a sheet to make another house. I wonder how long, though, he will put up with this change to his favourite place of play. I sit in the garden while they eat their picnic, making sure that all is well. Jonny sits next to me at the plastic table on the terrace and eats his lunch – all the bread first, then the ham, then the cucumber – methodical, not looking up.

'Drink,' he says, and I think it will probably be OK to go in and get him another. I won't be long and he's sitting some way from the girls.

'Hurry up, Hannah,' we hear. 'No, you must eat it all. Come on, it's my turn to be in the house.'

I'm tempted to put my fingers in my ears. Our garden is usually very quiet set, as it is, down from the road, large and private. I look at my watch; two more hours to go.

I'm standing by the tap in the kitchen, topping up the orange squash in Jonny's cup, when I hear it. I realize that there has been a very sudden silence, followed by loud howling. I run into the garden and see Virginia standing by the climbing frame, holding her face. A raw pinkish patch spreads from under her fingers. She is howling, tears rolling down her face.

'What happened?' I mouth to Hannah.

Jonny is still sitting at the table, completely unconcerned. He's drinking the squash I handed him as I hurried out. Hannah points at him.

'Jonny hit her,' she mouths back.

My hand comes up to my mouth.

'Was she still talking?'

'Yes.'

She's trying not to smile and I look away. We ring Virginia's mother, who hurries round to get her.

'Sorry, I don't know what upset him,' I lie.

'Never mind, he can't help it, I'm sure,' she says, closing the car door. Mother and daughter drive off.

'Isn't it lovely and quiet?' says Hannah, once Virginia has gone, still snuffling, her face red raw. She settles down in front of the television. Later on she has a bath with her brother.

'It's all right, Jonny,' she says. 'You can have the best pourer.' She smiles at him fondly.

On another summer evening, the house is busy. It's that time in the day when families are buzzing – everyone home, tea, television, and on this Friday evening, friends of Hannah's and Ben's staying over. They are in their rooms with their respective friends, with computer games or dolls and dressing up. The visitors have each been given their own toilet roll as they entered the house.

'Don't leave it in the loo,' I hear Ben say. 'Remember, keep it with you.'

The friends accept this strange admonition without a word of questioning or dissent, as if it were the most normal thing in the world. Jonny is in the bath. He'll play for a little while before bed.

'Go way,' he says to me when I look in.

He wants to be left alone to pour in peace. So I go downstairs to wash up. I come out into the hall from time to time to listen for his exit. But all is quiet. We've had heavy-duty vinyl laid in the bathroom, sealed to the edges of the bath and loo. Too many floods through the ceiling have taught us what we must do every time we move. Then I hear Ben's voice from the landing.

'Naked-boy alert. Naked-boy alert.'

I run up the stairs. All the bedroom doors are shut but Ben is standing on the landing making sure no one comes out, especially the little girl in Hannah's room. Jonny is an adolescent now. He's standing outside the bathroom, naked, dripping. I wrap a towel round him and take him into his bedroom. Hannah's face appears at her door.

'All clear now?' she asks. 'Rosie needs the loo.'

'Just a minute,' I say, 'Unless she wants to go downstairs?' I go into the bathroom and mop up the floor. 'OK,' I say.

'All clear,' Ben shouts.

Rosie comes out and looks around.

'Won't be a minute, Hannah,' she says.

I am proud of my children, of the way they make a family life in spite of all the difficulties they must cope with, of their enduring humour in the face of their brother's strange, and often difficult, behaviour. In our first house we have an old bed settee in the dining room, which is also their playroom. The children regularly unfold this settee to make a bed stretching across the floor on which they can lie to watch television. I come into the room from the kitchen one wintry Saturday morning to clear away breakfast and find all three children lying on this unfolded settee, side by side, on their tummies with their chins cupped in their hands, watching cartoons.

A few years later, we are living in the cottage. It has an open-plan staircase rising from the old dining room, with a wood-burning stove in the big stone fireplace. The wood burner isn't lit because it is summer, although the room is cool as it often is. The three children sit on the stairs, one above the other. They are all in school uniform and sit silently, completely absorbed in sucking ice lollies. Later on, after tea and bath, Jonny is in bed, clutching his boat. Ben sits on a little stool at the side of the bed, reading him a story, stopping every now and then to get him to repeat a word or say the one that is to come next. Hannah's lying on the end of the bed, listening as well.

'No, let Jonny say it, Hannah. It's his story time.'

'I hate that bloody film,' says Hannah as she and Ben come into the kitchen.

'What?' I'm busy cooking, absorbed in my thoughts, not listening.

'Yeah,' Ben agrees. 'People love it because he can say what day any date from any year is.'

'Oh, *Rain Man*,' I say.

'Yes *Rain Man*,' Hannah confirms. 'I hate it. I'm sick of people asking me what Jonny's special talent is.'

Ben agrees, 'Everyone thinks Jonny must be amazing.'

Idiot savant. The idea catches the imagination. People love it. They've never seen it except on television, but they know that autistic people have special talents – they play the piano brilliantly, draw buildings seen once from memory, do amazing calculations in their heads.

'I told them he can make himself invisible,' Ben says.

'What?'

'I told them my brother's autistic and they said "oh what's his special talent?" So I said, "He can make himself invisible whenever he wants to. It's really annoying. We never know where he is."'

They both laugh as they walk out.

Idiot savant. It's very, very rare. And ask yourself this – when someone can draw a building they've seen once, in the finest detail, but cannot sketch anything from imagination; when someone can calculate the day anyone's birthday falls but cannot tell a sad face from a happy one; is that special talent? Or malfunctioning of the brain on a massive scale? Or is it, perhaps, one of the saddest things you've ever heard?

Over the years my non-autistic children, who instinctively avoid drawing attention to themselves, become fierce advocates of a person's right to be different; to equality. They become suddenly eloquent – fired by anger – when they see injustice, especially towards disabled people. They themselves are relaxed and tolerant with others. They know what matters. They have enormous humour – just as their brother does – despite the fact that their lives are often troubled and filled with anxiety. I watch as Jonny turns away from the presents they have so carefully chosen and wrapped for him, and my heart bleeds for them. But I am also enormously proud of them for the strength they do not know they have, for their goodness.

Ben's away at university, but the rest of us are in a huge supermarket. Jonny's recovering from his toenail operation, so we get a wheelchair for him. He's delighted, hating to stand or walk when he could sit. I foresee trouble when we come next time. But for now we push him round in the wheelchair, filling our trolley. People smile sympathetically at us. How well we cope! How brave this boy must be. It's amazing the way a supposed physical disability provokes this benign reaction. When Jonny is just autistic, life isn't nearly so kind. At the checkout, though, he lets us down. He suddenly discovers that standing up on the footrest of the wheelchair and leaning forward is really good fun.

He does this once and we ignore him. The woman on the checkout looks surprised, but turns away. But Jonny thinks this is hilarious. He's laughing and laughing, watching me out of the corner of his eye. He stands again and again. People around us are starting to mutter and look at us. This is much more normal. I will the people in front to hurry up, so we can pack our shopping and get back to the car.

But then I hear

'It's a miracle!' and I have to laugh.

Hannah, my quiet little daughter, is looking round at our observers.

'It's a miracle!' she exclaims. 'Jonny can walk.'

On the way back to the car, we laugh and laugh. And Jonny smiles proudly at his clever trick.

Ben and Hannah dream that Jonny speaks to them. It's strange. We all dream it. We're sitting round the table, eating dinner. Jonny is away at school. Ben and Hannah are engaged in their usual repartee. I'm laughing so much I'm in danger of choking. Then suddenly:

'I dreamt Jonny could talk last night.'

'What was his voice like? I dream that too, but I can never remember in the morning.'

'No, I can't remember.'

'What was he talking about?'

'Oh, we were just talking about the TV – what was on. We were just walking along – just being normal.'

Of course Jonny has never been 'normal' in his life. But the wrench is terrible when I dream that Jonny talks and then I wake. I realize I was dreaming, that it is a fantasy, something that isn't true. The lovely chat I have with my son – the normal conversation, the relationship we have

in these dreams – will never happen. We will never have a
conversation like this as long as we live.

We've just come into the restaurant. Jonny knows it well.
We've come here many times over the years. The Italian
waiters are lovely – always helpful and kind to us. Jonny
has been staying for the weekend and he's going back today.
Hannah's with us, and Ben and his partner have come down
from London and are going to meet us here. We settle to
wait for them. Not too long, we hope. Jonny isn't good
at waiting. I ask Jonny if he wants pasta or pizza. He says
something that sounds like pasta, but I'm not sure. We order
lemonade for him and wine for us, just as the others arrive.
There's lot of hugging and exclamations of greeting.

'Hallo, Jonny,' says Ben.

'Hallo Jonny,' says Kirsty.

Jonny smiles, but not at them.

'Pasta,' I think he says.

'OK, let's get food.'

We all choose a meal. I choose a pizza, so that if I got
Jonny's order wrong, we can swap. The others chatter away.
Every so often, Jonny says:

'Go way.'

'Does he want us to go?' asks Ben, looking hurt.

'No,' I say, 'he's really pleased to see you. He's just finding the chatter a bit much.'

They stay quiet for a few seconds, but then inevitably
they start talking and laughing again, discussing a TV programme they regularly watch. Jonny smiles at Ben's partner.
His smile is sideways on – never direct. He repeats 'Go way'
periodically. But we ignore him, and he doesn't mind. When
the pasta comes, he wolfs it down.

'Slow down, Jonny,' I say.

He ignores me as he always does, but I repeat it from time to time anyway. He's finished well before anyone else.

'Take way,' he says.

'They'll take it away in a minute,' I say.

'Take way.'

He's getting agitated. I ask one of the waiters to clear his place and try to explain that 'no, the others haven't finished yet'. But we manage the meal. The others are going back to the house to stay but I'm going to drive Jonny home. The car is parked close by, on a yellow line. I have a disabled parking card for him. As we leave, Jonny looks out from under his lashes. His smile is for them and them alone. He loves them. When we get outside, he says 'Ben'.

At his home, he watches family videos over and over again. I make him a new one every birthday and Christmas. I also make photo albums – of himself and his family. He loves them. Sometimes, they tell me at the house, it is hard to get him away from them and out to do other things. He loves so much to sit and watch these videos. Sometimes he cries for us. Sometimes he says our names. Sometimes he says 'home'. But this is his home now. His brother has grown up and left, and so has he. That's what I tell people, but I know what Jonny thinks. He knows where his home is. It's where his family is. For my own part, I know that we all must have time without him. I know that I must take him back so that I can enjoy the company of my other children – and that everyone else can enjoy themselves too.

The family therapist who helped me so much still sees me from time to time. I ask her to help with my marriage, and she tries. But it's hopeless. I'm confused and exhausted. I feel so lonely, as if I am trying single-handedly to keep a sinking ship afloat. The other children do not swear at me, or argue, slam doors or flounce around. I know it's not normal behaviour for teenagers, but I can't help being relieved. There is a level of disconnection but I'm too exhausted to think about it. Keeping the family together has become an overriding obsession. Trying so hard to protect everyone from damage, all I succeed in doing is to give the impression that it's fine to leave everything to Mum. She can cope. They do have a lot to deal with, my children, maybe I shouldn't expect more? Alone with me again, the therapist says she thinks I should have some help. I don't understand.

'What do you mean?' I ask. 'You help. We have respite care. What more can there be?'

'You do everything,' she says, 'washing, cooking, housework – everything. The family should be helping you.'

I try.

'Come and help with the dinner, please,' I say.

My clever·son, absorbed at his computer making animations, looks at me as if I'm speaking a foreign language, then looks back at the computer.

'Just come and set the table,' I say.

He ignores me. Every evening we repeat this ritual. When Saturday comes, I do as the therapist recommended and say there will be no pocket money. He looks at me as if I am mad. Later, his father slips him a fiver. When his grandmother visits, she makes it up to 30. I give up – so very tired and not at all sure it's right. They have so much to cope with already.

I don't find out for many years, that the older son of the family who took Jonny for a night here and there – 'Family Support' it was called, an extension to the respite we already received – bullied Ben at school. That he mimicked Jonny in front of Ben's classmates. I think there are many things I am not told about, that they dealt with on their own. I know, though, that a particularly unpleasant teacher at Hannah's school, a teacher who terrorizes the children and causes them to cry as they go into her classroom in the mornings, has categorized us as a 'problem family'. On one occasion, she has reduced my daughter to tears for not knowing how to spell a quite unusual word. I go in to talk to her and she tells me this – that we are a problem family. When I ask her why she thinks of us like this, she looks puzzled. No reason except our autistic child, she explains, as though no more explanation were needed.

I am absolutely exhausted. Jonny's been home for two weeks of his summer holiday and I am feeling the strain. Also, I am worried – very anxious and stressed, not just from the constant activity, the seemingly endless washing, the broken nights. I am worried because we are going to a wedding. My brother is getting married at the weekend, and we are all going to the ceremony. I'd have preferred it to be when Jonny was at school, but it's in the holiday, and overnight respite isn't available now he boards. So, we'll drive to Hertfordshire, go to the wedding and then drive home again. I won't risk a hotel with Jonny, nor staying with family.

We used to stay with relatives; regularly go for the weekend and see everyone. When Ben and then Jonny were babies, it was quite manageable. Tiring, but fine. Then as Jonny got bigger and the autism more pronounced, things started to become more and more difficult. When Hannah was born, and Jonny was four and still in night-time nappies, we went to stay with a friend in Brighton. We had a good time, but when I got Jonny out of the bath on Saturday night, I looked at the faeces floating around in the water and thought 'we won't be able to do this for much longer'. A year or so later, we were staying with my father. Bob was getting Jonny out of the bath while I chatted with family. I heard him calling me and I ran upstairs, wondering what new disaster could have occurred.

'Can you help me? He's pulled the shower rail down.'

My heart sank. Between us, we managed to get it back up, but it was difficult. So was the constant vigilance, the removal of objects that could get broken, the averting of disaster before it became a reality. On the journey home I said, 'We can't do this any more. It's too hard for Jonny, and it's too hard for us.'

'Yes, I know.'

'He needs to be at home, where we can keep everything under control.'

'Well, they'll just have to visit us.'

'Um.'

In time, we stop having visitors to stay when Jonny is home. His wider family see very little of him for years and years. I cannot concentrate on what needs to be done for people who stay. I cannot give Jonny – or anyone else – enough attention.

But we will go to the wedding. I do not believe that Jonny will be happy to sit through the ceremony, and it's easily possible that he'll squawk or become distressed halfway through. Or possibly he'll start laughing and go on and on. None of these things would be good at a wedding – an event where many people won't know him. It's all so unpredictable. It could be fine; it could be terrible. So we decide that we will all go to the registry office in its beautiful grounds and meet the family. Then I will go into the wedding with the other two children while Bob takes Jonny for a ride in the car. After the wedding we'll all go to the reception, which is to be in a marquee in my brother's garden. I'm not sure what we can get Jonny to wear. By this time, he's a young teenager and very rigid about clothing. He wears comfortable trousers, trainers, a tee shirt and a sweatshirt. He's never worn a shirt – he'd insist on having the buttons done right up to his neck. And he takes a lot of persuading on hot days to remove the sweatshirt. Occasionally, he'll wear sandals and shorts. At night he wears full-length pyjamas – even in a heat wave. In the end I get a nice polo shirt, new trousers and a casual jacket. We try them out so they won't be new on the day, and he wears them quite happily. He won't undo the jacket, though, and he has the collar up. I hope it won't be hot – and it isn't.

It's a three-hour drive but we get there in plenty of time. We greet family and take photos. We manage to get some photos of the three children together, looking smart. Then the time comes for the ceremony and there is a general movement towards the building. I look at Bob.

'Come for a ride now, Jonny?' he says.

Jonny loves riding in the car with pop music playing. Often, it's very difficult to get him out when we arrive at our destination. So we are all surprised when Jonny follows us determinedly into the room where the wedding will be held. Ben and Hannah look at us – they are a little worried that it's not all going to plan.

'Shall we go for a ride, Jonny? A ride with music? That would be nice. Come on now,' says his father.

But Jonny walks in with everyone else and sits down in the back row.

'Will he be all right, Mum?' Ben is anxious, afraid his brother will do something outrageous in the middle of the wedding. I shrug my shoulders. I have no idea. But I'm certainly not going to risk cajoling him or telling him to do something that he doesn't want to do now the ceremony is starting. We'll just have to keep our fingers crossed.

'Don't you think we should take him out?' Ben asks me.

'No, he's decided to come to the wedding, and that's what he's going to do. It'll be far more trouble if we try to get him out now.'

Some music is playing – a CD – as my brother and his fiancée walk in. They smile, and so does everyone else, standing to greet the couple. Their little daughter toddles in with them and then runs into her grandmother's arms. I sneak a surreptitious look at Jonny. He's standing along with everyone else. No noise, no fidgeting. The ceremony is short and goes very well. My niece makes everyone smile, deciding that she'll sit with Mummy and Daddy while they get married. Jonny sits perfectly quietly. He sits when everyone sits. He stands when everyone stands. He doesn't put a foot wrong. He amazes me, as he so often does. He gazes into the middle distance, his head a mass of curls framing his beautiful blue eyes. He has resolutely zipped his jacket up as far as it will go. He behaves impeccably.

After the ceremony, we walk down to the river in the grounds of this one-time bishop's palace. Lots of photos are taken. My niece looks bewildered but very pretty. People smile, children run around.

'I thought Jonny was going for a ride,' my mother says.

'Yes, so did I,' I smile. 'We all thought that except for Jonny! He thought he'd come to the wedding like everyone else. He wanted to see his uncle get married.'

She turns to him. 'You wanted to come to the wedding, like everyone else, did you?'

'He certainly did.'

'Well, you were very good, Jonny.'

'He certainly was.'

Then we all drive to the reception. Jonny sits at our table and smiles. He doesn't make eye contact with anyone, but he is clearly happy. I take him up to the buffet to choose his food, and he puts plenty on his plate. I take pictures of my brothers with their families and marvel at my son. It isn't the first or last time that he rises so supremely to the occasion.

Many years later, Jonny attends another wedding. I'm 55 when I remarry. The night before the ceremony, my fiancé Will goes to stay in a hotel while Hannah and I settle down with a bottle of wine to watch one of our favourite films. In spite of this, I sleep very little and get up early to have a bath and stick patches under my eyes in an attempt to look as if I've had plenty. The last few weeks have been really hectic. My fiancé has moved in with us. Hannah has taken her finals and graduated. Ben has got engaged. I've been diagnosed with rheumatoid arthritis and feel very tired all the time. And there's been a wedding to organize. It's to be a church wedding, and a dear old friend from my days reading theology at Cambridge is to conduct the service in a beautiful little church tucked away up a narrow lane in Bath. I'll be wearing a silk dress made for me by a local dressmaker.

Earlier in the year I accompanied my fiancé on a research trip to China. It's very cold, wet and snowing, when one of our Chinese friends comes with me to the silk market in

Hangzhou. I'm wearing a padded coat with a hood, several thermal layers and two jumpers. The snow doesn't really settle for long, melting into dirty puddles in the road, but it's still very cold. For two hours we struggle with umbrellas, holding onto each other so as not to slip, in and out of the shops and covered stalls that line this street. My friend haggles gently with the shopkeepers for the beautiful things she and I want to buy. I cannot understand a word, although I repeat my Chinese 'thank you' many times. At one shop, I buy a peacock-blue jacket. It's absolutely beautiful. I have a tape measure with me, and know the extra, extra large jacket I've picked out will fit. But they shake their heads – I cannot be that big. Despite being five-foot tall and a size ten, the number on the tape measure I've shown them seems much too high. So I take off my padded coat and the stall-holder rushes to bring me a hot water bottle to hold while they unwrap the jacket. I hand him the hot water bottle when I put it on and they laugh good naturedly when they see that it fits me perfectly. Westerners – they're huge! At the end of the morning and the end of the street, my friend and I sit in a steamy noodle bar. Two delicious stir-fries, costing less than a pound each, are cooked in front of the shop and then brought to us while a young woman continually sweeps away the puddles of melted snow from the floor. We are laughing. On a chair next to us the bags of silk we have bought – presents for her family for the Spring Festival, presents for my children, the peacock-blue jacket, a beautiful pair of embroidered shoes and a length of silk in an 'auspicious colour' that will become my wedding dress.

We've planned the service, chosen poems and music, invited our friends and family, booked flowers, cars and a hotel reception. Now all that remains, on this July morning, is to do it. I decided early on in the planning that I would like my three children to walk me into the church – Ben and Jonny on either side, and Hannah as my bridesmaid. I'm hoping that Jonny will be happy and calm and so, in the weeks before the wedding, we prepare. Jonny stays with us overnight one weekend, and on Saturday we take him to the church with Hannah. We sit for a while in the pews, then show Jonny where Hannah will stand to read; where Will and I are to stand to make our vows, where his grandparents and cousins will be. Then we all go to the Parade Gardens for a picnic, sitting in deck chairs by the river, eating rolls and cold sausages. We take pictures in the church and make a little book of what will happen on the day for Jonny to take back with him.

He has the most wonderful key workers at this time – two young women he adores. They help us all they can. We decide that they will bring Jonny to Bath on Hannah's birthday, a couple of weeks before the wedding. We will spend another day showing him the church and hotel, telling him gently and repeatedly what will happen on the day. They arrive by train – Jonny's absolutely preferred method of transport at this time. We arrange to meet Jonny, Jan and Sîan at the station, where it's extremely crowded. People are milling around, taxis and cars picking people up are struggling to manoeuvre. We sit in the car, watching as people step out of the station and assume expressions of shock. They've travelled to this Georgian city for a day trip and come out of the station to find themselves in the middle of a massive building site. There are cranes and diggers, fences surrounding huge holes in the ground and a tortuous one-way system causing long traffic jams where an ugly 1970s shopping centre is finally being razed to make way for something more appropriate to a prime tourist destination.

Eventually, I spot Sîan and Jan guiding a very excited Jonny out of the door.

'Hallo, Jonny,' we call, waving to get their attention.

'Car later, car later,' he says as they reach us.

'In you get then, we're going to the church. Ben and Hannah will meet us there,' I reply.

We all cram into the car and drive off. It's been a terrible summer, but it looks as if the rain might hold off for a while. The church isn't far from the station, and soon we stop on a wide, leafy hill and ring the bell on a door set into a wall. A woman comes out, smiles and gives us a bunch of keys. We drive a little further up, turn into a narrow lane and then park up close to the wall of a manor house. To our right, the land rises up, and on this slope is a beautiful little church. There are grassy gravestones on raised lawns, overhung by trees on either side of the path to the door. There are flowers on the graves, among other flowering bushes. Through the trees the wooded hills that rise on every side of Bath can be glimpsed. It's windy, and every now and then a flicker of sunshine races across these distant hills.

'They should be here in a minute,' I say. 'Ben and Hannah are coming, Jonny. We're all going to look at the church. You can have another look at where you're going to sit and Ben and Hannah can see where they'll stand to do their readings. Then we'll all go to the hotel where we're going to have dinner on the wedding day. Then we'll go to the pub and all have our dinner today.'

'Car later.'

'Yes, car later.'

'Car later.'

At some point during Jonny's years of care, he's learnt to add 'later' to his requests, echoing of the standard response of someone who worked with him years ago. He doesn't actually mean 'later', we think. We think he wants to get straight back into the car now. He's barely been able to listen to one Blondie track in the short journey from the station to the church.

'Here they are,' Will says as Ben pulls up in his car and he and Hannah get out.

'Hallo Jonny, hallo everyone,' they say.

Jonny's head is down, but he is looking up through his long lashes and smiling. He's always very pleased to see his brother and sister.

'High five, Jonny.' Ben's hand comes up to meet Jonny's, then they make a circle of their forefingers and thumbs and join them together.

Will opens the church gate. I take Ben's arm and attempt to take Jonny's.

'We'll walk in like this,' I say, but he pulls away.

Still, I think he's understood and will probably be fine on the day. We unlock the heavy doors and go in. It's a beautiful little church, built in 1490 when this was a village on the outskirts of Bath instead of a popular area of the city for university lecturers to live. Inside the church is dark, and we fumble around till we find a bank of light switches. Brilliant pools of colour form on the floor and the pews, then disappear as erratic bursts of sunshine pour through the stained-glass windows and recede. All of the windows depict plants and flowers – there are no figures. The church will barely hold 90 people, so our wedding party will fill it nicely. Jonny immediately sits in the pew he knows will be his, and Sîan and Jan come in and sit with him. The rest of us explore. Will and I have been here a few times for services, but none of us has ever had the freedom of unlocking a church and having it to ourselves. We take some more pictures. Jonny won't move from his pew. Every now and then we hear 'Car later', and we reply 'Yes, car later'.

Once we've explored the tiny vestry where we will sign the register, Ben and Hannah have practised where they will stand to read and we've established where the loo is so that Jonny can go, we pile back into our two cars and crawl through Bath's Saturday-morning traffic to the hotel where the reception will be held. They are preparing for another wedding and are friendly and helpful. Ben establishes where his keyboard will go – he'll play a jazz set for us on the wedding day – and Jonny sits down at a table laid with a crisp white cloth and silver cutlery. Then Sîan hands him a parcel which he gives to Hannah, smiling. Inside is a birthday card he's scribbled in to show it's from him, and a beautiful silver bracelet. It's a wonderful birthday present. Jonny is happy to see Hannah's pleasure.

'He chose it himself,' Jan says. 'He'll like to see her wearing it.'

'It's lovely, Jonny,' Hannah says, 'really lovely.'

And it is. Then we drive off to find a pub, where we eat lunch. Jonny smiles a lot. Later, I drive them all back to the station, feeling very tired.

I leave it to Jan to find clothes for him to wear. She is so very, very good with him. I'm dubious about the possibility of his wearing a suit and I tell her that I just want him to be comfortable and relaxed. Over the next few weeks I tell the priest and the organist, the choir and my close friends, that Jonny may need to go out during the service, may make noises, may behave strangely during the wedding, but that it's incredibly important to me that he takes part, and that I want everyone to remain cool and take it in their stride. They are all fantastically positive, but as the day gets closer I worry more and more.

I am pretty sure Jonny will rise to the occasion, will play his part well. But there's always that little possibility, that nagging at the back of the mind, that something will go terribly wrong. Jonny can be violent and difficult to control when disturbed. At this particular time in his life he has a habit of smashing light bulbs when upset. I worry – am I asking too much of him? My friend, the priest, emails to assure me that he'll carry on unless I tell him to stop. The organist emails me to say he is the head of a very inclusive primary school in a deprived area. He's used to all sorts of noises – it won't bother him. Everyone is so kind. My fiancé and daughter reassure me, as do my friends – Jonny will have two people with him whose sole task will be to ensure that he is safe and happy and who will be able to take him out if he isn't. Just for once, they tell me, it will not be my responsibility to look after Jonny. My responsibility will be to enjoy my wedding day.

'This wedding's going to be fun,' says my daughter.

When the day arrives, despite the lack of sleep, I am completely calm and as happy as it is possible to be. It has rained and rained in the weeks leading up to the wedding and as I lie in the bath in the early morning, water pours relentlessly down the windowpane. But by mid-morning it stops and a watery sun appears in a pale-blue sky. I dry my hair and get dressed. The flowers arrive, three creamy-white buttonholes and two bouquets packed in a box. Drops of water glisten on petals that look as soft as velvet. Hannah gets up and dresses. She looks so very, very beautiful. Ben and Kirsty arrive, put on their buttonholes and say that the wedding cars are already parked in the road. I'm just thinking maybe I'll phone Jan and Sîan when there's a ring at the door, and they are there.

Jonny looks magnificent in grey trousers, a collarless shirt and a black waistcoat. I want to hug Jan, who has taken him out and persuaded him to try on clothes till they get it right, and has been inspired to think of this solution to the turned up collars Jonny insists on when he wears normal shirts. They have brought a large glazed pot and a climbing rose called 'Wedding Day' for a present. Hannah suddenly realizes she is hungry and makes toast. She makes some for Jonny and we all stand around as he eats it. The wedding is at noon, and lunch will be very late. I tentatively show Jonny his buttonhole – a cream rose – and tell him that the others will be wearing them and that he can wear it if he wants, or not if he prefers. He stands perfectly calmly as I pin the rose to his waistcoat – and he keeps it on all day.

We open the front door and go out of the house to the cars. I get into the first one with Hannah. As we drive through the city and people stop to look, I'm certain they think she is the bride – 21 and so beautiful in her cream dress. On her wrist is the silver bracelet from Jonny. The others follow in the second car, except for Jan, who drives behind with Jonny so that their car is close by and they can go if he cannot cope. At the church we all get out and the photographer starts to snap away. The rain continues to hold off.

Two of my friends sing in a very good little choir, and eight of the choir members will be singing for us today. One of them has come out for a moment and as she goes back into the church, she mouths that I look beautiful. I link arms with Jonny and Ben and we walk through the gate and up the path with Hannah just behind. Jonny has a key ring with photos attached to the belt loop of his trousers. The whole day is shown as it will be, in sequence so he always knows what will happen next. He is concentrating hard, incredibly focussed, holding my arm as I hoped he would. My friend waits at the door, looking magnificent in a white cassock with a golden-yellow stole. Jonny starts to express some annoyance at the photographer as he calls for us to turn just before we go into the church. Jonny's got a job to do and needs to get on with it! The organ rolls out the magnificent Bach I have chosen and the four of us walk into the church. I cannot smile any more widely. I feel as if I may float up to the ceiling, I am so buoyed up with happiness. Jonny, Ben and Hannah go into their respective pews and the service begins. It rolls along on music and poetry, hymns, prayers and laughter. Behind and around us, we feel a huge tidal wave of love. Everyone is smiling. During the service Jonny makes a few noises, requests 'Car later' a few times, but otherwise attends and watches.

In a beautiful Bath square by the hotel where we will have the reception, we take pictures and greet everyone. My niece and nephew throw confetti. Jonny stands patiently having his photo taken with us. He sits later, at the end of the top table, eating well and remaining calm. He sits through speeches and music. After the meal, Hannah leans over and kisses him. Jonny smiles, Ben takes a picture. Later, I'm told, he takes off his buttonhole on the way home. But, arriving at the house where he lives, he has it put back on again so that he can show people. The next day, Jan takes him to a musical film to maintain the high he is on.

People begin to leave the reception and so I change and

my husband and I get into the taxi we've ordered. We are kissed and hugged.

'It was the nicest wedding I've ever been to,' say four separate guests as they leave.

On our honeymoon in Rome, under a sky of brilliant blue, I replay the day over and over in my mind, especially the bit where my two sons and my daughter walk me into the church, where our friends all smile and my husband to be looks at me with all the love in the world in his eyes.

Autistic people often wander or run off. Jonny does it occasionally. It isn't a big problem for us, but it's enough of an anxiety to be very strict about locking the front door of our big house in the village which doesn't have a Yale. Jonny, who so often moves painfully slowly, or sits down on the pavement when he doesn't fancy walking any more, can move surprisingly quickly when he wants to. In the hall we have a cupboard for coats, and in the cupboard are some hooks for keys. Everyone must lock the door when they come in and hang the key on its hook in the cupboard. Sometimes I lie awake at night and worry about fires. But everyone knows about the key – except for Jonny of course. Unlocked, the door opens so easily it sometimes blows wide on windy days.

Jonny's sitting quietly on the chair in the hall as he often does. The chair is tucked under the stairs, by the phone. He shuts the kitchen door which is annoying because I can't see what he's doing, but he won't allow it to be open. Jonny always closes doors, even if people are trying to walk through at the time. We're all at home, in the kitchen apart from Jonny, chatting, cooking.

'What's that?'

'What?'

'It sounds like Jonny. Sounds like he's getting upset'.

My heart sinks.

'He's probably hungry. Set the table can you?'

I open the kitchen door. Jonny's agitated about something, muttering indistinctly. 'What's the matter, darling?' Indistinct noises. 'Are you hungry?' More, louder, but still indistinct noises. He goes to the front door. 'We're having dinner, now. We can go out later.'

He's standing by the door, saying something. I can't hear what it is and he's getting more and more frustrated. The others have come to look.

'What does he want?'

'No idea.'

'Does he want to go out?'

'Maybe. The door's locked, though. It's dinner time now, Jonny.'

Jonny's voice is getting louder and louder. He looks at us in frustration. Then he goes to the cupboard and pulls open the door. He looks in at the row of hooks, takes down the right, unlocks the door and goes out.

It's an exciting day. Ben's soon to graduate from the Royal College of Art. I love parking the car right by the Royal College of Music on this lovely summer's evening and walking along the imposing terraces to go to the degree show. The students here are so talented, so inventive. The building itself is unprepossessing, given the grandeur of what surrounds it, the Albert Hall virtually butting up against it and Albert, in his Memorial, glinting in the warm evening light, backed by the greenery of the park just across the busy road.

The college is buzzing with life. There are people everywhere, students in their 20s and 30s sporting red hair, stripy tights, hats or posh frocks, and parents and friends running the gamut from ultra conservative to aping trendy. Most people are clutching plastic cups, sipping indifferent wine. We wave when we see Ben and Kirsty and ease ourselves in. There are clothes, ceramics, paintings, films and installations to look at on the way to Ben's space. Here we pause to watch his latest films, look at the way he has used print, and read his book.

For his MA show, Ben has updated a book he made about Jonny for his BA. It's called 'I Have No Opinion on New York, dispelling the myths about autism', and Ben is wearing a tee shirt with the slogan printed on it. I sit on the edge of the white table where the book is tied so that it cannot be stolen, and read it. The noise around me recedes while a wave of pride swells inside me. Ben is a graphic design student and he has used a combination of imagery and words to paint a picture of autism. The book is absolutely brilliant. The autistic need for organization is shown by a page replicated in alphabetical order; the content is the same, but meaning has been sacrificed for order. The sense of repetition is achieved by printing a page many times. There are direction road signs only going to 'a place I have been to before' and an aircraft safety card indicating how play should be repetitive. Many people read this book over the week of the show. Many people, especially those who know someone with autism or work with autistic people, ask for a copy. We cannot afford to reproduce it for them. It takes about 15 minutes to read, and when you have finished it, you know more about what it feels like to be autistic than you would achieve by ploughing through many textbooks.

My new husband Will and I have just collected Jonny from his home. It's a bright autumn morning and we plan to be on trains for most of the day. Jonny has recently revived his love of trains, as I discovered when I picked up Will from the station with Jonny in the car recently and he said 'train' quite clearly. We try to reward speech with a result, and to give Jonny the sense that he can sometimes have control over his world. He's 25, after all, a time in most people's lives when they choose how to spend a sunny Saturday.

Jonny looks great in grey trousers and jumper. He is smiling broadly and, after the routine of switching off lights, closing doors and crouching to dip his fingers in the pool of water that gathers in one of the drain covers, we get to the car. As soon as Jonny is in, he says, 'Seatbelt'. After we're strapped in, he says, 'Sweets' and I explain that we're going round to the sweetshop now. Then he says, 'Moosic' and I put on a CD that Hannah has made for him, and start the engine. Sweetly high-pitched women's voices croon in harmony and Jonny rolls his head and claps with pleasure.

'Johnny Angel, Johnny Angel, Johnny Angel, Johnny Angel.'

And then the solo begins, 'Johnny Angel, how I love him. He's got something that I can't resist.'

We drive round to the sweetshop.

Chapter Six

———

THERAPIES

THERE'D BEEN A lot of publicity about it. Programmes on the television, a book, articles in magazines, Sunday supplements. It was all based on a silly idea – the old, frustrating, cruel idea – that autism is caused by withdrawal, by difficulties in family relationships. That it's a psychological problem. And of course, people who come up with miracle cures have a captive audience, a guilt-ridden, exhausted, desperate audience for their crackpot ideas. But what can you do?

What you may do – what I did – is try it. 'Holding' it's called. I'm dubious, but it's hard to get across the extent of my guilt and desperation in those days, my confusion and isolation. The idea of 'holding' was this – disturbed children who cannot relate to other people may have experienced birth trauma, may not have bonded with their mothers. To counteract this, you should hold your autistic child close by you, forcing him or her to stay in this position even if clearly unhappy about it. You must hold your child like this until he or she makes eye contact with you. This may take hours. If the child becomes angry or distressed, that may be good; it may lead to the catharsis that is a 'rebirth'. And then proper bonding – mother and child – can take place.

Oh dear. It's easy now to see how foolish this is, how abusive and distressing for autistic children. But it was thought up by a practising psychiatrist, and she was able to launch it in what was then a very different world for families with autistic children. Nowadays, you still get miracle therapies, maybe involving dogs or music – or maybe, in a time when wheat or dairy intolerances are all the rage, special diets avoiding certain foods. You get avoidance of drugs and administerion of drugs – some very dangerous.

Then, as now, the miracle cures were often surprisingly abusive. One such scheme involved isolating your child, keeping everyone else away except for a parent, friend or therapist who worked non-stop, one-to-one, to stimulate interaction. People had extensions built to their houses and employed round-the-clock 'stimulators' so that their child could experience this. Ideas about certain foods causing autism are stronger now but were promoted even then, when people had just begun to realize that it might be the artificial colouring in their child's sweets which was causing them to be hyperactive or difficult.

After publishing an article in a national newspaper about my experiences with Jonny, I received a number of letters. One claimed that a special diet would work wonders – a diet with a number of basic foods, certain nutrients regarded as essential for children's healthy development, left out. The woman who wrote the letter had put her child on it.

She'd been warned that it could lead to liver failure but, she explained, she'd rather let her child take that risk than continue to be autistic.

In the evening Jonny's bedroom, at the front of the house, is full of sunlight. It has a little bed, a bright-red cupboard and a sink; there are books and toys in the cupboard. The walls are covered in pictures – posters of trains as well as drawings done for him by his brother. He's had his supper and bath. It's a warm evening and he's just wearing his nappy, the nappy he shouldn't be wearing according to his teachers. But he has it on. I've had enough of changing sheets five times a night, of gathering up his turds from the floor, of putting my child to bed in a room that stinks, and watching him get more and more raddled with tiredness.

I sit on his bed, on top of the Thomas the Tank Engine duvet, and put him on my knee. He's quiet; his lovely curls rest against my chest and smell sweetly of shampoo. He doesn't mind sitting with me – he probably thinks I'm going to read him a story. Jonny isn't always happy to receive affection, but often he is quite relaxed about it. To be honest, his eye contact isn't that deficient either. It's on his terms, and he does have that obliqueness that's so typically autistic. But often what you get is a sense that something isn't quite right about his reactions, rather than a clear awareness that he isn't looking you in the eye. I tip his chin up a little so that we can look at each other, but he isn't having it and looks immediately away. He still has a slight squint at this stage, although it's less pronounced than it was. I wobble my face around, trying to force eye contact. He turns his face determinedly away. Then he starts to squirm. He wants to get off my knee, get into the bed. He wants his nightly routine to continue with the same stories we always read, with 'Night, night, sleep tight. Don't let the bed bugs...'

A pause, then 'Bite!'

I'm keeping him talking as long as I can – with lots of phrases he has to finish – however indistinctly they come out. But tonight, I won't go into the routine. Instead I hold onto him, quite determined to try the holding 'therapy'. He pulls away but I'm holding tight. Then he starts to groan.

'Tory, tory, bed, range juice.'

He's pulling my arms away and trying to get out from under them, repeating a string of half-formed words. The struggling gets stronger as he twists and pulls, trying to get off my knee. I hold on. He has red marks on his arm where my grip is tightest. I simply cannot get him to look into my face. How on earth do you force someone to look at you? I try to hold his face and he turns his mouth towards my hand and bites me. He's agitated and distressed. Just before bed too.

Eventually, we are both crying. I make a couple more half-hearted attempts to get him to look at me. And then, I'm proud to say, although I felt guilty about my lack of application at the time, I give up and put him on the bed. He throws himself around for a while and takes some time to calm. He's affronted – and quite rightly – by what I have done. But eventually he settles and quietly I start to read his stories.

'We're going on a bear hunt...' My voice is shaky but I make a huge effort to keep it steady. 'We're going to catch a big one. What a beautiful day. We're not scared.'

At first he won't look at the book, writhing away from me and continuing to groan. But eventually he calms and looks at the pictures.

'We're not...?' For a moment, he won't answer, finish the line as he usually does.

But then he mumbles, 'Cared.'

This is so much better. This is us, as we are, for better or for worse, doing the best we can for each other. What an appalling thing I have tried to do to my poor, poor little boy!

Later on, I read accounts by people with autism – assisted autobiographies. They are wonderful and enlightening things for people like me to read, parents whose children behave in a way so different from other children, and who cannot speak, who cannot tell us how they are experiencing the world. I read in these accounts of the torture of touch, of the overwhelming feelings it engenders if not regulated and controlled, of the sense of suffocation and being pushed under something terrifying, caused simply by a hand laid on the arm. I watch little films, read articles, start to hear for the first time, not of refrigerator mothers or of wilfully isolated children, of family scapegoats and intolerable pressure to succeed, but of sounds that rise and fall – some too loud to tolerate, some so quiet they can barely be heard; of noises that jump out and of others that fade away, making understanding virtually impossible. I hear about sight that causes some colours or objects to loom frighteningly large, of taste that is too strong, of touch that is too much.

I begin to understand why my son keeps his fingers in his ears for so much of the time; why he sometimes does this when everyone is speaking quietly, but laughs with delight at noisy fairgrounds or the rush of trains. I begin to understand why he looks at things sideways on, why his fingers are so often splayed out across his eyes to moderate the sight of things. And, of course, I understand how utterly abusive is holding therapy; how the sessions I did with primary school children on how no one has the right to touch them in a way they find disturbing applies to my child too; that everyone's body is their own and that to have it touched or held in a way that causes distress is an abuse of human rights.

There are other activities suggested for me to try, many of them much kinder and mainstream, that I later realize are completely inappropriate and very disturbing for Jonny. 'Time out' is a practice recommended for children who cannot control their behaviour, who are difficult or violent. I'm encouraged to try it and I do. The idea behind it is that bad behaviour is attention-seeking, so what you reward it with isn't punishment or anger but withdrawal of attention. It's still recommended for children who are genuinely disturbed, or whose behaviour is difficult to control. I think it's of little value for autistic children, because it's so hard for them to control their reactions. They aren't trying to get attention when their behaviour is difficult. They are usually distressed and frightened by what is going on, or how they feel. There's no way I can know if Jonny is feeling ill. If he has a sore throat, or is going down with something, he won't be able to show me and he won't understand either, that it's a temporary feeling, that there are things we can do to alleviate discomfort. What is now is forever for autistic children. The past and future do not exist. But I was encouraged to try 'time out'. When Jonny's behaviour becomes difficult or violent, it's suggested, I should try not to react, but I should make him go to his room. And there he should stay for a certain amount of time. Jonny won't go to his room, of course, so I end up lifting, or dragging, him there. Then I sit behind the door, or put something heavy against it, because he comes out again immediately.

It's a mild day in our isolated cottage, when Jonny throws his plate of cereal at the wall and bites his brother. I take him to his room, where he screams and throws things for a while. I sit against the door, heart beating, exhausted, angry, worried, until the noise stops. He seems quiet, so I join Bob on the terrace in front of the house for a cup of coffee.

'OK?' he says.

I shrug. 'Don't know. Quieter anyway.'

I sit at the white plastic table and flick through a colour supplement as I sip my coffee, shaking, unable to concentrate, ears tuned to the low groan emanating from the room above me. I can hear objects hitting the wall again, but Jonny hasn't tried to come out of his room. Suddenly Bob pushes me and shouts:

'Look out!'

I jump up and away from the table as a window falls from the sky. It crashes to the ground and smashes into many pieces. Jonny has shoved his window with so much violence that it has fallen out. If the table had been placed a few inches over, one of us might have been seriously injured or killed.

The truth is that if determination could cure autism, Jonny would have been a new child a long time ago. The energy and commitment I expend trying to help him with his problems are extraordinary. But, of course, it isn't about determination. Autism isn't curable. All anyone can try to do is manage it; attempt to understand it; try to make their child's life, their family's and their own, easier to bear.

And after a while, I begin to understand. I turn my back on attempts to force Jonny to stop being autistic, to stop him being himself. I stop trying to force him to get dry at night, to give up needing things to flap, to stop putting his fingers in his ears, to stop repetitive behaviours. I start to understand that this is his world and he needs ways to cope with it.

Gradually we start to understand what he finds frightening, what he needs to block out, how he imposes order on his chaotic world. We start to respect him for who he is and to understand how hard it is for him to cope. One day, when he is becoming violent and I am afraid I will get head-butted, I get close enough to feel the beat of his heart. And finally I understand. However bad I feel, however hard it is for his brother and sister to cope, however alarmed his teachers and carers become, nothing will ever come close to the terror he experiences. Jonny's behaviour may cause us worry or fear, but for him virtually everything that he experiences is unbelievably difficult. The world is a frightening place for him, and all our efforts must be harnessed in the attempt to reduce his terror, to give him support in managing this terrifying place.

I start to try gentler therapies, things that start from Jonny's perspective and work outwards from there. This I do instead of acting on ridiculous ideas from those who know very little about autistic people and have no respect for them at all. I get quite involved with the National Autistic Society and get elected onto their executive, where I meet a number of parents – some of whom have two autistic children. And I start to hear how real people cope in family life with an autistic child. I go to meetings and listen to educationalists or psychologists dedicated to autistic people talk about their research, what they have learned about the way autistic people experience the world, and their ideas to help make things better for all our children.

It's a sunny afternoon, but I have the curtains closed in our bedroom. It's a big room with beams overlooking our large garden. On the floor I've spread a duvet and pillows. Next to them is a tape recorder. Jonny loves music and I've made him a tape of what I believe he will find to be soothing pieces. It starts with one of his favourites – the Pachelbel *Canon*. Then there are some slow movements – from the Beethoven's *Emperor Concerto*, a Shostakovich piano concerto, some early choral music, and Mozart's *Concerto for Flute and Harp*. I'm going to try conditioned relaxation. The plan is that, when he is calm and happy, we will lie down together and listen to this music. If he will allow it, I will stroke his arm and head. The hope is that he will come to associate this music with feelings of peace and happiness. Then, I must make efforts to understand what triggers Jonny's periods of distress. When I recognize that Jonny is working up to a violent episode, I try to recreate the feelings of relaxation and calm by playing the music and lying with him.

I bring Jonny in and speak quietly. 'We're going to have a lie down, Jonny and listen to some lovely music.'

'Bub!'

He isn't keen. But I persevere. I lie down and put on the tape recorder. 'Come on, Jonny, lie down with me. It'll be lovely.'

He doesn't, and starts for the door, so I pull him gently down. It's 3 o'clock on a sunny afternoon, and he is disturbed by this odd situation.

'Sweetie, sweetie, pasta, bread.' Sometimes this listing of food preludes distress. But on this occasion it doesn't escalate and for a short time he lies down while I play a little of the music. I stroke his arm for the few minutes that we lie there, and feel that it was good start.

'Good boy, Jonny.'

He grits his teeth and pushes his face into mine. Sometimes Jonny finds praise unbearable, so I take him downstairs and give him a little bowl of sweets. He wolfs them down and runs out.

'How did it go?'

I shrug. 'Not too bad, I think. I'll try again tomorrow.'

I try a few more times. Sometimes Jonny lies for a few seconds, sometimes for some minutes. I can't say it is enormously successful. As soon as Jonny is seriously distressed and starts to scream, the music cannot be heard; and so often, I don't have a tape recorder with me when this happens. Recognizing triggers is also difficult. They change so often or are not obvious. None of my attempts to stop Jonny's distress really works – it seems to have a life of its own – but at least I start to try to see the world from his perspective, to understand his fear and be sympathetic to it, rather than trying to force him to be someone he could never be. I do get him to lie and listen to some of the tape, and I do play it when I think that he is starting to feel agitated. I don't know if it ever made any difference. It certainly didn't make things worse, and maybe just this shift of attitude – of wanting to help him fight his demons rather than pitting my will against something that is an essential part of him – starts a sea change in our lives together.

Jonny's periods of distress, I begin to think, last as long as they last, and I must wait them out. Later, I explain to people that I have sat with Jonny through many, many hours of screaming and violent terror and that, while my reactions might prolong these sessions, nothing will make them shorter than they were going to be. The imperative is to ride them and to reduce the suffering they engender to all involved, not least Jonny.

After this, everything gets a little better. I am not listening to people who want to blame me for my child's disability. I am not trying to force him to be someone he cannot be. I start to work as an equal opportunities trainer and in doing so, learn about the disability rights movement. I learn that the injured veterans who came home from Vietnam to find that they couldn't get into shops or cinemas, who suddenly found themselves, not heroes as they expected, but invisible men and women – were not prepared to tolerate the situation. They started a protest that became stronger and more sophisticated and then crossed the Atlantic. I read about medical and social models of disability, about the way society views disabled people, the need to cure them or ignore them.

So many of my experiences with Jonny fall into place. I start to see why doctors lost interest in us when they realized my son had a condition for which was there not only no cure, but also very little understanding of the cause or antecedents. I start to believe very strongly that the accusations of an inability on my part to let Jonny grow up and the assertion that he can be forced to stop being autistic – as though we were somehow doing it on purpose – is outrageously unjust; that attempts to blame me or to pathologize Jonny are an affront to ideas of justice or equality. I start to become passionate about his right to be the person he is, autism and all, and his right to experience a quality of life as that person rather than enduring endless attempts to force him to be someone he will never be. Instead of reading books, I watch my son and listen to him. I learn from him what causes distress, what is difficult. And conversely, what can help him make sense of the world.

From watching and listening I learn that Jonny benefits from sensory stimulation that is kept down to a minimum. I learn that if I watch and listen carefully, he will show me what is difficult for him to interpret. I learn that when he is distressed touch, words and even eye contact, are unbearable for him. I understand that he is already overwhelmed by emotion, that his senses are already heightened to an unbearable degree. I realize that everyday life is almost impossibly stressful for him and one of his most difficult challenges is the uncertainty about what will happen next. So I start to use photos and video to help him predict and manage what will occur, and his part in it. At the beginning of the day I run through, in very simple language, what will happen – what will follow what – and start to teach Jonny to manage experiences. We go to the supermarket and, slowly and carefully, I talk him through it. We do the same thing every time, and after a while, Jonny's face lights up with pleasure when we go in. You can see in his face the enormous relief and pleasure he experiences when he thinks 'I know this one'.

Every now and then, something or someone shows me that we are winning the battle. We're in the supermarket and I'm doing my usual thing – concentrating on him and his sister, not looking up, avoiding eye contact. It's a bad habit, but over the years it's become the norm for me. It's my way of coping with embarrassment, of fielding the stares and unkind comments about my son's behaviour. He's doing quite well today. He's learnt over the years how to cope with supermarkets, what you're supposed to do, what treats may be had. He stands next to a display of cakes, waiting, looking at me sideways.

'Yes, you can have one,' I say. 'Choose one.'

He smiles and picks up a gingerbread man, looking at me to check it's OK.

'Put it in a bag, then,' I say. 'You must wait till it's paid for before you eat it. Get him a bag, can you Hannah? Do you want one?'

She helps Jonny put his gingerbread man in a bag and chooses a doughnut for herself. Jonny's making quite a few strange noises, but he's content.

'Can you get a packet of cornflakes, darling?' I say, and he takes a box carefully from the shelf. 'Put it in the trolley,' I say, and he does. 'Well done.'

A young woman approaches me. My head is down and I don't notice her until she speaks.

'Excuse me. Sorry to interrupt you, but is your son autistic?'

'Yes.' I'm defensive already, waiting to counter the criticism; how I shouldn't have him out. Or the blatant curiosity – they've seen it on the telly. Isn't he good-looking? What a shame it is, but does he have a special talent?

She smiles.

'My son's autistic,' she says. 'He's only five, though. I couldn't think of bringing him to a shop like this. It's really given me hope seeing you. Doesn't he cope well?'

'Yes,' I say. 'Yes, I'm very proud of him.'

Restaurants and swimming pools, parks and fairgrounds are made manageable for Jonny in the same way – careful preparation to reduce uncertainty about what is to happen.

Jonny's fascination with pictures of himself and his family knows no bounds so I use that fascination to make books and films of events that have happened, and ones that are to come. When we go on holiday, I make a book – Jonny on the beach, Ben in the sea, Hannah on a roundabout. I type captions to go beneath each picture and read the book every night to Jonny. There are pictures of the house where we will stay, the sand dunes where he will play, the tables by the sea wall where we will picnic.

'What's this Jonny?'

'Holiday. Holiday.' He turns the pages quickly, looking for pictures of the sea, for boats, for streams, for water in all its forms.

'Who's this, Jonny?'

'Vannah. Vannah.' He continues to find words starting with an h very difficult, so this is his way of describing his sister. Sometimes he won't speak, but he will look intently at the pictures of his life – as fascinated as any of us by his own existence.

As time goes by, the aggressive nature of Jonny's care and education disappears, and he spends more and more time with people who genuinely care for him, love him, want to help him. More and more 'therapies' are based on the desire to help him manage his very high stress levels. He has foot massage and head massage – I never understand how these young men and women – often people who have not done well at school – get him to sit still while they perform these massages. I am full of admiration for them. I still cannot get Jonny to allow me to touch his head or feet. He has aromatherapy. And he discovers Snoezlen rooms, which he loves.

The carer puts her finger to her lips. 'Come quietly,' she whispers, 'he's in here. It's wonderful!'

I creep up to the door of the room. There's a little window in the door, and I hope to look in without the person inside being aware that I'm looking. Whatever is happening in there will stop if he knows he's observed. The music I hear is very New Age, like the sea sounds and soft ragas they play when I go for a massage. At first, the light is too dim for me to make out the figure lying on the floor cushions. But slowly my eyes become accustomed to the low light and I see him. Around the cushions, and wound around the low lamp and the pictures of the sea and quiet forests, are fibre-optic lights, changing languidly from purple to pink to blue to white. A lava lamp is on in the corner. Soft music plays, neither rising nor falling but steady and soothing. And on the cushions Jonny lies, almost asleep, mesmerized by the music and lights, quiet and relaxed. She moves back a pace or two.

'We try to get him in here before he goes home,' she says. 'And sometimes before mealtimes if he's not too hungry. It calms him so much.' She smiles broadly. 'He loves it.'

Chapter Seven

———

TRAINS AND BOATS
AND PLANES

It's 4AM WHEN THE alarm goes off. I'm in a deep sleep and for a brief moment I wonder where I am and what is happening. Then I remember. We're going on holiday and I must get up. It's dark, but as I drink coffee and wash, a line of pink appears on the edge of the horizon and light slowly works its way up the sky. I dress and start to wake the children. I've thought through this morning over and over again. Jonny will be last, and with a bit of luck I can take off the incontinence pad, dress him and get him into the car before he realizes what is happening. Breakfast has been packed – they can eat it on the way. I've told him we're going on holiday, and he loves holidays. Still, there's always the chance of anger and violence. It won't be easy for him to understand why he's being woken out of a deep sleep. We're going to France – by car to Portsmouth, a ferry and another drive into Brittany will get us there.

In Hannah's room I shake her gently and she rouses, looking confused for a second and then getting quickly out of bed. I help her on with her clothes and then wake her older brother. Bob gets them both into the car. We've put in pillows for them, but they are chattering excitedly – Ben in the front and Hannah in the back, where I'll snuggle down between her and Jonny, under the duvet.

'We're going to French France!'

'I know that Ben! We're going on a big boat.'

Everything is packed – wash bags, buckets and spades, sunscreen, shorts, t-shirts and swimsuits, as well as French money, passports and phrase books. I wash the coffee cups and go nervously up to Jonny's room. There's no sign of his head – just a large lump under the duvet. The sound of deep breathing indicates heavy sleep. There's nothing for it, though. We can't risk missing the ferry crossing.

It's surprisingly easy. I lay my hand gently on the lump.

'Jonny darling. Time for our holiday. You just have to get up, then you can sleep in the car.'

The lump shifts a little and I pull back the edge of the duvet. He opens his eyes. He's groggy, but I repeat myself, 'Jonny, darling. Time for our holiday. You have to get up, then you can sleep in the car,' and he sits up and gets straight out of bed.

I take off the incontinence pad with no trouble at all and wash and dress him. He doesn't groan or protest. Instead he smiles, jerking his head sideways three times. His hands are flapping at the side of his face as I hand him the clothes and help him on with them.

'We're going in the car and then on a big boat, Jonny.'

'Big boat!'

He constantly amazes me. It's like the way he can suddenly walk so well when we're on the way to the swimming pool. Jonny can wake from a deep sleep and get dressed when a big boat is in prospect!

After half an hour of Jonny watching the road from the
window and the other two chattering, they all fall asleep.
When they wake, I give them sandwiches and drink. Soon
we're queuing in a long line of cars to get onto the ferry.
It's still early and quite misty, but beyond the cloud there is
brightness. The sea looks calm behind the huge boats moored
alongside us. Just as we think that nothing will ever happen,
uniformed men arrive and start to marshal the queue. People
who have been standing around – Surrey fathers wearing
deck shoes with cashmere jumpers slung round their necks,
their well-spoken children in faded t-shirts running between
the cars in a way I would never allow, get back into their
Saabs and Volvos. The line begins to hum as engines are
started. When we get to the front of the queue, the car
bumps up onto the ramp and we're quickly directed in. The
uniformed men wave both arms – back, forward, stop, a
couple of centimetres forward, then stop again, until we are
all tightly packed into parking spaces. We're told to leave
the handbrake on, get out of our car quickly and get up to
the passenger decks. We squeeze out and weave our way
along the sides of the cars to the edge of the deck and then
up the metal stairs. We've been told clearly we won't be able
to get down here again, so we must take everything up with
us. Jonny gets out quietly with the other two. I clutch his
hand tightly but he does exactly what he's told to.

'Watch out,' I say as we reach the top. 'Hold the rail. Step
up high.' I hold Jonny's arm as we all step over the metal lip
and look down on the cars. There are a lot of people and we
all shuffle along, our footsteps clanging on the metal floor.
Jonny follows quietly, clutching his boat.

We've booked a cabin, even though it's a daytime crossing, just in case things don't go well. There are no portholes,

but there are four bunks and room to leave the bags with the toys, food and drink and a change of clothes for Jonny. We also have our own toilet, sink and shower. The children get onto the bunks, Ben playing with an electronic game, Hannah clutching her teddy and Jonny flapping the little fish on his boat close up to the side of his face. But they get bored quite quickly, and so we put on jumpers and go up onto the deck. I'm holding very tightly onto Jonny, despite his attempts to pull away from me. It's cold but exhilarating as the ferry leaves the shore. The children are holding tightly to the rails which have patches of rust and drips of water hanging from them. As we pull away, the foghorn sounds loudly and Ben and Hannah cover their ears. Laughing, Jonny flaps his boat and shakes in excitement, watching the sea sliced into white-tipped waves on either side of the boat.

We walk them round and buy drinks, sitting on plastic chairs on the deck with wind blowing in our hair. Then we retire to the cabin for a while before getting lunch – chicken and pizzas followed by wonderful fruit tarts – squeezed into the crowded cafe. There's a lot of noise with so many excited children on board, and Jonny is not conspicuous in any way. The four hours go quickly and soon we see the French coast on the horizon. Then we dock in Caen and join the crowds queuing to get down to the car deck. We squash into the car and are guided off. The gangplank bumps as we drive over it and onto French soil.

'It's France, Ben, it's French France.'

We crawl along in the line of cars until we join the main road, and then we are off.

My eyes are pricking now with tiredness, but I feel elated at how we've coped. A family holiday with all my children! A family holiday involving an early start, a ferry ride and a fortnight in France. I close my eyes for a second and hope fervently that all will be well. The sun is shining now, and children's songs are playing on the tape machine. I am covered in biscuit crumbs and cramped as I pour squash into plastic cups. As we leave the city, we find ourselves driving surprisingly quickly along quiet roads lined with poplars, surrounded by large fields and prosperous-looking detached houses with high pointed roofs and children's swings and slides in the gardens. We pass through villages where window boxes are full of geraniums and the glass in the doors of cafes are lined with cream lace and advertisements for Orangina. The sun is on its downward path again when we arrive at our campsite and find the caravan we have rented from friends of friends. We park outside it and get out of the car. Jonny has drifted into sleep again, so I leave him in the back with the car door open and find the keys I have been sent. We open the metal caravan doorand go in.

We are all quiet. It's very disappointing. We have paid more than we could really afford, or were expecting to pay friends of friends. We didn't expect luxury, but we did expect better than this. I smile determinedly.

'It's OK, we'll manage. Come on, let's get unpacked.'

It's easier said than done. There's virtually no cupboard space in this shabby brown interior. As I put sheets on Ben and Hannah's 'beds', I wonder how they will sleep on these hardboard shelves. We decide that Jonny will have the other bedroom to himself and I cover the flimsy mattress with a plastic sheet. We will sleep in the living area on what has been described as a pull-out bed, but is actually the two old, smelly and very thin cushions that cover the communal seating.

We unpack as best we can – most things will have to stay in suitcases, being moved each time we want to sit down, and a lot of things must stay in the boot of the car.

Then we get into the car and follow signs to 'La Mer'. It's too late to play for long but I sit by the sea on a mat with Jonny, who still seems to be content, as the other two throw stones into the water.

'It'll be OK,' I think. 'We won't be spending much time in the caravan. This is lovely.' I try not to feel angry with the friends of friends who have ripped us off. I hope everyone will all have a good time.

I've brought a home-made frozen meal from home – a shepherd's pie that they all like – which has been slowly defrosting during the journey, and which will be easy to heat up. We squeeze round the table to eat it. Then Ben and Hannah ask to go exploring, so I let them on condition they promise not to go far. I wash Jonny in the hip bath and see that he is confused and disorientated by this experience. But I press on, putting him in his pyjamas and incontinence pad and reading him his story.

'We're on our holiday, Jonny. Tomorrow, we'll go to the sea all day and you can play.'

I put on his tape and he drifts quickly off to sleep. Ben and Hannah burst in.

'We've met our next-door neighbours! They're nice,' they shout.

'Shh, Jonny's just got off to sleep.'

'Sorry, sorry. We're going out again.'

I look out of the window and see them running round with three children, a young girl and twin boys. They wave excitedly, and I relax a little.

Later, they're all in bed and we are drinking wine and reading. I feel so tired, it's hard to wind down. I try, as always, not to feel worried about what will happen, if Jonny will cope, whether *I* will if he becomes distressed. The children have responded with magnificent stoicism to their appalling beds. Jonny is the only one who will be even fairly comfortable. Ben slides off his tiny 'shelf' every night. Just as I try to get comfortable on my cushion on the floor, I hear the soft groaning that I dread so much, coming from Jonny's room. He has woken in terror.

'He probably doesn't know where he is,' I think, 'and not having a proper bath didn't help.' I try to stay calm, but I'm unsuccessful. As the groaning gets louder and thumps can be heard coming from the room – he is punching the flimsy walls – I start to panic.

'I can't cope with this,' I think, 'not tonight. People will hear. The children's friends will start to give them a wide berth.'

I go into the room – the bed completely fills it. There is simply no room for anything. 'It's OK Jonny,' I say, 'we're on our holiday, remember? Everything will be all right.'

The low moaning rises to a full-blown scream and he tries to head-butt me. I move away in time, but hit my head on the door, and feel tears prick at the back of my tired, tired eyes. Jonny continues to scream and starts to hit his head on the wall. I feel a wave of terror and anger wash over me and try to stay calm, to tell myself it will pass, but I cannot control the exhaustion-fuelled fear rising in me.

'Stop it,' I shout. 'Stop it, now!'

I know it won't work; it will make things worse. I know I will be consumed with guilt for days. The screams come faster and louder and Jonny hurls himself at me, sinking his teeth into my arm. I push him away and he hits the wall.

'Stop it,' I shout again. I shut his door as I squeeze back out. 'I'm taking him home tomorrow,' I sob. 'I should have known it wouldn't work. Tomorrow you must drive us to the ferry, and I'll go home with him.'

I repeat this many times until, after two hours, the wailing ceases and we all get to sleep.

'Are you taking Jonny home?'

I'm roused from sleep by the anxious face of my five-year-old daughter leaning over me. For a moment, I don't know where I am or why I'm sleeping on the floor. Then I remember and look at my watch – 9.30!

'Where's Jonny? Where's everyone?'

She looks at the door and I see the table covered in break-fast debris and hear Ben outside.

'Don't go home,' she says as she gets under the cover with me.

'No, don't worry,' I say. 'I won't go. I'm sorry. I was tired and worried. Did your friends say anything about Jonny?'

'No, they didn't hear.'

'Is he OK?'

'Yes. Can we go to the beach soon?'

'Yes, just let me get a cup of coffee.'

Our neighbours are lovely. We sit in their so much nicer living space and chat.

'Is it your caravan?' I ask.

'God no! Nothing would possess me to do this more than once. It's Joe's parents'. They thought it would give us a cheap holiday, but I can't stand being so cramped. Never again!'

It's ten times nicer than ours. They're both social workers from Manchester, and their children play happily with ours for the whole fortnight. No one says a word about Jonny's disturbed night, although I cannot believe they haven't heard. They are nice people, sympathetic; and Jonny settles down for most of the time. Our neighbours tell us where the best beaches are, and we spend some happy days on them. Every evening a van arrives on the campsite and produces frîtes that we often queue up to buy. Ben and Hannah find the swings with their friends and make the very best of their time.

We've arrived at the beach, as usual, just as many people are leaving for lunch. By the time I've got everyone up, sorted out Jonny and we've made and cleared up breakfast in the impossibly cramped space, it always seems to be about 12 o'clock. But we have our baguettes, our mats, towels, buckets and spades and inflatables, so we settle down happily. The beach is huge and white, with rocks and pools and the bluest of seas stretching into the horizon.

'Come on, Hannah. Hurry up!'

Ben runs to their favourite pool and jumps in. Hannah, doing her best but lagging behind, calls, 'Wait for me! Wait for me!'

She sits on a huge rock in her blue-spotted swimsuit, pink plastic shoes and rubber ring, waiting for her brother to swim over and help her in. I find a little pool for Jonny and give him his bucket and spade. His tubby tummy spills

over the top of his Thomas the Tank Engine trunks as he
leans over the pool and drops in pebble after pebble. After
a while, he changes to a new, but equally repetitive, activity – digging his spade in and bringing up the wet sand in
a muddy spray. He seems fine, but I go and sit quite close
when a toddler with his glamorous French mother, all glossy
curls and skimpy bikini, walk past him and stop. They are
collecting mussels from the rocks with an alarmingly sharp
little knife. Clearly very practised, they work together. The
little boy points and the glamorous mother cuts – snick –
and the mussel falls into their bucket. The little boy stops
to stare at Jonny, his spade hanging by his side, his wide
blue eyes mesmerized by the repetitive arc of wet sand. He's
probably not allowed to do such a thing. His mother is nice,
she doesn't think he should stare.

'Allez,' she says, pulling him gently. As they move away,
I hear her explain. 'C'est un petit idiot.'

A short ride away, there's another wonderful beach. At this
one, we walk across a wooden-decking 'bridge' from the car
park to the beach. Once again the sand stretches, white and
sparkling in a broad sweep, as far as the eye can see. Once
again the sea is a deep blue, chopped up and white fringed.
The beach is quite crowded with families, but there is plenty
of space for us to spread out our mats and toys. Jonny, in
his trunks and holding his spade, ranges up and down by
the water's edge, while the other two struggle onto an inflatable crocodile. From time to time I go into the sea to hold
Hannah steady for a few moments on this monster. When
I let go she inevitably falls off after wobbling for a couple
of minutes. We've been to this beach a few times, stopping
on the way back in a pretty old town for crêpes filled with

sugar which we eat sitting on the step at the base of the market cross. Anything to delay our return to the ghastly caravan. In fact we are very lucky with the weather, only suffering two days of rain when the children run around in their plastic macs, in and out of each other's caravans. So, most of the time we can sit outside, setting up our tiny picnic table for lunch and dinner.

On this day, all the children seem content on the beach. I look up from my book every couple of minutes, to check that Jonny is OK, that he hasn't disappeared as he did on the huge beach in Devon. He is very absorbed, though, clearing the beach! I watch him for a while, walking up and down, flinging seaweed into the sea. He seems perfectly content and completely unaware of anyone else. From time to time, the seaweed hits someone on its flight into the sea. I watch as a handsome French man, trim and tanned in his tight-fitting trunks, holding his young daughter as she jumps over the waves, turns to look, a puzzled expression on his face. Who is throwing seaweed at him? He scans the water's edge. How strange! No one is running away or giggling or look-ing guilty. No one is turning away from him. There is just a young boy with golden curls, paddling in the sea, looking completely unconcerned!

Back at the campsite, we unpack the car. I rinse through the swimsuits and start to cook our tea. Our field of cara-vans is separated by a hedge from the tiered plots for tents down below and Jonny seems quite content, throw-ing twigs over this hedge. He can't do much harm, I think, with a few twigs, and it's keeping him busy while I cook on the tiny Calor Gas stove by the open door of the cara-van. When I'm ready to dish up, I step out to call the children and see Bob holding Jonny's hand very tightly, talking earnestly to a man who is clearly very annoyed. Ben and Hannah stand a short way off, watching. They look a little worried.

'Hallo,' I say, approaching the two men. 'Time for tea. Come on.'

'Are you quite sure?' I hear the stranger say.

I don't like the look of him with his gold chain and arrogant manner.

'It's a TR7, I'm not happy about stones being thrown at it.' He looks disparagingly at our old Ford.

'I'm sorry,' Bob says. 'You must be mistaken. Our children have been playing quietly.'

'You better watch out,' he says, turning on his heels, 'I'll be looking out for you.'

Bob raises his eyebrows at me and releases Jonny's hand. Jonny looks completely unconcerned, flapping his boat, but Ben whispers, 'Jonny was throwing stones over the hedge!'

'Oh, never mind,' I say brightly, 'no harm done. Teatime!'

As we drive onto the ferry at the end of the fortnight, I feel that it's been a success. I am extremely tired, but Jonny's distress was confined to the first night. We've managed to give him and the other two a good seaside holiday, visited some lovely towns, seen the sea wildly crashing onto rocky cliffs, flown kites on the windy hills, shopped in French markets and eaten out a few times. We're happy, though, to have seen the back of the caravan and are looking forward to proper beds. We have a cabin again, where we leave our things and take a walk around the deck. I'm half listening to Ben and Hannah's excited chatter as I hold onto Jonny's hand. He's twisting, trying to free himself, and for a few minutes I let go. He seems to be watching the sea intently, making no attempt to run away or climb. Suddenly, as I look at Hannah for a moment, I'm aware of something being lobbed into the air behind me.

'Jonny's shoe!' my daughter cries, and I turn just in time to see one of his new Clarks sandals disappear below the foam.

For some crazy reason, I grab his other shoe before he throws it. Phew – saved one!

'Get back. Get back,' Jonny is saying.

'We can't get it back, darling,' I say.

'Get back, get back!' louder now.

Bob arrives.

'Jonny's thrown his shoe in the sea!' the children chorus.

'Silly boy, Jonny,' Ben says gently.

'Shhh,' I say, 'don't upset him.

'We're not allowed to go to the car,' Bob says, and I think I've brought a change of clothes for him, but not a change of shoes.

'He can't walk around in socks!'

Jonny's sense of what he should be wearing to be properly dressed is very acute. Any deviation from it will cause trouble.

'You'll have to go and ask them – explain what's happened,' I say, turning to take the children back to the cabin and to wait. I'm not hopeful, they are always so strict about not going down to the car deck during the crossing. We seem to wait for ages with 'Get back. Get back! Shoe. Shoe!' puncturing the anxious silence.

The other two look at each other. What a brother! Seaweed hitting people's backs, and new shoes thrown into the sea! The door of the cabin opens and Bob comes in brandishing Jonny's canvas shoes.

'They were great,' he says, 'once I explained. They escorted me down and let me get these!'

We don't try Europe again with Jonny for a while. Ferries are fine; planes definitely out. So, some years later, when I feel that Ben will soon be leaving us, we rent a gîte in Poitou-Charentes for our last family holiday. Because Ben wants his girlfriend to come, we end up driving two cars through the French countryside for the four hours it takes us to arrive at our village. Jonny, 16 now, sits happily with us on the deck of the ferry – we don't rent a cabin this time – while we play cards and eat French pastries.

The gîte is in a little village close to some pretty towns in a region that will definitely be sunny at this time of year. I am driving the second car with Jonny in the back, while the others are all together in the larger car. We arrive at dusk, turn into the gates and park the cars, to find the farmer who owns the gîte and lives next door, worried about the lateness of our arrival and quite incredulous that a woman – me – has driven this distance in a foreign country!

The gîte has a large living room, disconcertingly decorated in French rural style with the skins of many animals on the walls. There are three bedrooms and a strange balcony-style mezzanine overlooking the living room. The kitchen is capacious and the large garden, with its round swimming pool, slopes down towards fields. There are tubs of flowers on the pretty terrace, and under the canopy of a copse of high pines stands an old table, inviting us to sit and eat in the dappled sunshine.

As usual, I've done a lot of thinking about how to make this work. I feel quite certain that if there is a pool which we have to ourselves, then Jonny will be happy. In the event, he finds the unheated pool a bit of a shock, and only jumps in now and again and then gets straight out. He can't understand the idea that he will become acclimatized to the initial cold if he waits for a few minutes till the water feels comfortable, and he's a teenager now – no longer a child oblivious to the coldness of water. But the sun shines and he is calmed by the heat, sitting for hours by the pool watching the rest of us swim, play and float in the water. I spend quite a bit of time drifting round the pool on an airbed or reading by the side of it. Ben's girlfriend learns to swim. She, Ben and Hannah play charades, work up dance routines, ride bikes and laugh a lot. We visit the local market, wander round the village, eat out. It's a successful holiday.

One morning, we get up promptly. I wash Jonny's sheets and pyjamas and hang them out, knowing they'll be dry in an hour in the warm sunshine. We pack ourselves into the estate car – with me in the boot space to save us taking both cars, and set off. In a couple of hours, we arrive at our destination – a theme park of the moving image, called Futuroscope. It's hot and sunny, as ever, and the theme park is laid out with gardens, silver buildings, bridges, modern architecture and a huge stage set at the base of an amphitheatre – Hollywood Bowl style. Since I usually hate spending time at theme parks – although I hope none of the children ever realizes this – I'm agreeably surprised. We are given maps of the park and, after lunch on the terrace of a café with streams gurgling past us on all sides, Bob and I take Jonny exploring, while the others go off together to sample the 'rides' they have picked out. Jonny walks fast – a rare occurrence – and purposefully. He's very happy. In his Bermuda shorts and blue tee shirt he strides along, stopping every now and then. It's like a Jonny heaven. Water is the abiding theme. Huge modernist buildings stand glinting in the sunshine, with water running down them.

'This is how Jonny would like the whole world to be,' I say, and we laugh.

We find what we are looking for – a simulator that will recreate a famous car chase from a film. A few years later, when we take Jonny to the Disney theme park in Paris, I am organized and take his disabled parking card, which allows us to take him to the front of queues. But I haven't yet cottoned onto this, and I am full of misgivings about Jonny's ability to queue for the 40 minutes it will take to reach the front according to the notices along the snaking barrier. I know that Jonny likes simulators because he's tried them before, but queuing – that's not a favourite activity! Yet again, he amazes us.

'We have to queue,' I say. 'We have to stand for a while until we can go on the ride.'

He waits patiently. When we get to the front of the line, we go into a large room. There are many two-seater units filling it, all facing a huge screen. I get onto one with Jonny and strap him in as requested. He allows me to do this – to my complete amazement.

'It's to keep us safe, Jonny. 'It's going to be a great ride.'

Suddenly the huge screen, as wide as the very wide room, lights up. The room slowly darkens, and we find we are sitting in the front seats of an old Citroën, hurtling down through the narrow, cobbled streets of a French village. The seats we are strapped into move, swerve, judder and bump in perfect synchronicity with the film. I know it's a clever trick, but the sensation of speeding along, twisting and turning, avoiding collisions by a hair's breadth at every corner, is quite overwhelming. I believe I am there. The hall echoes with shrieks and shouts and I look anxiously at Jonny. But he is grinning, his face suffused with happiness; he is not frightened, he is completely exhilarated.

After this we take him on another simulator, a film of butterflies in the mountains – where we *are* the butterflies, lighting on flowers, flying on the breeze, a helter-skelter and a boat on the lake. His hands shake, held up beside his head, which he twists, once, twice, three times for each pleasurable experience. We meet up with the others and eat again, before going down to the amphitheatre to wait for the daily lightshow. We save seats for the other three, who go to get in a couple more rides. We are tired and content to sit with Jonny, watching a huge fountain rise and fall, changing colour every few minutes. As darkness arrives, the seats fill up and I look round anxiously for the other three. Suddenly they appear, waving and happy.

'It was great,' they chorus.

'Sit down now,' I say. 'It's about to start.'

The fountains start up again, but this time the colours and sequences change in time to music and suddenly we see figures in the fountains, or running across the lake. They move quickly, change and dance. I know it's an illusion, that the figures are projected onto the fountains, but it's a clever one. The show's all in French, but this makes no difference to us. The images are magical, enticing, international. I glance at Jonny, afraid that tiredness will kick in before this is finished, but I needn't have worried. He shakes his hands, twists his head and whoops in pleasure. His cries of amazement blend in with the 'oohs' and 'aahs' of the crowd. As the last glimmer of projected light fades, and the fountains grow quiet, fireworks start behind the lake. For 15 minutes they sparkle, whoosh, bang and cascade in ever more fantastic combinations. Jonny's excitement, if possible, grows even more at this display of his beloved fireworks. At last they stop, the crowd begins to move and, as the rush dies down, we get up too. In the car, Jonny and the others fall asleep. I bounce around in the boot, incredibly tired and completely triumphant.

We take Jonny to the coast for the day, whilst the others laze by the pool. We visit La Rochelle, wandering amongst the moored boats and stalls of jewellery and souvenirs. We stay till nightfall and buy lighted wands to wave in the darkness by the glittering harbour. We buy bags and necklaces from African vendors, listen to street musicians and drummers, eat crêpes or bags of frites sitting on the sea wall or on benches by the boardwalks. We climb the steps to the castle. After returning from all our excursions, Jonny sleeps in a room with Bob and me. He settles quickly and sleeps through the night. In the daytime I look round for Jonny and, not seeing him, walk through the garden to a bench shaded by hibiscus and jasmine. He can very rarely be persuaded to part with his sweatshirt, so has found this little, quiet place to lie to get cool. We all lunch at the table under the trees. Jonny sits quietly, enjoys his food, smiles at his brother and sister and at his brother's girlfriend. In the mornings, he climbs into bed with me for a cuddle. It is one of the happiest times of our family life.

Some time before this, on a cold, sunny Sunday in November, I think I have found us the perfect holiday destination. Ben isn't with us – he's busy taking his driving test, doing gigs with his band, studying, clubbing, spending time with his friends before they all disperse to work or university. But the rest of us drive down to the Devon coast for the day. It's cold, but we've brought a picnic and toys to play with on this shingle beach with its red-earthed cliffs rising behind, set in a stunningly beautiful bay. We are alone on the beach, watching massive, white-capped waves pound the rocks that litter the beach. We shelter behind one particularly large one, where Hannah plays with her little people and I get out a kite for Jonny to fly, holding my hand firmly over his on the plastic handle.

'Can I have a biscuit, Mum?'

'Sandwiches first,' I reply and, ignoring the scowl, give Hannah a small ham sandwich. 'D'you want squash?'

'Yes please.'

She's wearing an old red anorak bought from a church jumble sale, and her long curls blow across her face in the wind. I get a hair elastic from my bag and tie it back for her. Jonny's anorak is blue. He's eating heartily – no resistance to sandwiches with him, his hands flapping in excitement at the food, wind and sea. I pour them both drinks in plastic cups. Jonny downs his in one and gives me back the cup.

'Way', he says and watches me carefully to check that I put the cup away in the picnic bag and zip it up completely.

No matter that we'll have to open it again in a minute for cakes, crisps or more drink. It must be closed properly each time. I eat my sandwich quickly – it's not a relaxing way to eat, but finally I have a chance to look around me properly and notice the pine chalets all the way along the bottom of the cliff. They are actually set on the beach in some places – perched above, tucked into the cliff, in others. All have long verandas; all have an undisturbed view of the magnificent sea. I wander along to the shop and ask about the chalets.

'Oh, yes, we own them. They're closed for the winter now – we rent them out from Easter to October. They've all got heaters, but it'd be too cold after that. Be quick if you like them! We've got people who rent them year after year – they book for the next year as they leave.'

The woman is plump and wrapped up in a woolly hat and scarf, her permed hair escaping at the sides. I wonder how it can be worth it to open today, although I can see that the nicely refurbished old coal depot – God knows how they managed to unload in these fierce seas – must be a thriving shop and restaurant in the summer. It's a popular spot for day-trippers too – the coast path is stunning and the fishing productive. I thank her for the brochure she gives me and return, with sweets and coffee in paper cups, to the others.

'Look,' I say to Bob, 'I think it'd be perfect for us with Jonny. They look really robust and plain – and he could go straight out to the sea. We'd be able to watch them really easily. Imagine opening your windows every morning to this!'

And a couple of weeks later, I ring and book one for a week in the summer.

By the time the four of us arrive, having wound down the long narrow valley and through the village, past the church where a clutch of doves fly up from the dovecot, their white wings catching the sunlight, past the pub, the working blacksmith's, down an ever narrowing lane with high hedges and sudden glimpses of the sea, we are very excited. The car is crammed with the accoutrements we need for a week's holiday – clothes, towels, boules, books, a TV and many, many beach toys, including an inflatable dinghy and paddle. We've had to bring bedding – lots for Jonny – and food from a supermarket in the nearest town some miles away which we have somehow managed to pile on top of us for the last few winding minutes.

We drive through the barrier, park and go into the little office to announce our arrival. Soon afterwards, a tractor backs up to our car. Between us, and with the help of the tractor driver, we load our possessions before following the tractor across the shingle on foot. We pass the upturned boat, the stream that feeds into the sea, families on their beach mats, our feet sinking into the shingle, feeling the pull on our thighs, till we arrive at our chalet. It sits on a grassy mound about three feet above the beach – we can easily get down and, during the week, Jonny takes to clambering over the verandah fence and jumping down onto the beach. It is also perfect inside – wooden walls, with a bath not shower, living room with a tiny kitchen tucked into the corner and French windows opening across the whole width of the room to a spacious verandah. It has two small bedrooms – one containing two single beds, and the other a double bed and a hanging rail. There is a coffee table and bench seating which can be used as beds for more people, and a heater. The walls are plain and solid. There are no ornaments – nothing that can be broken, nothing to worry about.

The air is sparkling – light glinting off the sea and the blue of the sky – and the sound of the sea is ever present. During the day, curious people look in as they trudge across the shingle, and occasionally ask to look inside. But as evening descends and the sky is streaked with pink and orange light, the day-trippers leave the sea, the sky and the magnificent sweep of the bay to us. It is gorgeous. Jonny plays with stones and water, paddles, sits just watching the sea. He bathes happily and it doesn't matter how much water spills over onto the floor. We breakfast on the verandah and sit there at night watching a path of silver move across the sea.

The chalets are identical and we hit on the idea, after Jonny has wandered into one of our neighbours', of attaching the rainbow windsock that friends gave him for his birthday, to our verandah. It blows in the constant wind and shows the children which home is ours.

'Swimming time!' Jonny says and I help him off with his tee shirt and shorts and into his swimming trunks.

I change too and pump up the dinghy for them. I pull him and then his sister around in it until I am tired out. Huge waves crash in on most days, pounding the shore and rising into massive walls of white foam. The seabed slopes dramatically, echoing the steep drops on the beach, which the children skid or roll down. They can splash around and watch the waves crashing, in between watching TV, playing, buying ice creams from the shop, flying kites and throwing balls. We come back to this place time after time – in autumn as well as summer.

I'm woken from a deep sleep by unexpected noises. My daughter is calling out, but she doesn't seem to be in her room. It sounds as if she is just outside our bedroom door. Bleary-eyed I get up, open the door and look into the living room. Light spills from the children's bedroom door, which is open. Hannah – barely five years old, is on the floor blinking at her sudden awakening, bewildered and disorientated. She sits on her mattress on the floor – as if she has been bodily lifted with her bedding – surrounded by her Barbie dolls and tapes, to which are added, second by second, her toys, clothes and duvet.

'Jonny,' I cry. 'What are you doing? Stop it at once!'

He is moving determinedly in his blue pyjamas, to and from their bedroom, heaping more and more of Hannah's things around her on the living room floor.

'Go way, go way,' he says.

'No, Jonny, stop it now, NOW.' I grab him and take a pile of Hannah's storybooks from his hands. 'Back into bed, NOW!'

He looks surprised, but stands still. A wail erupts from his sister as her father appears.

'What on earth's going on? It's 2 am. Why is Hannah in the living room?'

'He must have picked her up in her sleep and moved her.'

It's not at all funny, but I feel my mouth struggling not to smile.

'Into bed, Jonny, now. You share this room with Hannah while we're on holiday. Don't you dare do this again. Come on darling.' I scoop Hannah up into my arms and indicate with my chin her mattress lying on the floor. 'Put her bed back, can you?' and my sleepy husband does this.

They are both back in bed before they have time for much reaction and I sit outside for some time while a story tape plays, until I can hear regular breathing from them both.

In the morning, Hannah asks, 'Did I dream it?'

'No,' I say, 'Jonny thinks he should have the room to himself!'

'Will he do it again?'

'No, I don't think so,' I reply, with my fingers crossed. And he doesn't.

So, in spite of it all, we manage a semblance of 'normality'. We have seaside holidays and ferry crossings, fairground rides and ice creams, parks and playgrounds, boat rides and slot machines. Every event has its own quality – something quite different from what most other people experience, but we are out there, visible, holidaying like the others. We manage a plane once, when Jonny is still tiny – strapped to me with a baby seatbelt – before autism has its name, before we are a different sort of family. We fly to Ibiza with our two sons, and enjoy a week of sun. Jonny still isn't walking and spends his time shovelling sand into a bucket, propped up on the beach, or wobbling his arms and legs up and down whilst sitting in his buggy, watching his brother swim. But after this, we never try a plane again. There would be nowhere to take Jonny if he became distressed – and when the pressure built in his ears, I would expect this to happen. We couldn't really afford this type of holiday anyway, so we return year after year to the one or two places in Devon we have claimed as our own.

At another, earlier time, in the north Devon house we rent year after year, we wake to hazy sunshine and decide to visit one of our favourite attractions. It takes a while to have breakfast and get into the car. In this time, the sun fades and ominous grey clouds pile up. But we put on a tape of fairy stories and set out anyway. In the back the three children eat biscuits, and Jonny, head pushed up against one window, flaps his boat. We drive along a fast road, with farms to each side, hills in the distance and, after half an hour, pull into the car park of the tourist farm we visit every year. The car halts and I get out and open the back doors, child-locked against unauthorized exits. We like this place – it's just the right mix of farm and adventure playground for us. Hannah and Ben tumble out of the back seat.

'Come on, come on. Can we see the sheep?'

'Yes,' I reply, 'we'll go and see what time the feeding is. Come on Jonny.'

His face is still pressed against the window, now misted up. He seems miles away. I open his door gently, which seems to wake him from his trance. The other two are running around now, but Jonny is slow this morning. I unstrap him and gently ease him out.

'We're here, darling, shall we go and look for the lambs?'

He allows one hand to be taken by mine and flaps his boat with the other. Bob reappears – I'd been too absorbed with Jonny to notice him go.

'Hurry. They're doing the lamb feeding now.'

The other two run off with him and Jonny pulls his hand from mine. He has blue tracksuit bottoms on and a cream tee shirt. Eight years old now, he still loves animals. Later he becomes wary of dogs, and even of his beloved horses, but at this time there's still the affinity with beings to whom there is no need to speak and no fear of incomprehensible talk back. This silent communication is just what suits him. Although he's pulled his hand away, he walks with me round to the pens where the lambs are kept. Under a high, clear corrugated roof, and sitting on a circle of hay bales, excited children wait. A man appears with a bucket of feeding bottles and hands them to the children. I sit with Jonny and we watch as the lambs are brought in. Hannah's having the first turn, and she laughs as she wrestles with the bottle, pulled and pushed by the lamb she is feeding. Her curls tumble round her face and I fish an elastic band from my bag and lean away from Jonny to pull back her hair. Jonny is looking sideways at the fun. There's no other expression on his face, but his boat flaps faster and faster.

Ben's turn is next and then it's Jonny's; I sit with him as the lamb is brought to us. He pulls away as the animal gets close and the keeper looks at me questioningly.

'Will he be OK?'

'Yes, in a minute. It takes a minute for him to get used to it. He's done it before.' I take the bottle and put it into Jonny's hand, holding my hand over his. He doesn't resist, although he's still looking away. 'Look at it, darling,' I say gently, 'look at the lamb. He wants some milk.'

I guide the bottle into the lamb's mouth, and suddenly Jonny is watching, still sideways on, but intently. He pushes my hand away and for a minute feeds the lamb quite well. Then he drops the bottle and I ease him up as I look round for the next child in line.

We go into the café for a cake and drink.

'It was great, wasn't it, Ben?' Hannah says. 'The lamb drank all the milk.'

'Yes, Hannah.'

They eat their cakes and ask, 'Can we find the rope swing?'

'Yes, can we?'

I look doubtfully at the window, where the sky looks even more overcast. 'Better go now, then,' I say, 'it's going to rain soon.'

The rope swing is attached to a tree, where the children can swing across a small ditch. It's situated on part of a nature trail, across a couple of fields, and I make sure I have a bag with their macs in. But the rain holds off, and Ben gets to the swing first. He's swinging back and forth by the time I arrive with Jonny.

'My turn, my turn,' says Hannah and her father lifts her up.

'Ready,' he says.

'Yes, let go, let go!' she cries and off she swings, all courage and excitement.

'Jonny's go now,' I say. He stands there making noises and flapping, but not rushing to the rope. 'Come on, Jonny. Hold on tight.' I lift him on, prise the boat out of his hands and put them onto the rope. 'You've got to hold tight. Don't let go.'

'Will he be all right?' Ben, as usual, is nervous about his brother's safety.

'Yes,' I say, with a confidence I don't really feel. But I don't want Jonny to miss out on these experiences, and he's managed this before. He swings across and back successfully, shrieking, and then scrambles off. I catch the rope just in time to stop him landing in the ditch.

By the time we get back, the first spots of rain are falling.

'Trampoline, trampoline,' Hannah sings.

'It's starting to rain,' I say doubtfully. 'It'll get slippery.'

'Never mind. We'll be all right.'

They both bounce on the round blue trampoline, clutching each other and laughing. Then they scramble off, their wet hair clinging to their heads. I think we will go home now, but Jonny clambers determinedly onto the trampoline. I take off his shoes and socks, and he bounces, lost in happiness, up and down, up and down, his boat flapping at his side, oblivious of the falling rain.

The next day, the weather is better, and we bounce over the cattle grid at the nature reserve backing onto the beach Jonny once got lost on. We bang the poles of the windbreak into the beach with one of the huge pebbles that form a ridge behind this mile of sand, secure it with more pebbles, and sit behind it. The rain has stopped but it's still windy. White clouds race across the sky and a continually eddying fine layer of sand hovers over the ribbed beach. As the day progresses, the wind drops a little and the sun gets stronger. Ben and Hannah build a castle, paddle, eat sandwiches, kick a ball around and chatter. We're there for four hours and for the whole of that time, with only a few minutes break to eat a couple of sausages and some rolls, Jonny sits a short way from us, by a little pool, dropping pebble after pebble into the water.

'Is Jonny all right, Mummy?'

'Yes, I think so. It's what he wants to do.'

'Jonny never wants to play!' she cries.

'It's playing to him,' I reply. 'He watches the splash every time the stone plops in.'

Every half hour or so, I sit down by Jonny and gently ask, 'Jonny? Do you want to go in the sea? Do you want to come with Mummy and see the big waves?'

He ignores me completely and continues with what he does want to do. Pick up a stone, hold it high above the water for a few seconds, drop it and watch the big splash. Repeat the action. He is completely absorbed, not looking up at all during the ritual. I regularly squeeze out some sunscreen and do my best to apply it to his back, tummy and arms while he tries to push me off. At the end of the afternoon, I start to put things away and tell the other two to get dressed and collect their things. When we are ready to go and I have given Jonny his ten-minute, five-minute and one-minute warning that we will be going soon, I prise him away from the pool, take off his trunks, pull on his shorts, tee shirt and sandals and take his hand ready to return to the car. As I dress him, I see that he is pink down one arm, one cheek and one half of his stomach. On the other side, he is completely white.

The big attraction of Longleat for our family – far ahead of the lions and boating lake, the maze and glasshouses, and even outstripping the brilliant adventure playground – at least for one of our children – is the Dr Who exhibition. Ben's bedroom is full of home-made models of daleks and tardises; his duvet and pillowcases, tee and sweatshirts, feature characters and monsters from this programme. He draws, models and makes films of his favourite adventurer, and we regularly visit this attraction at our nearest theme park. We've seen the exhibits and played with the interactive games on many occasions. Jonny is patient under the circumstances. He's only seven, and will love the high walkways and slides of the playground, the little train and an ice cream by the lake. But he manages to tolerate the queuing and slow progress round the exhibition. Until that is, some excited children in front of us, out with their father, stop for so long in front of the tardis console that he becomes impatient and pushes at them to move on. They turn to stare at him and look up at their father. I am all apology.

'Oh, I'm sorry. You're not hurt are you? Jonny, you musn't push – you'll hurt people.' I look at the father. 'Sorry, my son's autistic. He doesn't understand that he mustn't push.'

'Then he shouldn't be out,' he says in a strong Irish accent, 'you should keep him at home if he can't behave.'

I take Jonny out and we sit and wait for the others, before moving on with relief to the adventure playground. People stare a lot. Sometimes they tut. At the swimming pool, which Jonny loves and to which I take him regularly, every visit is a battle of wills between the attendants and me. Jonny likes to stand by one of the short ladders going into the shallow end of the pool and jump in over and over again. His joy knows no bounds as he repeatedly submerges himself, water cascading around him. He never seems to experience the discomfort of going under water that bothers his brother and sister so much. There are no cries of distress when water goes up his nose or into his ears. Jonny and water form a seamless whole, a perfect marriage of two attracting halves. I stand close by, asking him to pause if anyone wants to use the steps to get into the pool. He is good, although the impatience of an interrupted ritual is clear, and waits till I tell him he can start again. He isn't hurting anyone, I think, and it's good for him to learn to wait for other people to get in.

But it's always the same. After a while an attendant always comes up to us. I think I know what is happening. They're disturbed by the oddness of it – not that he is doing anything more dangerous or anti-social than the toddlers or teenagers in the pool. Just that it is odd and disturbs them. I don't suppose they think any more deeply than that. I see a young man in the leisure centre tracksuit approaching.

'Can you stop him doing that, please?'

'Why?'

He looks surprised at being asked. 'Because it's danger-ous.' 'How is it dangerous? He's just jumping in.' I look around me and wave a hand. 'Lots of other children are jumping in.'

He looks at me doubtfully and hesitates for a moment before replying. 'People might want to use the steps.'

'He stops every time someone wants to come down the steps.'

'You must stop him, I'm afraid. I think it's dangerous and I can't guarantee his safety unless you stop him.'

Mostly, though, people are kind. Some go out of their way to come and talk to Jonny, although he generally ignores them. On a boat trip in Bath, his charge is waived and he is helped sensitively to get on and off. At Center Parcs they keep a close eye on him, but don't stop him jumping into the pool from the steps, or otherwise harass him. The whis-tle is blown frequently to tell other children to get off the rocks at the side of the pool but he doesn't try this, and it's a relief to watch other people's children being asked to stop something, rather than my boy. At Weston super Mare, the owner of a Thomas the Tank Engine beach ride waits patiently while Jonny displays his ritual hesitation before climbing on. At Tintern Abbey, people smile as this 25-year-old indulges in his favourite activity of jumping in puddles.

'You like puddles, then, do you?'

Silence.

'He likes puddles.' This to me.

'Yes he does. He loves them, don't you Jonny?'

He ignores me, grinning broadly, and the stranger and I smile politely at each other before moving on.

At restaurants, other diners ask him, 'Are you enjoying that?'

I answer for him, but it's nice that they are kind.

It's a cool day in February, and Hannah and Jonny are on their half-term holiday. Jonny is 15 and Hannah is 10. Bob is away somewhere, and the week has been dragging. I've been asking myself – going over and over in my mind – if I can manage to take them on the train to London by myself. I'm nervous – if Jonny gets distressed it might be very tricky without another adult to help or to take Hannah away from the trouble, and it might turn out to be very hard for her. I run it around in my mind for a couple of days, unable to make a decision, until my daughter says 'Come on, Mum, let's try it.'

So we do. I make sandwiches for the train, talk Jonny through what we are going to do, check that the London Aquarium will be open, study the tube map, make sure the disabled parking card is in the car and get Jonny and Hannah up in plenty of time to drive down to town, park and get tickets for the train. I factor in time for searching for a parking place but we find one straight away; for Jonny to hesitate getting out of the car but he gets out straight away. The lure of trains! I factor in time to queue for a ticket but there is only a short line of people and plenty of time to get up the stairs to the platform. Jonny is in his stride by this time and mounts them quickly. In the end, we catch an earlier train.

'It's coming, Jonny. The train's almost here.'

He flaps the wrapper from a packet of sweets, looking up and sideways, head rigid, excited, then quickly tears the wrapper into little pieces and gives it to me. He's unhappy that I've stuffed it into a pocket – really it should be washed and put in a bin – but as the train is coming to a halt, he accepts that proper disposal must wait. The train door opens, I hold Jonny's arm and tell him to get on. We step up high into the train and I turn round for Hannah, extending a hand for her. The station is crowded with children and parents, but we get on without incident and find a seat together.

'OK, love?'

'Yes Mum, I'm fine.'

As the train pulls out, and we pass quickly through the Box Tunnel and out into the countryside, I take off Jonny's jacket, step up onto my seat to reach the rack where I put all our coats, and get out the sandwiches and squash. I hold the bottle carefully as I fill their cups and the train speeds on. Hannah gets out some little dolls to play with and Jonny, once he has checked that I've put all the lunch things away properly, presses his face against the window where a sticky patch of condensation soon forms.

We arrive into Paddington and I let other people get up and crowd by the door before I tell my reluctant son it's time to get off. Stepping out onto the platform, Jonny stares up at the vaulted glass above him, where the sounds from the station tannoy, guards' whistles, the beeping of trucks and the calling of passengers whirl and echo round. We walk slowly along the platform. A train pulls out and Jonny stands and watches intently. My daughter looks anxiously at me, but I tell her 'He's just excited by the train. Don't worry. Everything's fine. Jonny's having a lovely day.'

I'm hiding my anxiety about the tube. I don't think Jonny will have a problem with it – I once took him up to the Maudsley Hospital for a consultation with a doctor who was an expert in autism, and we did the whole day together without mishap. Jonny had enjoyed the tube trains, except for one moment when some pigeons flew into the carriage. He's a lot bigger now, though. Then, I had a buggy with me and could push him along when he got tired. Had there been a problem, I could have swept him up in my arms. Now I would have to negotiate, and there are times with Jonny when we are far beyond negotiation. It's Hannah who's always been nervous of underground trains and she looks a little stressed as we make our way downwards again after a brief stop to look at Paddington Bear. But she does well, as does Jonny, quietly getting on and off escalators, on and off trains till we emerge onto Westminster Bridge.

Here, traffic rushes by, and looking around at Big Ben looming above us and the river boats below us, we are all excited. It's still overcast and cold, but there is no rain and as we make our way across the bridge I realize that there are also too few children for a school holiday. The crowds I am expecting in the aquarium, with their shrieks and cries and demands for sweets, have caused me a great deal of worry. But when we arrive, after a slow walk across the bridge and lots of stops to look at boats, it is almost deserted. The London half-term was the week before. What luck! We join a very small queue, but an attendant approaches us and Hannah and I look anxiously at Jonny, expecting something to go wrong after this easiest of journeys. But he is a lovely man, London through and through, and says, 'Come in this way, love. It's priority for disabled. Need any help?'

'I think I should take him to the toilet. Do you have a disabled loo on this floor?'

'Just there, love. I'll open it for you. You and your brother up for the day?' he asks Hannah and she nods.

After we've been to the toilet, we go into the aquarium and spend the most magical two hours. It is almost deserted – no crowds, no echoing shrieks, no difficulty in seeing everything. We can spend as long as we like by each tank and move on quickly if it doesn't interest us. Jonny is very, very happy.

I realize that the aquarium holds enormous tanks that go down through the building and each floor winds round them so that you see the same tank again and again from a different angle and height. We sit in the semi-darkness at one level and watch as sharks come repeatedly up to the edge of the glass and nudge their noses against it. Hannah grabs my hand the first time, but laughs in relief when she realizes what is happening. Jonny watches and watches – the bubbles and weeds and fishes and sharks. He can sit on the floor if he wants or stand with his face against the glass without getting in anyone's way. At one small tank, the action of waves is simulated and, after a while, I wonder if we are ever going to leave. Jonny's face, against the part of the tank where each wave crashes against the glass into white foam, registers delight over and over again. Finally, we are able to leave it and, walking under the arch of an illuminated tank, looking up at the undersides of rays and small sharks, he stands, mesmerized by light, water and movement. He sits quietly on a bench while Hannah feeds another lot of rays in a large circular, open tank, where the staff describe the fish, how they live, that the 'eyes' are not eyes at all but designed to frighten predators.

In the café, we sit at a table and eat flapjacks with juice for them and coffee for me.

'Like it?' I ask Hannah.

'It's great and Jonny's being brilliant,' she replies.

'Yes, we're really lucky the London children's half-term was last week. Jonny's having a great time. Thank you for getting me to come.'

She looks pleased, but doesn't reply. In the shop I buy her a book and a plastic fish, and then we emerge in the mid afternoon. We walk along the embankment and across Charing Cross Bridge. Our progress is slow now. They are tired. But we make it to Trafalgar Square and watch the pigeon feeders and fountains for a while. Suddenly, I realize I am exhausted and that they are both flagging.

We've had enough, I think and, in an uncharacteristically spendthrift moment, hail a cab and get them both in. The cabbie is another diamond geezer.

'Hang on, love, I'll give you a hand.' He holds out an arm for Hannah, lifts out our bag and helps me with Jonny.

On the train going home, which is much more crowded, we encounter our first crosspatch of the day. I can only find one table with three free seats and a youngish woman has already settled in the fourth. Despite the fact that there are plenty of empty single seats and Hannah has to sit next to her, across from us, she huffs and puffs at every movement, grimace and noise that Jonny makes till, thankfully, at Swindon she gets off. Other people look askance at her as she sighs and raises her eyebrows. I want to tell her to stop frowning at Jonny every time he makes a strange noise or tears up some paper, but I don't really care. Provided we manage this last leg without incident we will have had a trouble-free, happy day – an achievement of no mean proportion, under the circumstances.

Several months later, at Jonny's review at his boarding school, I tell the people round the table about our trip.

'You took Jonny to London and to the aquarium on a train by yourself?' asks an incredulous educational psychologist.

'No, I had my daughter to help me,' I reply.

Center Parcs work well for Jonny. The villas are robust and undecorated. Despite the fact that they are cheek by jowl, they are designed to be private. As Jonny gets older, he starts to love the television channel where music videos are played, and will sit and watch one while I get our picnic lunch ready. Then we sit, in more or less the same place for most of the day, eating the lunch, watching the wave machine and enjoying the water. Jonny visits our nearest Parc over many years, with different combinations of people. When he is young, he will still go outside into the warm pools, even at night, even in snow. As he gets older he becomes more sedate, less adventurous, more passive and more fixed in his routines.

Hannah and I take him again when he is 24 years old. As we drive in his eyes light up and he says quietly 'Holiday.' Inside the villa, we unpack and eat our first meal. There's time to get down to the pool for our first session and Jonny, looking handsome in his leather flying jacket, walks well under the dark trees and along the pathway with lights at the edges, avoiding adults and children on bikes, till we get under the dome. We change in the cramped cubicles, cram our clothes into the lockers, put in the pound coins I have been careful to bring, and splash through the footbath. We find a plastic table and chairs right by the edge of the pool, and settle down. The darkness outside the curved glass roof is contrasted by the lights under the water and by the sides of the pool, and turns the great roof into a giant curved mirror. Jonny wants to sit and watch, but Hannah and I sink into the warm water and float, looking up at the magical portrayal of our world below, blue water, huge green leaves, rocks, lights.

When Jonny was younger, he would be in in a second, but it's easy to keep an eye on his older self. I get out and sit by him. He is grinning, calm, watching. I get out a book and read peacefully. A siren sounds and Jonny's face lights up even more.

'Waves, Jonny,' I say, 'want to go in?'

He doesn't, but he watches with greater and greater excitement as the wave machine begins. The peacefulness of this time, after toddlers are in bed, is broken by people rushing from the chutes and rapids, smaller pools and cafes, tables and sun beds, to jump in the waves. Hannah gets out – it's too crowded and we sit and watch.

'Doesn't he want to go in?'

'No, seems not. Maybe a bit tired. He's enjoying watching, aren't you Jonny?'

There can be no doubt of this. The wave machine sends higher and faster arcs of water towards us, crashing onto the rocky sides and sweeping up small children in the currents created. Despite the screams and shouts and the little children crying, Jonny becomes more and more excited, whooping with joy until suddenly, it stops as quickly as it began, and people drift away.

'Bubbles', he says. 'Mummy.'

This never fades, the love of the Jacuzzi. We get up and move to it, shaded by foliage. Down the steps, holding the rope. Children stare at Jonny, but he is very focussed. We move to the side and sit on the stone bench in this small, circular pool. The water is very warm – it spoils you for the other pool, but I know we'll be in here now for a very long time. The water is still and the pool uncrowded.

'Bubbles.'

'They'll start soon,' I say.

As a low rumble sounds, Jonny look excitedly down into the water. He takes a mouthful and spits it out.

'Don't do that,' I whisper, but he is distracted now.

The bubbles rise up from the bottom of the pool and spread round the circle, getting stronger and stronger. More people get in, but I resist their attempts to make us squeeze up. I avoid eye contact and keep our space. Jonny is very happy. I sink back onto the bed of bubbles, pushed from my seat by their force. I see Hannah appear at the top of the steps and mime taking a picture. She nods and goes to get the camera. She stands at the top and clicks away – pictures of Jonny, absorbed and smiling, surrounded by the white movement.

Hannah gets in with us as the bubbles stop and we wait again in the calm few minutes before they start again.

'Bubbles.'

'Soon.'

The mouthful of water, looking at me for a reaction.

'Don't,' I say without confidence. He doesn't. After an hour, I look at my hands – wrinkled with exposure to water. 'We'll get out soon,' I say, 'Jonny?'

'Bubbles later.'

'We'll go back to the villa. Ben is coming tomorrow.'

Back at the villa, Jonny moves into water again. Despite his hour or so in the Jacuzzi, he still must have his bath. But it's easy here, the bathroom with nothing to flush down the loo, which is in another place, anyway. Radiators up the wall will get the swimsuits and towels dry. After the bath, I read to him and then I settle down with my daughter, a welcome glass of wine in my hand.

In the morning, I am dragged from sleep by the sound of movement in Jonny's room. No sound from Hannah's. I make some coffee and sit up in bed with the door open, waiting for him to be ready to emerge. A blissful half-hour later – time in which to get washed and dressed – he emerges. I've brought, as I always do, his waterproof duvet and pillow, lots of sheets and many pairs of pyjamas. Jonny, though, has slept through the night – a new development and one that gives me much relief. I still sleep, as my second husband tells me a few years later, with one eye half-open, ready to spring into action.

The stink, once he does emerge, is grim. I get him into the bath as quickly as possible, having pushed the stinking sheets and bedding, which Jonny assiduously removes before he will think of going to the bathroom, into a plastic tub brought for the purpose and out into the lobby. It's tiled and brilliant for this purpose. Once out of the bath I help him to dress, put out some breakfast for him and then fill the bath with strong detergent and the sheets. Wash and rinse, then I squeeze them out and drape them onto the wonderful radiators. By this time, Hannah is up and she gets dressed while I make the day's picnic and Jonny watches semi-naked girls bump and grind to pop music on the video channel. He smiles.

'God, he loves this, doesn't he?' Hannah says. 'It's awful!'

'Yes and yes.'

After a few hours in the same place by the pool, punctuated by the eating of sandwiches and crisps, and followed ritualistically by the hour in the Jacuzzi, we drive out of the 'forest' to the nearest railway station to pick up Ben. I'm very glad for the company of my two other children. I had planned this trip with a man who seemed like a permanent fixture, but turned out to be temporary. I wander in a permanent state of guilt about this, feeling that Jonny shouldn't be exposed to temporary relationships, but he, and the others, about whom I also feel guilty, don't seem to mind at all. Back at the villa Ben and Hannah disappear as usual, into her room and their own world of laughter, music and references I do not understand, to films and TV I am not familiar with. I light a paper-covered briquette in the fireplace and sit with my glass of wine, half listening and drifting off into the joy of stillness.

The next day we repeat the day before, except that this time Ben and Hannah disappear for long periods of time, going down rapids and splashing in the hot and cold outdoor pools. Ben is worried that Jonny is watching rather than doing. He remembers him as a younger child, in the water all the time. And I wonder if I have wasted my money. But Jonny is happy and we are together, so I think not. Does it matter if you watch the water rather than get in it? It's what I do mostly when by the sea. From time to time, I try to encourage him to get in, but he is quite clear about what he wants to do – watch, especially the waves, and then get into the bubbles for a very long time with me.

The next day we take Ben back to the station. It's the first time I've been to Center Parcs and left the site – driven back and forth to pick people up. I'm very tired, but I think it's worth it to have them together, for Jonny to spend time with his beloved brother and sister.

'Jonny doesn't seem pleased to have seen me.'

I'm driving through poorly lit country lanes, with both sons in the car. Hannah has stayed watching a video.

'He's pleased to see you,' I say. 'He's pleased, aren't you Jonny?'

'I don't think so.'

'No, please don't say that. Jonny loves you, don't you Jonny?'

Jonny remains impassive. We arrive at the station.

'Thanks for coming, I say. See you soon.'

He gets out of the car and goes into the station. I start the engine and start the 45-minute drive back. It is peaceful and Jonny dozes off. As we pull into the car park, under the fir trees, I say, 'Back at Center Parcs, Jonny. Let's go and find Hannah.'

'Ben,' he says.

Packing to go home is hard and I feel angry. Whenever we've been here before, our blue disabled parking card has given us the right to park by the villa, to unpack and then leave the car there until we have to load up again. I applaud the policy of no cars at Center Parcs, of the walking and bikes and little trains you can catch. But on the rare occasions when Jonny has absolutely refused to walk, it has been great to know that I can get him to the pool in the car or away from difficult situations. There are maintenance vehicles around anyway, and the cars belonging to disabled visitors must drive very slowly. But under this new management, and in the age of the Disability Discrimination Act, this right has been taken away. Stopping the car by the registration window to be given our villa number and keys on the way in, the woman obviously felt sorry for me and arranged for me to be allowed to park the car at the villa for some extra time.

'Don't worry,' she said, 'you won't need your car on the Parc. We've got cars to transport disabled people now. You just tell them at the pool to ring for one.'

But this turns out to be a little economical with the truth. On our first evening, after arriving, unpacking and then going for a 'swim', Jonny seems very tired. So I go to the main desk and ask for a car and they tell me there will be a 45-minute wait for *the* car.

'Is that a joke?' I ask.

But their faces tell me it isn't.

'You tell me I can't use my car for a disabled man, even though we've been here many times, and always been able to use the car. You tell me that you will arrange transport and then when I ask for it you tell me there's a 45-minute wait?'

They nod. Hannah and I manage to get Jonny back with the aid of a packet of sweets and lots of stops, and realize that the conversation I have just had means that there is *one* car on the site for disabled people. It seems to be an obvious message. You are no longer welcome here.

On Monday morning, after we pack to go home, Hannah stays with Jonny while I walk to the car park and crawl back in the snaking queue with the car. Without her I couldn't have managed, and we have never been back. It's sad, because we are customers who pay good money; because we have fun; and because it's important that our sons and daughters are out there, visible, taking their place in the world. They have a right, just like everyone else, to take part in what the world has to offer; to be seen; to be people in their own right, joining in. They might experience things differently, look a little odd, need support to manage, but it matters that they are there, amongst us, reminding us that homogeneity isn't real or possible or even desirable; that difference is OK and an important part of this world in which we live out our lives.

Chapter Eight

OBSESSIONS

IT STARTS WITH 'traffic jams', one of the few phrases that Jonny still uses. On one day among the days; on one morning among the mornings of playing with toy cars, buses and trains, of pushing them round tracks, down the ramp of the toy garage and whizzing across the floor; on one normal day, after Ben is at school and we are back home with the washing and the washing up, I turn from the sink and see a line of toy cars and lorries snaking almost beautifully across the carpet. Was it on that morning or on a later one that my accidental disruption of the line produced rage and distress, shaking Jonny's chubby little body? When does this barely perceptible shift from something approaching normal play to the obsessional lining up of toy cars and lorries take place? Was it about the same time that we no longer read through books, cuddled up together on the cheap canvas chairs? When, instead, one page is open at a picture of food or of a digger or tractor, and we are not allowed to turn it over? How was I to tell that the building of 'towers' of bricks – so normal in toddlers – would become an activity governed by strict sequence and to which deep feeling is attached? That it must happen in the same way over and over again?

Later on, I categorize obsessions into rough groupings of what I think they provide. There are obsessions that use order and repetition to manage a chaotic world, a world where you do not know what may happen next. There are obsessions that filter sensation and block out frightening or unmanageable sensory input. There are obsessions that create pleasurable sensation to replace what has been blocked. There are obsessions that complete – finish off things so that you can move onto the next activity in safety. All of this makes the unpredictable and frightening world into a much safer place.

The 'traffic jams' create order. They are satisfyingly under control, and soothing to look at. Morning after morning, immediately after getting back from taking Ben to school, Jonny lies on the floor with his tub of cars and happily sets about this task. I look down on his mass of golden curls and quietly watch. His plump little hands work quite quickly and deliberately; his blue eyes are intent. He is completely absorbed. Once the line – each toy nose to tail with the one in front – is completed, he sits vacantly, thoughts apparently far away. The line must stay – by this time his anger has started to become ungovernable – until he goes to bed. He does not seem to mind that each morning the ritual must recur. Indeed, as the years go on, it becomes clear that the repetitive nature of these activities is an intrinsic part of their value, that it provides its own comfort.

The traffic jams are troubling because they are odd and can be mildly inconvenient, when, for instance, other parents visit and their children pick up the cars to play with, resulting in a volcano of emotion. Some of Jonny's obsessions are unpleasant – like being slightly sick after every meal, on the carpet or a chair if access to the bathroom is denied, but they do not, on the whole, make life impossibly difficult. Some people have autistic children who can only eat foods of a certain colour, or who must wear the same clothes put on in the same order every day and who must start over and over again if the slightest variation occurs in this ritual. Sometimes, though, Jonny's obsessions have to be managed if they are not to inhibit everyday life and curtail enjoyable experiences.

One changeable March day, we are visiting a friend in Devon. The journey involves three trains, one of which runs right along the seashore. I make sure that Jonny sits on the side where he will see the waves; when they crash up against the railway line, he and Hannah, are as excited as I expect them to be. When we arrive at our destination, we get off the train and sniff the salty air. Our friend waits on the platform and Hannah, clutching a toy rabbit, runs to her. We all walk up through the town, slowly, at Jonny's pace, and stop to sit in a little park and watch swans mill around the stream that flows through it and down into the sea.

'Here it is!' our friend announces proudly and we enter the beautiful little cottage she has bought.

Jonny sits quietly flapping his boat, while we toast the house in Prosecco and orange squash. After lunch, we are able to sit in the garden for a while. Jonny wants to sit inside and, as always when we are with company, I check the accommodation to make sure we can get through without incident. I look in on him regularly and he seems fine – quiet. The day has gone remarkably well – no wet pants or tantrums. I look at my watch and say, 'We probably need to get going now. Jonny might be slow walking back to the train.'

And we go inside. My friend has had a sofa and armchairs made for her little sitting room. They sit angled into a comfortable semicircle in glorious red Persian-patterned splendour amongst her customary muted decoration, books and plants. Except that they are now all lined up against one wall. I catch my breath when I see that my eight-year-old son is pushing and shoving them in increasing exasperation because the wall is not long enough to line them up perfectly. Jonny has also closed the curtains in an attempt at imposing order on what is to him a ridiculously chaotic room, and I quickly start to push the furniture back where it should be. Jonny is agitated, but we manage to get things back roughly to the way they were and get out of the house.

The next time Jonny visits this cottage, he is in his 20s. We negotiate the mass of motorway traffic and drive down to Devon where I have to tell my friend that my marriage is on the rocks. While she cries apparently more for the upset to her than to us, Jonny slips inside from the garden decking where we have braved the aggressive seagulls to have lunch, and quietly sicks up on her beautiful settee. I clean it surreptitiously. We do not have cause to go there again.

Jonny's bedroom at home is stark – short on decoration and bits and pieces, although there are plenty of photographs up in safe Perspex frames or pinned to a notice board. Jonny likes photos. There are a few books in neat piles carefully set exactly parallel to the walls. Sometimes Jonny spends minutes pushing and shoving these books, rearranging and reordering them in increasing agitation. It seems as though there is some golden standard that they never attain in terms of order. His tape recorder, parallel to the edge of the chest of drawers and pushed up against the wall, must be unplugged and put into a particular holdall on his shelves when he finishes with it, however late that is. His bathrobe must be hung from its hook by the edge of the collar, not the loop provided for the purpose; lights must be on or off, curtains open or closed in some sort of sequence that I still haven't quite fathomed.

Jonny is 19 when he goes to live at his current home. The first time we come to take him out for the day, it takes 20 minutes to get out. Several of the residents are sitting watching television in a large sitting room with sturdy furniture – leather sofas on solid wooden frames all pushed against the walls – the large television in a strong wooden cupboard, blinds and flowery curtains. Jonny sits among them. He sees us in the doorway, although he doesn't react. After a short pause, he gets up.

'Hallo Jonny,' I say. 'Ready to come out?'

He hesitates.

'Come on, we're going out in the car,' I coax. 'We'll have music and sweets.'

Still he hesitates. Then suddenly he runs to the windows and closes the blinds. Before I can reach him, he yanks the curtains closed.

'Jonny!' I protest, 'what about the others?'

He pushes the settee even closer to the wall. He turns off the TV and closes the doors of the cabinet. He walks to the door and turns off the light. The other people in the room sit impassively, not reacting at all to this performance, even though their TV chart show has been abruptly brought to a close. Then Jonny slams the door closed and stops in the corridor. The look of intense anxiety has left his face and he almost runs to the outside door. His key worker raises his eyes to the ceiling.

'Jonathan,' he says, 'has left the building!'

The spinning and flapping of objects wears them out, but very effectively blocks and filters sensations of sound, touch, light and generally perplexing activity. Fingers in the ears help as well – Jonny can do all kinds of things with his fingers firmly stuck in his ears. Clapping, sometimes used to express delight, is also an effective barrier and self-stimulator. Jonny claps a lot. Obsessions creating pleasurable sensation include the stretching and swinging of 'slinkies', requiring that we keep a large supply of these plastic or metal springs to replace each one as it becomes impossibly tangled. We also keep light sticks, children's 'musical' instruments, jointed snakes, streamers, plastic pots of bubble mixture, coloured windsocks, balloons and anything else that can be shaken, spun or flapped.

Fireworks are wonderful – the bangs don't seem to cause distress in this context – as are disco lights, especially when coupled with harmonious pop music. Movement in cars, trains and boats brings high levels of excitement. Water will always please. Just watching it flow, sprinkle or spurt will do. Pouring it oneself even better.

It is 4am in the morning in the middle of February. I sleepily go downstairs, put on a coat and unlock the back door. I wait for my eyes to become accustomed to the dark garden, illuminated only partially by the light from the bathroom. Stars are hard and bright in a clear dark sky and the frosty ground sparkles. It is freezing. Everyone else in the house is asleep, as usual.

I find the pillow and duvet frozen solid on the ground. The sheet, pillowcase and pyjamas are draped across a bush below the window from which they have been thrown. I'll find the flannel, dish and cup in the morning. I take all the bedclothes in and drape them over the banister. In the morning, I'll put them over radiators to get them dry for the next night. I return wearily to my bed. Jonny is 15, home for the school holidays and his nights – and mine – are regularly punctuated by this ritual washing of bedclothes. When he wakes in the night he wets the bed, strips it, gives himself, the bedclothes and pyjamas a bath and then throws the wet debris out of the window. While he simultaneously baths and does his laundry, I remake the bed, spraying the plastic sheet with antibacterial liquid and wiping it down first. The ritual allows him to go back to bed and to sleep, for which I am very grateful.

Other things are regularly washed and disposed of in this way. They mark the change from one activity to another and allow Jonny to move on. In this same holiday, he comes home from respite care and walks straight into the kitchen. His face is determined; he is quite clear about what needs to be done. He takes off his sweatshirt and runs it under the tap. Then he opens the window and throws it out. As he takes off his shoes, I grab them. A look of annoyance passes across his face, but he allows me to take them and put them in the cupboard. On some nights he must creep down to sort them out, because I find them soaking when I open the cupboard in the morning. Then he runs upstairs and I watch as jeans, tee shirt, pants and socks, all dripping, fall past the window to the ground. Once I'm sure everything has been washed, I go out, pick them up and put them in the washing machine.

Ben, sitting at the piano, looks exasperated. 'How can you stand it?' he says. 'Can't you stop him?'

'No,' I say. 'He needs to mark changes. It's his method of self-management. It's a compromise. I don't let him do coats or shoes if I can help it. But he'll become distressed if he can't do something. They all just go into the washing machine, anyway. It isn't a problem.'

He shrugs and goes back to his jazz.

Later, the whole family sits round the table eating dinner. Jonny gobbles his and then starts to clear up – washing his plate, cup and cutlery rather inadequately and putting them away in the cupboard and drawer. Sometimes he can be persuaded to put these things into the dishwasher. But often he is agitated until the programme finishes and the dishes are put away. Once he goes back to school, we find plates encrusted with food in the cupboard for several weeks. Jonny is often careful to put these objects down near the bottom of the pile. We are all rushed when we try to have a meal. In restaurants, we must take away the cup and plate as soon as his meal is finished. If we can't achieve this, then increasing agitation is the result.

Jonny always needs to finish things off. It doesn't sound much. It sounds quite easy, and perfectly sensible for a person who finds the world horribly chaotic, and hard to get a grip on. Make beginnings and endings. Make the endings clear. Get life a little organized. For this reason, we need to have plenty of equipment for unblocking sinks and toilets. For this reason, preparing for a school holiday involves removing all soap, shampoo, towels, flannels and toilet paper from the bathroom. It looks very bare. Everything we need in the bathroom must be hidden in a cupboard on the landing. We must arm ourselves from this cupboard with everything we need before we go in. Or, what we need may be found in the locked corner cupboard, made to our specifications, provided we have remembered to get the key from the landing cupboard first. No use realizing you need toilet paper if you have forgotten to retrieve this key. Woe betide anyone who leaves the half-full roll in the bathroom. They will be responsible for the blocked toilet when Jonny puts all the paper down. He doesn't like unfinished rolls. They are disturbing and untidy. He'll 'tidy up' anything left lying around. Shampoo? Let's pour it down the sink and throw the empty bottle out of the window. Towels – well they need washing first, but once dripping, are fine to go the same way. Soap – well that can go down the toilet too; the same with cotton-wool pads and buds. We once called out a plumber on a bank holiday to retrieve a large apple from our blocked toilet.

On another occasion, soon before Christmas, I go into the kitchen where Jonny has been suspiciously quiet for a while, and find that all our Christmas drink – except for the wine, which he couldn't open – has been poured down the sink. On the work surface is a neat row of empty bottles. The floor is sticky with sherry and lemonade.

One Christmas holiday there is an apologetic note in the book that Jonny brings home from school. 'Jonny made up planters for you for Christmas but when he'd finished them, he threw them out of the window and they broke. Sorry. They were lovely!'

Jonny's nocturnal activities are often announced loudly and suddenly when our bedroom door bangs open and the light is switched on. I often think it must be like this when the secret police arrive in repressive regimes – waking so suddenly to find the light in your face. He has often rushed out again by the time I am fully awake. But on one night he returns quickly, bearing a heavy computer in his arms. He dumps it on the bed and leaves again. I am really worried. I have a job where I work from home and the charity I work for has provided me with a computer, monitor, phone and printer. Jonny has always accepted that this office is a place he doesn't need to bother with, but tonight he's decided that it needs clearing up and that this computer really shouldn't be in there. The wires are trailing where it's been yanked out. But in the morning I manage to reconnect it and breathe a sigh of relief as it springs into life.

It's a sunny afternoon when there's a knock on the door. Our elderly neighbour is standing there holding a dripping sweatshirt.

'I think this is yours,' he says.

'Oh, yes, thanks, it's Jonny's,' I reply.

At least it's only a jumper today. Sometimes large toys or gardening items get thrown over. I'm always worried that some terracotta pot is going to land on someone peacefully sitting in the sun.

'Just go through it one more time,' my new husband, Will, says. 'I want to make sure I get it right.'

Jonny is staying with us and we are moving on with our programme of slowly increasing the range of things Jonny can trust his stepfather to do. The plan is that I will have a lie in and he will manage the morning routine.

'The plastic tub must be outside his door,' I reply. 'Once he wakes, he may lie in bed for a long time. You'll hear when he's ready.'

Indeed, the turning off of the tape recorder, unplugging it, putting it in its holdall and the stripping of the bed all produce a disproportionate amount of noise.

'Then the door will open and he'll start to put the wet bedclothes in the tub. But he'll keep his wet pyjamas on. Once the bed is stripped, he'll go into the bathroom. You must put his plastic bottle and flannel in there and run the bath before this.'

Will nods. 'Do I take the tub of sheets to the washing machine then?'

'Not quite. Wait till he hands you the dripping pyjamas and the plastic cup and bowl. He'll go to the loo, throw the plastic bottle over the shower rail into the bath, get into it in his pyjamas, then get out, remove the pyjamas and hand them to you. Then you can put the washing on.'

Jonny spends an hour in the bath, pouring from the bottle and running the taps. Happy squawks and laughter can be heard from the room.

'Knock and look in from time to time to make sure the bath isn't overflowing. While he's in there, put out his clothes in his bedroom – if he doesn't like them, he'll get some others from the drawer. When he comes out of the bathroom, he'll have put on his bathrobe. Give him his towel, take the bottle from him and put it away. He'll check that it's been put right away – so don't just hide it behind your back. Once he's in the bedroom you can get breakfast.'

Once Jonny is dressed and is downstairs with his step-dad, I go into the bathroom. The bath is empty, although the floor is quite wet. The toilet brush has been pushed against the wall and the loo roll holder is empty. We keep a supply of almost finished loo rolls specifically for these visits. The soaking cardboard inner of the roll has been torn up and put into the bin. Downstairs I can hear the breakfast ritual being played out. Jonny has asked for his favourite cereal, which Will has put on the table with a jug of milk, a dish and a spoon. I know that Jonny will have lined up the tablemat against the very edge of the table and the mat for a cup adjacent to the larger mat. Jonny pours the cereal and milk into his bowl, and I hear Will say twice, once for the cereal and once for the milk, 'Steady, Jonny. Now it's all over the table.'

The cereal packet and the milk must be taken out, even though we know that a second helping will follow. It comes in again, is taken out again and then bread and jam follows. After this I hear the drawer banged shut several times, and I know that Jonny – once Will has removed all crockery and cutlery from the table – has asked for a wet cloth and is squeezing water from this cloth onto each of the place mats, before wiping them, putting them in the drawer and slamming it shut. And I know exactly what will follow. Jonny will go into the kitchen to check that the washing and wiping up has been done properly and that everything has been put away. He and his stepdad often complete this task happily together. Jonny puts the butter away in the fridge even on the coldest day. He will hover around looking pointedly at objects or putting them away himself till he is satisfied with our efforts. Once he's checked that all has been cleared away correctly, he is able to relax and watch television.

Water – as well as being one of the best things in the world to watch, pour, sprinkle and get into – is a great completer of rituals and a marker of change.

'Here we are, love. Back at the house.'

I park the car and open Jonny's door for him. He gets out,

stamps in a puddle, then walks towards the gate clutching my hand.

'Washa, washa,' he says. 'Wash hands.'

'Yes,' I reply. 'You can wash my hands.'

It is dark and we have had a good day on trains and boats. We've had 'steakchips' in a nearby pub and are delivering Jonny back. We ring the bell and open the door. Jonny's face is serious and focussed. These rituals are immensely important.

'Washa.'

'Yes.'

'How did you get on?' The night staff member smiles at us.

'Very well,' I say. 'He's had his tea, been very happy.'

Jonny is impatient. 'Wash hands, wash hands.'

He pushes open the door to a toilet and pulls me in. He turns on the tap – fully on. Water splashes onto my jacket and I turn the tap a little to reduce the flow of water. Jonny thrusts my hands under the running water.

'Go way,' he says, 'goobye.'

'Goodbye, darling.' I put my face close to his and he gives a token kiss.

'Go way.'

'I'm going,' I say. 'See you soon.'

On the best day, he pulls his stepfather into the room and washes his hands as well. Walking back to the car Will kisses me, beaming.

It's been a long drive, and it will be a long drive back, but I was determined that Jonny should come to his grandparents' surprise 8oth birthday party. Hotels are difficult with the changing of sheets required during the night. So I grit my teeth, stick to orange juice and plan to do the return journey in the evening, back to our house where Jonny will feel secure. My brothers and their families and I have been planning the party for months. There is a marquee in the garden. There are collages and old photos. There are balloons, posters, a dance floor, disco lights, tables and decorations. I have made two cakes, which have been packed into the boot of the car with coats, towels and bubble wrap to keep them safe.

We've tried to prepare Jonny in the usual way with a photo story sent to his house to be read regularly before we go. His key worker drives Jonny over on the Friday night and he seems happy. But, after our usual tea of bacon pasta, he sits on the settee and repeats 'five minutes, five minutes' over and over again – an all-purpose phrase meaning 'Leave me alone for a bit, I need some space to deal with all this'. You'd better hope you don't hear this when he's sitting on a loo in a friend's house or a public convenience. You could be there for a long time. Jonny eventually goes to bed at 2 o'clock on Saturday morning, after repeating 'five minutes' over and over for four hours. I feel exhausted and think it very unlikely we'll get him up and on the road in time to get to the party.

But I'm wrong. In the morning he gets up, has breakfast and gets into the car. We get to my brother's house in plenty of time and with the cakes intact. Jonny has never been to this house before and as soon as we arrive he starts the 'five minutes' routine again, refusing to get out of the car. I go in with my brothers, nieces, nephews and great-niece and we wait for the arrival of the surprised 80-year-olds. Jonny's stepfather sits in the car with him.

For two hours they sit there. The surprise is successful, producing shrieks of pleasure. People chat and laugh and look at the photos. I take drinks out to Will, who sits in the car and does the crossword while Jonny repeats his mantra.

Then, as food is ready to be served, and with no great hope in my heart, I go out to the car, resolutely open the door and say, 'Come on Jonny, come in to the party.' And he does!

We get as far as the stairs, then up them to the toilet where I rush in ahead of my son and remove the full roll of paper, replacing it with a few sheets torn off and put on the dispenser. Jonny goes in and locks the door and I hope against hope that he will not stay in there for two hours. But he comes out, makes it into the marquee, sits with a bowl of crisps and a drink and suddenly smiles. Made it! I feel so proud of his achievement.

My youngest brother hugs me. Jonny's family is delighted to see him. He sits with his grandparents and uncles, aunts and cousins, touching hands, giving maybe a very small kiss and smiling broadly. He doesn't seem worried by the absence of his brother and sister, who have decided not to come. Later, as the light fades, there is music – old numbers by Glenn Miller and Frank Sinatra, as well as Beatles and other easy pop, accompanied by disco lights. With this and a plate of pasta and several chunks of bread, Jonny is in seventh heaven. When my three brothers and I stop the music to make a speech, Jonny calls out, 'Moosic, moosic,' and everyone laughs.

When we get home, I flop onto a chair and drink a huge glass of wine. Jonny gets into bed, fully clothed including shoes, and goes straight to sleep. We are all happy and flushed with success. Obsessions have to be factored in. They have sometimes to be manoeuvred round. We have to negotiate with them. But it is possible sometimes to do this, to accommodate autistic necessities. And when you can, then participation, family, love, enjoyment and – most of all – music, can ensue.

Chapter Nine

———

SECRETS, LIES AND
VIDEOTAPE

'I THINK THAT'S AWFUL,' he says. 'You shouldn't talk about Jonny as if he were dead.'

Was it then that I began to realize that this relationship, following the break up of my first marriage, was a big mistake? How could he be so insensitive? I'd never confided my feelings of grief about Jonny to anyone else. You aren't allowed to grieve for people who are alive. And that's right in a way. But anyone who has an autistic child, however much they love them, will spend some time grieving for their son or daughter, and for themselves.

My beautiful son with the huge blue eyes and shock of curls would never be able to talk to me; never be in a permanent relationship, have sex or children; never go to university, have a job or live in a flat with friends. He would never go clubbing or get drunk, read a book, surf the net or write a letter. He will always be dependent on others, especially after my death. How will he cope then? Who will make sure that he is looked after properly? The vulnerability of our children is something we hate. We are worried when they go to school and we can't be there to make sure that everything goes well. We hate it when we can't protect them from bullies and illness. But autistic people are very, very vulnerable, child and adult. They are, and always will be, easy to hurt.

The feeling always comes when something else is happening. There's a row, or a disappointment, some other sadness. I feel too much, too strongly about it, I do not know why. Then the waves of it wash and wash over me. I cry and cry. My other children, should they see it, hate it and later blame me for upsetting them; suggest that it shows I am unstable. I can't explain. Either you know what it is like or you don't. It is a deep and ineffable sadness that will never leave me. One minute I'm shouting at my husband that he doesn't listen to me or I'm listening to someone criticize me unfairly at work, or I'm watching a film where someone dies, and the next moment I am drowning in a sea of grief that will never give me up, never flop me out onto the shore. I must learn to live with it because it will never, ever go away. As long as I live, it will hide there, in the crevices of my life, unseen, waiting for me. It will never end.

Grief will always find some way out. If you don't allow it to be what it is, then it will poison some other well in your life. If you have a disabled child, it will always be there, a shadow at your shoulder, waiting to stick its finger into your heart. You might as well learn to live with it. It doesn't mean you don't adore your child – even when you wish she or he was dead – it doesn't mean that. Even when you wish your own life would end, it doesn't lessen your love. You must accept the shadow at your side, if you are to survive. Grief, like autism, must be integrated into your life.

The best advice I ever got was from my family counsellor
– the woman who, on occasions, I felt had quite literally
saved my life.

'Does it interfere with your life?' she asks when I explain
about the crying that will not stop.

'Only if I try to suppress it. My husband and children do
not like it. My mother-in-law says it shows that I'm mad.'

'But if you accept it?'

'Then it is hard, but eventually it stops and I feel better
– sort of washed clean. I suppose that is what they mean by
catharsis?'

'Yes, it's your way of dealing with it and it's better for you
to do what works for you – as long as it doesn't interfere too
much with things. This is what I think you should do. When
you feel it coming, if you can be alone – and as soon as you
can if you are busy – you should run a bath, lock the door,
get into it and cry till you have finished. You have a right to
your sadness and the relief it brings.'

I want, like Jonny, to put my fingers in my ears. I want
to screw up the newspaper and throw it into a fire. I want to
throw my shoe at the television, for that odious man is on
there again, or he is being interviewed in the paper. If I manage
to ignore all this, then a friend will ask me what I think
about it and I must be politely reasonable, although I want
to scream:

'What do I think about it? I would like to kill him! Does
he have any idea how much harm he does, how he twists
our hearts inside out? How we lie awake at night, year after
year, wondering what caused it, what we did, what bad,
bad action resulted in our darling babies being afflicted in
this way? Having your child vaccinated is what responsible

parents do. Could a responsible action like this have set in motion such a terrible chain of events?'

Of course, in reality, I am calm and reasonable.

'I don't think Jonny's autism was caused by the MMR vaccine,' I say and change the subject. Later, many children become very ill with measles or mumps. Some die, some have their sight or hearing affected. And it all turns out to be tosh, just as I expected. Of course, they must go on, the scientists and the doctors. They must try to establish what it – or more likely what range of factors with what range of triggers – can cause a child to be born with autism. But this irresponsible attempt to bypass proper scientific scrutiny? This use of our children's suffering to build a career? We hurt every time it is in the papers, on the television – even the good articles and programmes freeze our blood. We are frightened. It makes us go back over and over the painful road – the conception, pregnancy, birth, early childhood. It makes us go back along the lines of our families, the food we ate, the things we did – even at times, our thoughts – trying to find the answer we will never find. Why? Why me? Why him or her? How did this happen?

Programmes about miraculous cures hurt just as much. Nobody wants to think of random illness or disability. Nobody wants to accept that a child cannot be cured. We all crave hope. But autism cannot be cured – not by isolation or diet or dogs or singing or strange drugs or holding against the will. It isn't caused by coldness or scapegoating or childhood trauma. We do our children a disservice when we give in to easy answers. Maybe one day there will be a cure or, more likely, an effective screening process. Maybe. Until then, the people who work quietly, helping us to understand or to educate; the people who don't take shortcuts for their 15 minutes of fame, but beaver on with research into autism and the best way to care for people who experience it – these are the people we should listen to.

Jonny has cycles of sorrow all of his own. After he has hit and screamed and bitten and headbutted; after he has torn the tee shirt of his ever-patient key worker, smashed light bulbs or windows, knocked holes out of the wall or ripped down the curtains; once the intense violence is played out the remorse comes, the ritual of putting it right.

'Sorry, wite, wite,' he says anxiously and you must answer correctly.

'It's all right, Jonny. It's all right.'

Sometimes this will go on for hours, maybe punctuated with 'finish' often accompanied by a throat-cutting gesture.

It's another ritual, but he *is* sorry. What does he feel about the violence he cannot control? How much does he know about what makes him different? Something I'm sure – something that makes him sad on occasions, watching his brother and sister joking together, sitting up late into the night watching films. Don't ever be pulled into the lies about autism. Don't ever let them tell you that autistic people don't feel pain or sorrow; don't love or hate; don't have respect for some people and contempt for others.

Once I am over the first few years; over the belief that I can eradicate the autism; that it might, in some way, be my fault; then I turn my determination to understanding my son and ensuring that he has the best life possible. He has, I know, a right to his life, to be part of a family, to be listened to and loved. I go to enormous lengths, over the years, to make sure that this happens.

It's Easter Sunday and I'm out at the crack of dawn hiding Easter eggs. We have a huge garden, so I have plenty of scope. The air feels fresh and new. It's a wonderful time of year. The garden is full of daffodils and the promise of warmth and new life. Once I have finished, I go in and drink coffee. I don't allow Jonny's brother or sister to start the egg search till he is dressed and breakfasted. They can go out in their pyjamas, but for him it would be unthinkable. We are finally ready, and go into the garden. Ben rushes round, finding egg after egg. Hannah protests 'Mum, Mum, Ben's finding all the eggs. There won't be any left for me and Jonny!'

I'm fully absorbed with my autistic son, leading him round, helping him to find the eggs. 'Ben,' I say, 'slow down. Stop when you've found six. There are six each.'

I nod at Bob and he helps our daughter. Finally, we have all the eggs on the garden table. Jonny is happy. He has chocolate, and he found some of it himself.

Three months earlier, the garden was covered in snow and the children were inside the cottage, by the Christmas tree, ripping open wrapping paper and shrieking with delight. We have waited for Jonny to get up and have breakfast. The rest of us are in nightclothes. Jonny doesn't seem to mind what we others do – except leaving open zips or buttons on our clothes, of course. He is not a person who extrapolates from his experience to others. Most of his obsessions concern himself only, except when we have crossed legs, untidy arms, glasses or gloves not on correctly. Then he will put us right. The fold of skin that gets caught in a cardigan zip pulled up abruptly hurts a lot, and it's worth tidying yourself up before he sees!

'Here you are Jonny,' Ben says.

I feel a slight sinking of my heart, a creeping anxiety. Jonny is looking away from the proffered present. He is sick of the whole process. I've tried to leaven it with balloons, bubbles and things that spin or whirr – presents he can relate to, as well as sweets, but he is like a dead weight on the excitement. Presents for him are a kind of torture.

'He doesn't like it, Mum,' Ben says, dispirited. 'Why doesn't he like it?'

'He does, love, but this is too much for him.'

'No, he doesn't like it, he doesn't.'

I can feel Ben willing me to make Jonny behave properly – show due gratitude for this gift. But it isn't something that's possible for me to do. Jonny isn't interested in presents and you might as well get used to it. Later I get Jonny to at least hold the present from his brother and I take a picture before he can throw it down. I struggle so hard to make it all right for them.

It's a warm evening. We drive over to the theatre in the small market-town where my ex-husband once worked. I have my new partner with me. He is a mistake, but I don't know that yet. He is making a tremendous effort to understand Jonny and succeeding pretty well. Jonny likes him and he likes Jonny. We park the car and walk into the theatre. I'm crossing my fingers that Jonny will be OK. I think he will. Over the years, I've taken him to a few shows at the theatre. This is to be a performance by an Abba tribute band. We shuffle into our seats and wait for the show to start. I'm relieved to see that there are a number of people with learning disabilities in the audience, scattered amongst the platform-wearing, blue eye-shadowed, tight-jumpsuited fans. There isn't going to be anything demure about this audience. We should be OK.

The lights dim and the music starts. A wonderful light show begins. Dry ice pours from the stage. 'Waterloo' at a powerful volume belts out. The dry ice disperses, and there they are, impersonating Abba for all they're worth. Behind us, a young man with Down's sings every song with them. His mother keeps 'shushing' him but his enthusiasm is infectious. In the interval, Jonny has an ice cream. He is shaking with excitement and pleasure for the whole evening, grinning, laughing, mesmerized by the show. Sometimes he gives me so much happiness that I can hardly contain myself.

Jonny is sitting next to me on the settee. I feel nervous. He takes my hand – quite roughly – and pulls it towards his lower leg. He has rolled up the bottom of his trousers. He wants me to stroke his shin. I never know what to do when this happens. As is so often the case, an argument rolls back and forth inside my head. 'Everyone needs touch,' I think. 'I cannot expect this young man to go through his life without affection of any kind. We are lucky that an autistic son wants physical touch.' That's one side. The other is the sure and certain knowledge that Jonny will get an erection when I stroke his leg. Then I will become worried that I'm doing something wrong, and he will become aroused and agitated, trying to rearrange his trousers. We're very lucky that Jonny doesn't strip off or drop his trousers in public when he's sexually aroused. Many autistic men do. Jonny seems to have acquired some sense that sexual arousal is a private matter.

At one of Jonny's annual reviews there seems to me to be some awkwardness that I can't quite unravel. We are talking about Jonny's attendance – or not – at his day centre – the fact that sometimes he takes an awfully long time to get up in the morning. His key worker – a young man – is looking uncomfortable as he tries to explain without explaining and I am becoming increasingly worried about what I am about to learn. Suddenly, I realize what the coyness is about and feel enormous relief.

'Oh, you mean he's masturbating?'

'Yes, well yes. It's just that sometimes it can take… well he gets impatient and frustrated.'

'Oh, well that's normal, I think. I mean, we're lucky he knows it's to be done in private, aren't we?'

Nervous laughter relieves the tension.

Jonny masturbates, like most young men, usually first thing in the morning, sometimes last thing at night. He gets frustrated when it doesn't go right. When he has finished, he wets the bed and then strips the sheets; a different kind of wetting, but a closure of activity all the same. Perhaps he doesn't distinguish between the two kinds of bed-wetting? I'm not sure what is going on. It's hard to talk about these things, to admit them. But it's better than not saying them.

I'm sitting with Jonny at the edge of the pool. The wave machine is on and he is very excited, watching the water crash in over and over again. The excited screams of the bathers don't seem to bother him. Once the wave machine stops, many people go back to the chutes and rapids and the pool quietens again. I am reading, keeping an eye on Jonny. He takes my hand and puts it against his bare leg.

He moves it up and down along his shin. As usual, I don't quite know what to do. I don't want him to become violent in this crowded place, but neither do I want him to become aroused. As far as Jonny is concerned, swimming trunks are swimming trunks and shorts are shorts. I'd never be able to get him to wear what most men are wearing in this pool. He'd be fine in France, where shorts are not allowed in the pools, but here he looks different and there is no disguise for sexual arousal. I try to pull my hand away as I see that this is exactly what is happening. Suddenly he runs into the water, and I feel a great sense of relief. For a moment. He is lying in the shallow end, by the long, low steps, when I see the water suddenly change colour. He's weeing in the pool – maybe OK when you're three, but definitely not when you're 25. He's doing what he does after feeling aroused, but in public, in the pool.

Jonny has a whole range of unpleasant rituals: being sick after most meals, smearing saliva, spitting out food so that it sticks to the walls and furniture, scooping up water from drains and drinking it, washing things in the toilet, taking things out of his mouth and giving them to me or, on occasions, attempting to put this half-chewed offering directly into my mouth! Managing these things discreetly can be really difficult when you're out in public.

Jonny looks away from the camera. It's incredibly frustrating. He loves photos and videos of himself and his family, but obstructs the production of these things whenever he can. Later on, we sit and watch the film. He is completely absorbed in it. Sometimes we sit together and watch old videos of the family. I have one on now. In the film it is summer and we are in the garden of our first house. Jonny is about six years old, clutching his boat with the blue plastic fish and jumping off a garden bench over and over again. He is concentrating very hard and making strange noises – quite high pitched. The other two children are playing on the sloping grass in the evening light.

The video switches abruptly to the next day. It is a bright sunny afternoon and we are all in the garden. Ben is reading funny poems to his grandmother. Jonny and Hannah sit in the little paddling pool. Jonny pours water from a plastic pot over and over again. Hannah, in her bathing suit and an old-fashioned sun bonnet, tries to engage him in play, but he isn't interested. He gets annoyed when splashed with water and suddenly my back appears in the film, as I try to intervene. I am wearing a sundress from the Oxfam shop. My voice is gentle, but I remember quite clearly that I was always afraid, always anxious that I would have my back turned at the wrong moment and that my toddler daughter would get hurt.

The film jumps again and Jonny is on the swing beneath the apple tree. His hair is still damp from the pool and he is wearing light grey shorts and a yellow tee shirt, trying to hold onto the rope of the swing and clutch his boat at the same time. Ben is hovering nearby and so am I, trying to get Jonny to count and Ben is encouraging him in a piping voice. I feel ashamed now when I watch this piece of film. It seems that I couldn't leave him alone to relax, was always trying to prove to myself that the teachers and doctors who had told me that he couldn't learn were mistaken.

'One,' I say. Silence. 'One, two…'

Jonny makes an irritated sound.

'Come on, Jonny,' says Ben. 'One two…?'

'Th-three,' says Jonny, pushing himself backwards on the swing, irritated.

'That's good,' I say. 'One, two three...?'

'Four, five,' he says and pushes me away.

I walk out of the room but big Jonny stays, watching his little self being irritated by his mother.

Sometimes the staff members where Jonny now lives tell me that he asks to watch these home movies, but often becomes sad and cries or gets angry. I'm not sure if they're suggesting that I stop making them. The same, they tell me, happens with the photo albums. But Jonny frequently wants to look at the photo albums and videos. What does he understand of what he sees, I wonder? Does he connect himself now with what he sees on the screen and in those old snaps? He wants to look at them, whatever the reason. I think he gets home-sick for his family when he is away, that sometimes looking at these things makes him sad. But which of us doesn't feel a sense of loss or of poignancy when we look at the pictures of our past? Isn't it good that Jonny has enough of a connection with us to feel something strong when he looks? I don't know the answer to this question.

But videos and photos certainly help Jonny place himself somewhere that matters to him. They also help him to cope with the future and bring it into some kind of order. They help him to make links between past and present that are difficult for him to understand. 'Album' is one of the few clear words he uses. Grief, sex, memory – these are complex and difficult things for us all. For Jonny there are extra difficulties.

I realize, when I watch these old films, or look at the albums, that I felt a dead weight of guilt and responsibility during most of Jonny's childhood. I rarely took the easy way out if there was a more difficult path I could follow. Sometimes this paid off. I painstakingly 'taught' Jonny supermarkets, cafés, swimming pools, parks and theatres. I taught him to choose what he wanted in shops and then wait for the change. I taught him to queue for rides and for buses; to change trains and to hold someone's arm near busy roads. Sometimes I used photos or video to reduce stress and fear; to make the future less frightening. Always, I tried to help him make the most of the world he lives in. Maybe some of it was a punishment for me. Maybe some of it made life hard for the rest of the family. Maybe though, it gave Jonny the chance, a life, a place in the world despite his autism.

Chapter Ten

———

A DIFFERENT WAY

'HE'S IN HERE. He's very happy.'

She knocks on the door and opens it onto a small lounge. It's Jonny's favourite place, used mostly by him. In a corner is a shelf unit with boxes of games, jigsaws and books that Jonny uses. A bay window looks over the lovely garden – once an orchard. Jonny is sitting on the settee.

'I'll just go and get his shoes and coat,' she says.

Jonny has no shoes or socks on – he'd probably wash them if he had. He looks smart in cord trousers and striped jumper. His hair is short, just curling slightly against his head. His hands flap once, twice – the indication that he is pleased to see us. We are quiet, just standing, waiting for a minute. Jonny smiles – not at us – but definitely smiling. We wait another minute.

'Hallo, darling,' I say very quietly. 'It's nice to see you. You look nice.'

Another smile flits across his averted face. Another flap. More quiet. The door opens.

'Here we are,' she says softly and hands him the shoes and socks.

He puts them on and I pull the socks round so that the heel is in the right place. Don't want him uncomfortable today. He pauses several times during the putting on of the shoes but he's smiling more, even looking sideways on at us. He takes his coat and puts it on, pulling the zip up tight to his neck and turning the collar up. Then suddenly he stands up, turns quickly to the television and leans over it to the floor behind. He pulls out the plugs, then puts them back in again, then removes them again. He closes the blinds, pulls the curtains across then looks at them and says, 'Curtener.'

'OK, you can open them,' I say.

He opens them, throws open the door of the room and strides out. The door slams on us and we open it. He pulls us through then locks it on the outside.

'Light.'

'OK.'

He switches it off and then turns quickly to the garden door, opens it and strides through. He stops, looking at a plastic chair outside the door, straightens it, walks away, returns to it and straightens again, walks down the ramp and stoops to a drain where a small puddle of water has formed. He dabbles his fingers in the water, scoops up a mouthful, wets his face and hair, gets up again and smiles broadly.

'Car later.'

'Yes, car,' I say. 'It's out here.'

Jonny stamps in a puddle then gets into the car. Jonny's stepfather and I get in and I hand Jonny a bag of crisps.

'Seabelt, seabelt.' His is already fastened.

'Yes, seatbelts. We're doing them now.'

We fasten our seatbelts and I say, 'We'll drive to New-port, darling, then get a train, have our picnic and then go for a boat ride. Then we'll come back on the train, drive to the pub and have steak chips before we come home. OK?'

A moment to absorb this. Then 'Moosic, moosic. Car later.'

I turn on the CD player, Blondie starts being 'Atomic', I start the car and the day begins. Jonny sits in the back, impassive, and then as we turn into the one-way system and the music plays, he turns his head to the side, clicks his fingers close to his eyes and smiles. Will squeezes my hand. Jonny's happy and so are we.

There are ten of us in the room, the new head of the residential service, Jonny's key workers past and present, his key worker from day service, Bob and his partner, Will and me and the local authority social worker whose job it is to monitor Jonny's out-of-county placement. Every year we have this review. For the first few years I am terrified that somehow we will lose this place. But as the years go on, it seems less and less likely. We had previously held the review without Jonny. I could not see the point of his being there, not understanding – as I thought – the sometimes good but also quite difficult things said about him; he would find the whole thing boring and distressing. But I was wrong. This is the second year that Jonny has taken part completely successfully in his person-centred review. There are photos all round the walls of him taking part in a range of activities. Some are of him with his brother and sister – the first time they've visited him in his own home. I am surprised, not having known of the visit.

'Did Ben and Hannah come to see Jonny?' I ask.

'Yes,' Bob's partner replies. He is prone to long explanations, so I'm surprised by the brevity of his reply.

We get through the medical questions and the reports of 'incidents' of challenging behaviour before Jonny arrives. When he comes in he looks around at us, less surprised than last year. His key worker speaks very quietly and economically to him, indicating his seat, and Jonny sits down calmly. He eyes the food on the table – crisps, biscuits and fruit – and is told he can have some.

'Hand some food round, Jonny,' I say to him. 'Give some to other people.'

There is a pause. He picks up a single grape and puts it into Will's mouth. The staff and Will and I all speak quietly and infrequently. Jonny gets up to wash some plates in the sink and then looks round.

'You can put them in the cupboard, Jonny,' says his day centre worker, barely audibly.

Jonny puts things away and then sits down again. After a while, the social worker says, 'You're all very quiet.'

'Low arousal,' replies the key worker before silence falls again.

'Ah,' she says, 'I see. I never thought of that.'

I know all about children, I think; have always had a natural rapport with them. I love their smallness, their eagerness, their lack of cynicism, their excitement in what they see and do. I had three younger brothers and lots of baby-sitting jobs before volunteering, as a teenager, for several children's holiday schemes. Some of my free time was spent as a youth club leader – an attempt to provide some structured leisure for anarchic children from Hornsey – and then later for a similar group of children from the deprived estates on the edge of Cambridge. I started teaching as soon as I could, and then later worked for a voluntary organization providing a multicultural toy library and anti-racism training to nursery schools and childminders.

I love children's books, good-quality children's television, their art and music and have written about them for childcare publications. I had children of my own as soon as I could. I know, I think, quite a lot about children. You give them unqualified love and affection, affirmation and fun. You read to them, talk to them, 'bathe' them in language from the moment they are born. You kiss and cuddle them, tell them they look good, are doing well, are clever and kind. You give them as stimulating an environment as you can. You fill their worlds with colour and with tactile experiences. If they fall over, you scoop them up in your arms and kiss it better. If they are quiet and sad, you talk to them gently, you listen, you comfort. You give them words to describe the world, words to reason with, the tools to manage difficult situations. Unless, that is, they are autistic. Then, everything you know about children is turned on its head.

It is a long learning process, one where you must forget what you know, listen, watch and learn and think. This is a different world – or at least the same world differently experienced. I have seen the damage caused when you try to force 'normality' on autistic children. I will, till my dying day, feel guilty about Jonny's first school. You expect yourself to protect your children and I let down my darling son, the most vulnerable of my children, very badly. Now we are a little better informed about disability. We have been taught by disabled people themselves in their fight for equality that the infantilization of them and the description of their impairments as some kind of terrible disaster are unacceptable. People are people and what we all want is access to what society has to offer us and what we have to offer it. The world is a better place for us all when we see disabled people on their own terms and learn from them. We've come a long way. We still have far to go.

So, over the years, and with help from people who actually *like* my son, I move from punitive regimes that try to force him to be what he cannot be, to understanding his world and trying to provide what he needs to live the best life possible for him. I learn that words are hard for Jonny to process and that too many of them are distressing to him. I learn that he needs time and peace to make sense of what is happening. I learn that his senses are strong, different, that he likes to be affectionate, but that forcing touch on him when he is not ready is a cruelty to him. I learn that my son's distress is not assuaged by cuddling and talking, but by quiet and listening and by giving the space necessary for the world to turn the right way up again.

The children have friends round to visit. Altogether there are six youngsters – five of them noisy and boisterous, one of them sitting quietly with his fingers in his ears. Jonny is seven years old. It is a sunny summer's day and the children are keen to be out in our huge garden. Jonny is pleased to see them. A casual observer might not pick up the quiet smile and the quick, flickering, oblique observations of our guests, but I do. They would see a lovely-looking but somehow odd child sitting in the corner with the top of an old plastic boat, intent on flapping the little plastic fish attached to it and ignoring everything else. They might describe him as being shut away in his own world if they didn't watch carefully, but I know that he is acutely aware of what is going on around him. What I think he is doing is screening sensation in a way that makes it manageable for him. An intelligent solution to his situation, I think.

The five other children run out into the garden and head straight for the climbing frame.

'Come on, come on. I'm first.'

I look out and see that the older ones are taking care of the little ones, lifting them to reach the bars and pushing them on the swing. I am pleased.

Jonny, who loves the climbing frame when he's in the garden on his own, and also occasionally when his brother and sister are out with him, continues to sit on the settee flapping his boat. I watch for a minute, establish that he isn't distressed, and then go to get some squash and biscuits. Outside, on the terrace that runs across the front of our beautiful cottage, is a plastic table with four chairs round it. I put the tray with five plastic beakers, a jug of orange squash and a plate of biscuits on this table.

'Drink and biscuits here,' I call above the shrieks of delight.

'OK, Mum,' Ben calls back, hanging upside down from the climbing frame. 'Thanks.'

Behind him a bank of trees rising to the front gate shivers gently in the breeze. The two little girls, Hannah and Emily, have gone into the playhouse next to the climbing frame. It is a small wooden house with a sloping roof and window boxes on the front, which we have filled with pansies. I walk across the lawn which is sprinkled with daisies, and peer into the house through the door that they have left open. They are squashed in, under the little ladder which takes you up to the top if you are small enough, sitting on red plastic

chairs at a table. Dolls and teddies sit with them and they
have a china tea set on the table.

'Would you like some real drink and biscuits?' I ask.

'Yes, please.' They barely look up.

I fill the teapot of the set with squash and hand it and
some biscuits to them. They all seem OK.

Going back into the cottage, the sudden darkness diso-
rientates me for a minute. I look, once accustomed to the
dimmer light, towards the settee where Jonny was sitting
and see that he has gone. I still feel a wave of panic when
this happens, although I ought to be getting used to it. It's
the fact that I never seem to see him go that's worrying. He
must slip away so quickly and quietly. I go into each room
of the house, but he's not there. Neither is he upstairs. Looking out of a bedroom window, I see that the gates are still
securely locked. So I go round to the back of the house, and
I hear straight away the unfocussed noises he makes and
the flapping of the little fish. There is a low wall here, and
he is on it. He flaps the fish quickly, then leans forward till
he is almost falling and then jumps off the wall. A second
of intense flapping follows and then he climbs back up and
repeats the exercise, over and over again. He is, I think,
excited by the presence of our guests. This repetitive activity
is his way of managing his excitement. He can just catch a
glimpse of them from the corner of his eye if he glances up.
I don't see him do this but I think he does. He's got his companions where he can manage them – at a suitable distance,
slightly hidden, their noise much fainter from this distance.

'Do you want some drink and biscuits?' I ask him, speaking quietly and not making eye contact. A direct gaze seems
to unsettle him as well, as if the intensity is too strong for
him. He continues the repetitive jumping and the noises he

makes get a little louder. I wait for a few seconds and then repeat my question.

'It's on the table at the front, if you want some. Come if you want.' You wouldn't have thought that he'd heard a word, but I go round to the terrace and sit at the table. I can hear the jumping, flapping and squawking continuing and then suddenly he is beside me.

'Drinkbiscuit.'

'OK, here they are.'

He sits on a chair and pours some squash from the jug. He's watching it intently but shows no sign of stopping as the cup becomes nearly full.

'Jonny, stop pouring now,' I say, but it's too late and he continues to watch in fascination as the liquid flows from the table to the ground. I get a cloth and clear it up.

So – a different way. Take what you think you know about children and turn it on its head. Keep words to a minimum. Keep stimulation down. Don't make eye contact until you know there is calm. Don't fan the flames of distress and anger by touch, emotion, sound or gaze. Wait. Wait. Wait. Understand the fear, the rapidly beating heart, the overwhelming sensation of touch, the intrusion of the eyes. Understand a world full of confusion and danger. Understand that to be quiet is to be kind, to give time – even if it is hours and hours – may be necessary for the world to come the right way up again. Remember, there are different ways of experiencing the world; different ways of thinking and feeling; different ways of being frightened; different ways of showing love.

Chapter Eleven

———

A SENSE SUBLIME

H E STANDS ALONE right in the middle of it. It is a huge space. Massive walls surround us, towering up to the place where the roof should be. Before and behind, they point upwards in a sharp, upended V where the gable ends of the huge chapel would have been. From the middle of the ruin wings fan out on either side, making the building into a disproportionate cross. He is wearing blue jeans and a fleece jacket. His hair is short and curly, his eyes very, very blue. He stands looking up, feeling the soaring walls, the hugeness. He is very happy.

'Up, up up!' he cries, 'up, up up!'

His head and hands are shaking with excitement. His arms are raised. High, high above him, white clouds race across a sky of blue. It is muddy underfoot. Rain has fallen for several days, but today the puddles are full of light and cloud, fragmented by each joyous stamp as he moves from one to another. His shoes are getting wet. I watch and smile – something I haven't done in weeks.

In this deep valley, the brown, broad River Wye coils sluggishly by in one of its many bends. Rising sharply all around are steep wooded slopes. It is held in, separate, a world away from the world. It must have been terrible in winter. Down here – we drove up first through curling, wooded roads and then down, down, down – the ruin of Tintern Abbey sits, wrecked and dignified, huge like a conquered giant. To us it is an old friend. We two have sheltered among the half-fallen walls where the old kitchens and dormers once stood, on a midwinter's day, alone in swirling snow. On summer days, we've sat watching busloads of tourists catch their breath as they see for the first time the soaring heights appearing to sway against the blue sky and brilliant sun. Today, we are here again, on a Saturday in April, two of a few visitors walking round as sun follows cloud and wind follows sun, all reflected in puddles of light.

I'm full of foreboding when I pick Jonny up and drive here for the first part of this routine we repeat again and again. My personal life hasn't been going too well and I'm worried how it will be today. A 27-year marriage has collapsed under the weight of repressed sexual incompatibility. A subsequent relationship has been smashed to pieces, leaving me bruised and shaken among a great deal of glass. The man who I thought would be constant at least, has driven off into the night, and this time I do not respond to the ritual of remorse and forgiveness. This time, I put an end to it. How will I explain this to my son? How could I have introduced this gone-away man into his life? I've been running around – rushing, rushing, packing up a home, alone, frightened, sad, not sleeping. I've been filling box after box after box, remnants of a life taped shut and labelled, rarely stopping to eat or sleep. The man from the removal firm seems genuinely worried about all five foot of me and my ability to complete the huge task before me. He arrives regularly on the doorstep with more flattened boxes and stands for a few minutes, looking helplessly at the diminishing floor space between the ones I've already filled. I've been struggling up and down the loft ladder with old televisions and broken chairs. There are bruises on the bruises. I've been selling things, giving away possessions, taking old bunk beds and bookshelves to the tip, dismantling our family life, drowning in memories, assailed by grief. I need to take Jonny out, but it is an interruption, a distraction. I don't really have time for it.

All the plans for buying a new house, plans that I now realize were never real but a fantasy into which I was sucked, disappeared over night with my companion. And this collision of the fairytale with the reality of a time for selling up and moving ended in an explosion of violence. I have had to start all over again, searching for a new home with very little time, and much less money. But my daughter and I found a house, smaller but full of light and wonderful views, and now I must shed possessions to fit into this place. The sense of rushing, the terrible fear that it is simply not possible to complete this task in the time available, has left me stressed and distracted. I'm afraid it will communicate itself to Jonny and leave him as unnerved as me.

Arriving at his home, I open the squeaky gate and scrunch across the yard. I press the bell and push open the door. I say 'hallo' to the staff and to the other residents who greet me in their own way, flapping the sock a bit harder, jumping up and down, telling me I'm Jonny's mum. I walk down the corridor to the little lounge where Jonny sits waiting for me, smartly dressed and watching television. His face lights up with a sideways smile when he sees me. We go through the routine of television off, television on, television off and unplugged, curtains and windows closed, lights off, doors closed, chairs straightened, water scooped from the drain and sprinkled over his hair, puddles splashed in before we get into the car.

'Seabelt, seabelt.'

I put it on.

'Moosic, moosic.'

'OK Jonny.'

I put in a CD and we drive off, round the one-way system, through the small town, back onto the motorway, through Chepstow and to the abbey that we love. I turn off the engine and we sit for a moment.

'Jonny,' I turn to look at him, 'Jonny, I'm on my own today. Tom has gone away. He doesn't live with me any more. We'll be going out on our own again now.'

He smiles. That is all – a smile of pleasure that he has me all to himself! I open his door and we go through the entrance shop and into the ruined monastery. He has linked his arm through mine, unconcerned with the loss of someone who was here for a short time, happy to be with his mum who comes and takes him out, always when she says she will, regularly, whatever may be going on.

And now he stands, arms raised in the windy ruin, bathing in happy sensation.

'Shall we go up the steps?' I ask him and he reluctantly leaves his worship of the racing sky.

The goblin drives me on. I cannot slow down. At the top of the steps, we look across the site, to the hills behind, where trees are filling up with green. Jonny is still, watching.

'Come on,' I say. I am not still at all.

Back through the roofless walls shadows race and my

poor brain pushes on. We step through and past some low walls to some benches where we often sit. The sun gets stronger, birds sing. The gentle hand of the day lies upon us. Jonny sits as still as the surrounding stone. It is amazing how still he can be. He's like a radio switched on and off, from perfect stillness to extreme movement with the passing of a second. I feel the warmth of the sun on my face. It has felt like an ice age, like a war, like a car crash and suddenly all is soft and peaceful.

'Shall we go, Jonny? Shall we go on and have the picnic?'

Jonny, so often the one driving us forward, unable to rest till the list of activities has been gone through, does not speak and I repeat the question as if I think I can move time forward with all this rush.

'Shall we go and have the picnic now?' I am jagged and taut.

He turns his face to me.

'Stay here,' he says, quite clearly, 'Stay here.'

And we do. We sit together in this gift of a day, softly warm and bright, an armistice, in the grace of light.

With all calmed and slow, we drive on to Symonds Yat, where we eat our picnic beneath the budding trees in companionable silence. With the picnic bag back in the car, we walk up to and across the wooden bridge. Jonny stops for a moment to watch the road below and then turns abruptly and almost runs up the uneven path to the rock. At the top, the trees part and we are on a stony mound protected by a wall, which is all that keeps us from the huge drop to the river bank below. We stand by the wall for some minutes, our chins resting on our arms, looking over the unspeakable height and beauty stretching away, away to the horizon.

Far, far below, the sky is reflected in the river, winding sinu-
ously round a hill. In the far distance, there are light-tinged
buildings – the town of Ross and then to the side and farther
still, Hay. But up here there are only people mesmerized
by the view and twitchers watching nesting hawks through
RSPB telescopes.

Later, after we have driven through the Herefordshire
orchards, bright in the sun, and eaten in a restaurant, we
sit on a bench in a bend in the road above the river at Ross.
All is now peace and companionship in the evening light. I
sit with one of the people I love best in the world, watching
the Wye again, broad below us. I think of the house I must
return to, empty of almost everything except brown boxes
and echoes of the past, and I realize what a gift my darling
son has given me in the midst of all this loss.

'Give me a hug, Jonny,' I say, half joking, knowing that
this simple request is an enormous and dangerous thing
to ask of him – an impossibility. I've never asked this of
him in his whole life. I don't believe he can do it. A hug
is something that might crush and suffocate him. It repre-
sents unbearable and overwhelming fear – of touch that
cannot be controlled, of feelings you do not understand. He
turns to me and gently, deliberately places one hand on my
back. I am mesmerized, holding my breath for fear that this
miracle will end if I breathe. He places his other hand
carefully on my shoulder, as if meticulously following an
instruction manual. He leans in to me, his face against
mine, and for two seconds, on a bench looking down on the
River Wye, for the first time in his life, he holds his mother
in his arms.

EPILOGUE

WHEN WE REACH Tintern Abbey, Michael parks the car and we all get out. The fine drizzle that has accompanied us shrouds the site in mist, but detracts nothing from its poignant grandeur. I have been sitting in the front passenger seat of the car, navigating, but now I get out and open Jonny's child-locked door. He gets out and looks up. Will and his son also get out and slam their doors. Jonny hesitates by the entrance, looking obliquely at his driver who probably does not catch the brief, sideways smile that I see, then strides up to the entrance of this place he knows and loves. We all follow quickly. By the time we have paid and moved out of the entrance hall the rain has stopped, the clouds have parted and watery sunshine bathes this grand ruin.

Michael is an archaeologist and I hope I am repaying his kindness today with an interesting itinerary. He stops to look at some large sculptures, worn away by the years, labelled and laid out under a canvas awning, while Jonny sits on a nearby bench. He looks at Michael from time to time – quickly and with a soft smile on his face. This is his stepbrother and a new friend. Jonny has watched him from the back of the car with quick, darting glances. He's been told that Michael will come today with Mum and Will to take him out and get to know him. He's been shown the pictures of the wedding when he last saw his stepbrother, so he knows who will be coming today. He's looking good in jeans, a leather jacket and a contented smile. He has a new friend who's quiet and drives him around with his mum and stepdad, playing the ska CD he has made for Jonny. Life is good.

I am often ill now with a chronic and painful disease, and cannot drive for hours on end. We take Jonny out on trains, an old passion of his, newly and conveniently revived. Somehow, during all the difficulty and exhaustion of divorce and new life, my two other children have moved away from me, decided they do not wish to be part of this new arrangement. Maybe this tangle is too hard; maybe it will right itself someday? But on this day, the grief of their loss can be laid aside in the wonder of unexpected kindness, the amazing twists and turns of love.

We all sit on the bench where Jonny once forced me to be still. Chinese tourists click away. A family from the north laughs as the children jump from the ancient walls and play tag, and I remember a poem by Wordsworth, written looking down on this ruin. The poem describes a 'sense sublime' and 'elevated thoughts' felt in this place, sense and thoughts which join with the round ocean and the blue sky and the setting sun to roll through all things. And here and now, in the place that was the inspiration for that poem, with my

son and my stepson and my husband, I feel it. Something
more than joy; something more than love, some sublime
sense that joins us all together, whoever and wherever we
are, and rolls on through the universe.